THE MIRROR AND THE WORD

Texts and Contexts: volume 5

ERIC B. WILLIAMS

The Mirror
&
the Word

MODERNISM,

LITERARY THEORY, &

GEORG TRAKL

University of Nebraska Press

Lincoln & London

© 1993 by the University of Nebraska Press
All rights reserved
Manufactured in the United States of America

The paper in this book meets the minimum require-
ments of American National Standard for Information
Sciences – Permanence of Paper for Printed Library
Materials, ANSI Z39.48-1984.

Library of Congress Cataloging in Publication Data
Williams, Eric, 1950-
The mirror and the word: modernism, literary theory,
and George Trakl / Eric B. Williams.
p. cm. – (Texts and contexts)
Includes bibliographical references and index.
ISBN 0-8032-4756-7 (alk. paper)
1. Trakl, George, 1887-1914 – Criticism and interpretation. 2. Modernism (Literature) –
Austria. 3. Literature – Philosophy. 4. Mirrors
in literature. I. Title. II. Series.
PT2642.R22Z95 1993 831'.912 – dc20
92-24242 CIP

To Herb, Bev, Bill, Marilyn, and Hapaki

Contents

ACKNOWLEDGMENTS

I would like to acknowledge and thank Otto Müller Verlag in Salzburg, Austria, for permission to quote the critical edition of Trakl's works, *Dichtungen und Briefe*. Though phrases and formulas are insufficient to express my appreciation and debt to my wife, Susan, I would like these words to mark my gratitude for her years of patience and assistance in seeing this book to its conclusion. Earlier versions of sections of Chapters 6 and 7 appeared in my essay on Georg Trakl contained in the anthology *The Dark Flutes of Fall: Critical Essays on Georg Trakl* and published in 1991 by Camden House, Inc., in the series Studies in Literature, Linguistics, and Culture.

In the history of the poem Trakl's books are important contributions toward the liberation of the poetic figure.

RAINER MARIA RILKE

And we all, with unveiled face, reflecting the glory of the Lord, are being changed into his likeness.

2 CORINTHIANS 3:18

Georg Trakl's manuscript page for the poem "Landschaft." Courtesy of the *Forschungsinstitut Brenner-Archiv* at the University of Innsbruck, Austria.

Introduction

Ein Wort—ein Glanz, ein Flug, ein Feuer,
ein Flammenwurf, ein Sternenstrich—
und wieder Dunkel, ungeheuer,
im leeren Raum um Welt und Ich.
—Gottfried Benn[1]

MANY MODERN thinkers have vociferously despaired—some quite eloquently—at the insufficiency of the word. Others, like Gottfried Benn, have celebrated its luminous power. For Benn, the word is ephemeral, a mere *Sternenstrich* in the infinitely dark space that surrounds *Welt und Ich*. Without *words*, Benn's words seem to say, we would be lost in a monstrous night. Although modern critics of language are quick to point out that words are incapable of producing mimetic pictures—verisimilar representations—of what is (*die Welt*), it seems equally true that their fleeting *Sternenstrich* brilliance does occasionally illuminate the darker regions of the human psyche.

Gottfried Benn was, as many other artists and thinkers of the twentieth century have continued to be, deeply concerned, if not obsessed, with the world of words. In this century language has

1. "A word—a flash, a flight, a fire, /a thrust of flame, a fleeting star—/and then dark again, monstrous / in the empty space surrounding the world and the ego" (Benn, *Das Hauptwerk*, 1:208). Unless otherwise noted, all translations from the German found in this book are my own.

become an important issue in itself: there is hardly an intellectual discipline that has not woven in some manner a reflection upon the function of language into the fabric of its discourse. The world of words has become a new frontier; it is, strangely, the very familiar terra incognita in which we carry out our lives, pervasive but to a large extent mysterious and as yet uncharted. It is ironic that our preoccupation with language, born of an awareness of the word's insufficiency, has led to a new and profound appreciation for the linguistic dimension of human existence. The psyche and our understanding of it, we have come to assume, are literally unthinkable without words.

This book takes as its point of departure our century's profound ambivalence toward language, our "discovery of the word in its impotent power."[2] In the first part I examine various aesthetic and philosophical texts from the past two and a half centuries and elaborate a psychological perspective of the developments in philosophical discourse that culminated in the so-called crisis of representation at the beginning of this century. I then, in the second part, bring this perspective to bear on the difficult poetry of the Austrian writer Georg Trakl (1887–1914). By reading the verse of this modernist poet—Trakl was one of the first modernists to write in the German language—as a poetic convergence of certain psychological, epistemological, and aesthetic determinants, I suggest a model for reading that does not depend on the "negative categories" so often invoked to characterize modernist poetry—"obscure," "unintelligible," "disjunctive," "esoteric," "dissonant," or even "antihumanistic."[3] Such negative categories, I believe, are largely the result of false expectations, of an anachronistic mismatch of premodernist aesthetic values and modernist poetry.

2. Foucault, *Order of Things,* 300.
3. See Friedrich, *Die Struktur der modernen Lyrik,* 15–23.

The Crisis of Representation

Ein Bild hielt uns gefangen. Und heraus konnten wir
nicht, denn es lag in unserer Sprache, und sie schien es uns
nur unerbittlich zu wiederholen.—Ludwig Wittgenstein[4]

It has long been assumed in Western thought that the perceived
world serves as the foundation for rationality, knowledge, and
certainty. Insofar as visual perception is considered to be the primary mode of perception, theories of knowledge have entailed in
one form or another the basic assumption that "seeing is believing." This primacy of visual perception has, at least since Plato's
Allegory of the Cave, generated various optical and visual metaphors
for characterizing the acquisition and analysis of our knowledge
about the world. In the seventeenth century this metaphorics of
visuality crystallized in the image of the mirror: human cognition
was believed to function like a mirror that reflects the world at the
end of our gaze. This book investigates how both poetic theory
and epistemology have, since the German Enlightenment, gradually broken away from this deeply entrenched epistemology of
specularity and how, in particular, this shift is manifest in the poetic production of the early twentieth-century expressionist poet
Georg Trakl.

Beginning with the German Enlightenment, I examine the rise
of language philosophy and the parallel development of literary
modernism by interweaving a discussion of selected texts from the
fields of aesthetics, philosophy, and poetics. Central to this historical perspective is the distinction between the classical and modern
periods elaborated by the French philosopher of intellectual his-

4. "A *picture* held us captive. And we could not get outside it, for it lay in our
language and language seemed to repeat it to us inexorably" (Wittgenstein, *Philosophical Investigations,* 48).

tory Michel Foucault in his seminal study *The Order of Things*. Foucault's structural approach to European intellectual history counters the "impression we may have of an almost uninterrupted development of the European *ratio* from the Renaissance to our own day" by describing two major "discontinuities" or "mutations" in scientific-philosophical thought. These two historical breaks, seen in a quick, cross-disciplinary transformation of the preceding era's underlying conceptual scheme, gave rise in the middle of the seventeenth century to what he calls the Classical Age and, in the closing years of the eighteenth century, the Modern Age.[5] Foucault argues that between 1775 and 1825 the cornerstone concept in Classical thought—representation—lost its explanatory power and ceased to function as the unproblematical foundation for human knowledge and cognition. Scientists and philosophers were no longer satisfied, as they had been in the Classical Age, with classifying the visual orders of things into complex representational grids and tables of taxonomies. They turned their attention to the "organic" functions that underlay or made possible the apprehension and representation of surface "visibilities." Such thinking gave rise, for example, in philosophical discourse to the Kantian critique, which posited a dynamic relationship between mind and world. The Kantian transcendental subject synthesized its view of the world by projecting its own inborn structure (the a priori "concepts of synthesis") onto the manifold of perceptual experience. This transcendental subject thus supplanted the more static Cartesian Ego, which, it had been assumed, passively mirrored—re-presented—the world. Thus in post-Enlightenment thought, knowledge of the world carries the indelible mark of the human mind; understanding and cognition become as a result more a function of projection than representation.

5. Foucault, *Order of Things*, xxii, 217.

Using Foucault's epistemological model, my historical sketch relates more specifically the rise of language philosophy and aesthetic theory over the past 250 years to their convergence in the semiotic strain of contemporary literary theory. I argue that both the early twentieth-century philosophic crisis of representation and the contemporary question about the referential status of poetic language are rooted in late eighteenth- and early nineteenth-century speculations about transcendental subjectivity. I also argue that such a rethinking of representation and subjectivity enabled the romantic poets and theorists to speculate about what they called the *Nachtseite* of the human mind—a powerful but unknowable psychic dimension which expresses itself in and through poetic creativity. In trying to understand the subjective conditions of poetic creativity, the romantic generation began to articulate, and, in a sense, invent the modern discourse of the unconscious. The notion that, as one recent critic put it, "the structure of literature *is* in some sense the structure of the mind" is not exactly new.[6] It has its roots in the aesthetic speculations of the romantic era, which explicitly formulate the inseparability of literature and mind and, ultimately, the reciprocity of literary analysis and psychology.

In an important sense—and here I may diverge somewhat from Foucault's structural analysis—the early post-Enlightenment conceptualizations of a transcendental subject can also be viewed as a response to the Cartesian philosophy of doubt. Although Descartes believed he could ground philosophy in the indubitability of the thinking (conscious) subject—that which he felt could not be doubted—his influential speculations indirectly served to institutionalize the philosophical method of doubt. In positing a transcendental subject whose inborn structuring principles would be logically prior to the conscious subject, Kantian philosophy was a product of such doubt in that it sought to establish an indubitable

6. Brooks, "The Idea of Psychoanalytic Literary Criticism," 148.

foundation for the thinking subject, which, it would seem, had been rendered problematic by an incipient failure of representation.

The increased interest in questions of semiotics and language philosophy in the aesthetic and philosophical tracts of the German Enlightenment, between roughly 1720 and 1780, is itself the product of a growing doubt about the reliability of representation. Motivated by a subliminal need to counter the incipient failure of representation, thinkers such as Georg Friedrich Meier went to great lengths to defend the assumption that human cognition is at its most fundamental level constituted by an innate representational capacity. Metaphors of visual reciprocity—mirrors, reflecting surfaces, and even the mimetic surface of the painted canvas—abound in descriptions of man's cognitive faculty, which was characterized in representational terms as a kind of mirror of the world. Conflating representation and perception to describe the "painterly" character of the human mind, Meier wrote in 1752 that "an idea [*representatio, perceptio*] functions like a picture, which demonstrates the inherent painterly dexterity of the human psyche."[7] This specular-visual function runs even deeper, as the recent work of the American philosopher Richard Rorty would suggest. The Cartesian mind, Rorty shows in his *Philosophy and the Mirror of Nature,* was thought to possess an inner eye that, in its internal mirror, saw reflections of the external world.[8] In any case, these thinkers struggled to demonstrate that language was fundamentally representational and referential, that it was a graphic representation of a mental *representatio, perceptio,* and that language was truly meaningful and valid only when it was causally linked to and represented the mental images of man's primary visual encounter with the world. Words, understood in this way,

7. Meier, *Auszug aus der Vernunftlehre,* par. 10.
8. Rorty, *Philosophy and the Mirror of Nature,* 17–69, esp. 46–52.

had a quasi-picturing function that served not only as an epistemo-logical anchor but also as a guarantee for the efficacy and deter-minacy of language in general.

The interest in metaphors of visual reciprocity underlies the important mid-eighteenth-century *ut pictura poesis* debate, which revolved around the question of whether poetry should emulate the picturing function of painting. Those in favor of the *ut pictura poesis* dictum generally believed that poetry should conjure in the mind of the recipient a phenomenological experience practically indistinguishable from man's primary visual experience of the world. Poetry should, in their view, produce mental images with the clarity and indubitable certainty of those produced in visual perception. To accomplish this, the material or graphic qualities of language must recede so as not to interfere with the desired imagistic effects: the recipient must "see" images, not individual words. Some thinkers of the German Enlightenment thus specu-lated about a transparent or natural form of poetic discourse which could present (or re-present) to the "eye of the mind"—the *an-schauende Erkäntnis* (literally the viewing cognition)—the world in its full visual plenitude. In grounding poetic language in a quasi-mirroring function, they tried to provide it with an objective and rational basis firmly rooted in representation.

Speculations about such a transparent form of verbal mimesis, what I term *absolute visual mimesis,* led some thinkers to posit the superiority of verbal over visual art because they believed that the visual effects of linguistic representations could be manipulated in such a way as to convey an intangible something that can never be portrayed by the sensory quality of the painted canvas. It was thus possible to believe, as Françoise Meltzer has pointed out in her study of literary portraits, that a "prose 'portrait'" was more effica-cious than a "painted portrait" because "the entire man can be visualized through a verbal description that 'captures' his essence."[9] The imagistic effects of words were, then, superior to the "mere" optical effects of painting.

The ardent desire for a transparent and natural form of poetic language whose representational power is superior to that of painting suggests that these thinkers shared an uneasiness or skepticism about man's representational capacity. In speculating, moreover, about an ideal (natural) form of poetic mimesis, these thinkers were in effect positing a model discourse that would overcome the troublesome, abstract effects of representational language in general. Being ultimately a representation of a representation, ordinary (nonpoetic) language tended in the final analysis to put its speakers and listeners at an abstract remove from the privileged (and desired) realm of visual experience. Ordinary words, these thinkers felt, were obtrusive because they wedged in between the subject and its primary visual encounter with the world. Troubled also by the nonvisual effects of graphic signs in general, the thinkers of the German Enlightenment began to see language as a problem in itself. It was a problem, I argue, in which a growing concern about man's separation and estrangement from nature began to take form: it parallels Rousseau's critique of civilization and is thus an adumbration of the romantic generation's explicit lament about the alienating effects of human rationality.

It is my contention that all these speculations about visuality and the need for an absolute visual mimesis in this phase of the German Enlightenment reveal a deep-seated obsession with establishing an *unmediated and pure visual* link to the world of experience. Such an obsession with vision and visual reciprocity, which was motivated, I believe, at least in part by what was considered to be the alienating abstract effects of language, brings to light an intriguing parallel between these eighteenth-century tracts and the

9. Meltzer, *Salome and the Dance of Writing*, 127.

recent analysis of visuality and language found in the theoretical writing of French psychoanalyst Jacques Lacan. Axiomatic to Lacan's analysis of the formation of the human ego or self is the belief that the psyche has an inborn "mirror disposition."[10] Expanding on the notion of a "looking-glass self" found in the early work of American social psychologists,[11] Lacan suggests in his influential "Mirror Stage" article that the human psyche contains a "mirror apparatus" which is instrumental in the formation of the concept of self or ego. To overcome the fragmentary character of its experience in the early months of existence, the developmental period Lacan designates as the "mirror stage," the prelinguistic human subject begins to form, with the help of its intrapsychic mirror, the concept of a unified self by making visual identifications with its phenomenal world. The so-called mirror-stage infant thus enjoys an undifferentiated visual symbiosis with its mother and environment. This visual connection, however, is broken by the acquisition of language: in learning to speak and say "I," the infant becomes increasingly aware of itself as opposed to the surrounding world rather than a (more or less) undifferentiated part of it. Because this transformation, what Lacan describes as the "deflection of the specular I to the social I,"[12] is always, to a certain degree, associated with trauma, it can produce feelings of anxiety, paranoia, and aggression and even a regressive longing to return to the prelinguistic security of mirror-stage visual identifications with the phenomenal world.

One could argue that, seen in this light, the frequent occurrence of metaphors of visual reciprocity, mirrors, and other reflecting surfaces in the aesthetic and philosophical tracts of the German Enlightenment is a compensatory gesture or subliminal attempt to

10. See Lacan, *Ecrits*, 1–7, 16–22.
11. See Muller and Richardson, *Lacan and Language*, 37.
12. Lacan, *Ecrits*, 5.

counter an incipient modern skepticism about language, which, some 250 years later, is reformulated in the discourse of Lacanian psychoanalysis. The poignant discontent with the abstract effects of language emerging in these mid-eighteenth-century texts would reveal a deep-seated desire to reverse the alienating effects of language so as to (fancifully) recuperate the unitary world of visual plenitude and security which characterizes the human subject before the acquisition of language, before the traumatic "deflection of the specular I to the social I."

Pictures and Poetry

Und da ich über die schweigenden Wasser bog,
sah ich daß mich mein Antlitz verlassen [hat].
—Georg Trakl[13]

Though the problematics of representation had become an important philosophical issue over 250 years ago, Western philosophy is still in the process of working out the details of what epistemology and the sciences of man might be without the discourse of pictures and mirrors. Indeed, it was not until the early twentieth century, when the problematics of representation became the acute crisis of representation, that various forms of philosophical discourse and semiotic analysis began to unpack the metaphorics of pictures which had for so long been so deeply entrenched in the Western discourse of ideas.

The development of Ludwig Wittgenstein's philosophical writings is exemplary of how the crisis of representation at the beginning of this century led to a dismantling of the epistemology of pictures. In 1922 Wittgenstein published his first major philosophical treatise, the *Logisch-philosophische Abhandlung,* or *Tractatus,* as

13. "And as I bent over the silent waters, I saw that my face had left me" (1:169).

it is known in the Anglo-Saxon world. Under the guidance of Bertrand Russell at Cambridge, Wittgenstein here presented a complex logical analysis of language—his so-called picture theory—which, he believed, answered once and for all the growing skepticism about language. The key to his picture theory argument is the notion that language and reality share a "logical form." "That which any *picture* [*Bild*] . . . must have in common with reality, in order to de*pict* it—whether correctly or not—is the logical form, that is, the form of reality."[14] This quotation indicates—though the full argument cannot, of course, be presented here—that Wittgenstein assumed language to have a picturing and representational function that tightly (logically) binds it to reality. Wittgenstein, not unlike his predecessors in the German Enlightenment—and perhaps for similar reasons—privileged man's "mirror disposition." His attempt to preserve the objectivity of epistemology by grounding it solidly in representation suggests that his earlier work may also have been under the sway of a subliminal wish to counter the effects of a (traumatic) acquisition of language.

In any case, sixteen years later Wittgenstein published his second major work, *Philosophical Investigations,* which, as he indicated in the book's preface, was a response to "grave mistakes in what I wrote in that first book."[15] In this later work he spurned his earlier project and any related attempt to understand language in terms of pictorial models and strove to articulate a nonvisual (nonrepresentational) model of language. Language, he had come to believe, has no single function that determines or underlies its many and varied uses: it is, rather, an aggregate of diverse "language games" (*Sprachspiele*) whose flexible rules generate the sense of the game or play (*Spiel*). The point is simple but laden with implications: deter-

14. Wittgenstein, *Logisch-philosophische Abhandlung,* par. 2.18; the English translation appeared as *Tractatus Logico-Philosophicus.*
15. Wittgenstein, *Philosophical Investigations,* vi.

minate meaning does not, strictly speaking, exist, because what an utterance means is always relative to any number of "language games" embedded in various cultural and behavioral "forms of life"; meaning is not a picture, but rather the product of use. Summing up in his trademark aphoristic style, he writes: "*By itself,* every sign is dead. *What* gives it its life? In use it is *alive.*"[16]

Taken as a whole, Wittgenstein's philosophy, with its shift in underlying metaphoric analogy from picture to play-game, exemplifies a definitive break with the epistemological discourse of visuality. But there is more to this metaphoric shift. In dropping representation out of philosophic discourse, Wittgenstein's work registers a concept that emerges almost everywhere in twentieth-century thought and might even be considered fundamental to the human condition in the modern and postmodern eras: relativity. Without the representational synchronization of words and world—words and pictures or words and vision—the conscious subject loses its epistemological anchor and is set free in a sea of relativity where meaning and truth are a function of, in poststructuralist terminology, the indeterminate free play of differential signifiers.

In the second half of this book I explore how the difficult poetry of Georg Trakl also registers this relativity. Here I work to articulate how his densely imagistic verse, replete with metaphors of visual reciprocity—mirrors, reflecting surfaces, and eyes—is firmly rooted in the problematics of representation which have transformed the epistemological horizon of our century. It is my contention that Trakl's fascination with the mirror, what likely prompted Rainer Maria Rilke, one of Trakl's first critics, to characterize this work as a "mirror-image world" (*Spiegelbild-Welt*),[17] closely aligns his work not only with certain strains of twentieth-

16. Ibid., par. 432.
17. Quoted by Storck, "Arbeitsgespräche," 158.

century language philosophy but also with the psychoanalytic discourse that has articulated what could be called the mythology of the mirror stage. By focusing on the psychological implications of Trakl's (narcissistic) interest in images denoting vision and visual reciprocity, I argue that the metaphoric function of the mirror is of central significance in his particular "poetological" exploration of the wellsprings of poetry.[18]

My analysis of Trakl's poetry focuses on a small selection of poems which highlight certain phases and trends of his short career. I follow generally the periodization of his work that links his aesthetic breakthrough around 1912 to an intense reading of a German translation of the late nineteenth-century French poet Arthur Rimbaud. I argue that Trakl's encounter with Rimbaud's symbolist poetry provided him with the vocabulary and poetic model to develop his own, nonlinear style. This breakthrough, which I characterize in broad structural terms as a paradigm shift from the narrative-representational (syntagmatic) axis of language to the associative-connotative (paradigmatic) axis, also marks Trakl's definitive break from the dominant nineteenth-century German tradition of confessional poetry known as *Erlebnislyrik*.

In his earliest writing—well before the breakthrough—Trakl's work shows clear signs of a problematic relation to language, which, I argue from a psycholinguistic standpoint, engenders various images of visuality and visual reciprocity (or their absence) and fanciful notions of a prelinguistic realm of harmonious sound and luminous colors. Recorded in the linear structure of confessional poetry, these images are, in the main, descriptive and egocentric first-person pronouncements. Following his Rimbaud breakthrough, this pronounced egocentric character markedly drops off

18. The term "poetological" corresponds to the German critical concept "poetologisch" and designates any aspect of a poetic text which reflects upon poetry, language, or itself.

as the paradigmatic axis begins to dominate. From 1912 on, Trakl becomes increasingly accomplished at using the impersonal paradigmatic axis and is able to tap into something like what Julia Kristeva refers to as a preconscious "semiotic" language, an impersonal dimension, which, she claims, is "a heterogeneousness to meaning" and opposed to the "symbolic" language of the conscious, social ego.[19] This paradigm shift may move Trakl's poetic production closer to a fanciful prelinguistic realm of pure sound, but it can do nothing to satisfy his longing for a prelinguistic state of visual reciprocity. The underlying stress associated with language is not resolved, and so visual images continue to flow right up to his very last poems. It is, moreover, this particular problematic of visuality, I believe, which underlies the profound ambivalence expressed in the many optical images of (good or bad, frightful or reassuring, sinister or divine, broken or whole) visual reciprocity found in his writing. It is as if Trakl's psyche creates or imagines the narcissistic security of a prelinguistic mirror-stage visual link to its environment, only to recognize this as a wishful projection, a beautiful but impossible myth engendered by the estranged state of a human psyche that must renounce the sensory in favor of the symbolic.

Though my analysis of this paradigm shift is essentially philosophical in nature, I believe that one cannot read this poetry in total (New Critical) isolation of the poet's trauma-filled existence—of clinically diagnosed schizophrenia, drug addiction, alcoholism, and ultimately suicide—without missing a psychological dimension that is essential to the understanding and appreciation of his writing. Trakl's work, I show, warrants and in fact necessitates a loosening of the often strict methodological separation of biography and poetic production. The basic thrust of my readings is thus synthetic, in that it works to elaborate how his linguistic break-

19. Kristeva, *Desire in Language*, 133.

through is a unique convergence of intellectual history and personal trauma. I do not, very importantly, attempt simplistically to derive poetry from pathology or symbol from symptom, for such approaches miss, among other things, the effective *poetic* power and the sensuous aesthetic allure which this dark and repetitive poetry of richly melodious assonances and alliterations holds for its readers. Rather, by tracing out various strands in a web of frequently recurring but always slightly different paradigmatic ties between words, phrases, images, and the like, I try to demonstrate how the sensitive reader can begin to grasp a level of linguistic-psychological significance, which, though rooted in Trakl's psychobiography and historical situation, belongs, strictly speaking, neither to the reader nor to the text in itself; his "disjunctive" and "obscure" poems present a potential field of significance, a potential psychological meeting place for reader and text. Trakl's poetry may, as one critic put it, resemble scars,[20] and it may even begin in sickness, but this is not where it leads. Its destination is, to borrow Roland Barthes's term, the "zero degree" of modernist literature in which poetic words become "an act without immediate past, without environment, and which hold[] forth only the dense shadow of reflexes from all sources which are associated with it."[21] Trakl's mature verse issues from the "shadow of reflexes" associated with, among other things, his life and era; it is a poetic speech act that engages its readers in a highly productive psychological dialogue.

If one reads Trakl's poetry as one would the *Erlebnislyrik* of the German classical-romantic tradition, expecting to find a unifying narrative moment, this verse will seem unintelligible and obscure. The difficulty encountered in reading Trakl's poetry is the result of a modern poetic diction which has incisively disengaged itself from the representational epistemology of mirrors and has become, to

20. Graziano, "Introduction," in *Georg Trakl*, 10.
21. Barthes, *Writing Degree Zero*, 47–48.

borrow Kristeva's term, a "heterogeneousness" to the symbolic meaning of everyday social discourse. It is, as such, a poetic response to the early twentieth-century crisis of representation, a response that demonstrates the psychological power that can be tapped when the dichotomy between vision and speech is no longer seen as a debilitating insufficiency of words but rather as the possibility of saying and experiencing something else. Trakl's verse will seem less uncompromising if one approaches it with positive values, asking not what it fails to do, but rather what it succeeds in doing in the space opened up by the visual dis-synchronization of words and world.

PART ONE

Poetics and the Mirror

CHAPTER I

Prelude on Difficulty

"Let's hear it," said Humpty Dumpty. "I can explain all the poems that ever were invented—and
a good many that haven't been invented just yet."—
Lewis Carroll, *Through the Looking-Glass*

BECAUSE HUMPTY DUMPTY is so clever at explaining words,
Alice decides to solicit his help in understanding a *difficult,* in her
words, a *"rather* hard" poem, which, as she muses, "seems to fill
my head with ideas—only I don't exactly know what they are!"[1]
Hearing such a humble confession, this egg-shaped bundle of
words cannot resist demonstrating his exegetical acumen and so
he invites her to recite the poem. Alice begins,

> 'Twas brillig, and the slithy toves
> Did gyre and gimble in the wabe:
> All mimsy were the borogoves,
> And the mome raths outgrabe.

Here Humpty interrupts her recitation to interject some interpretative commentary, blustering, "There are plenty of hard words
there. '*Brillig*' means four o'clock in the afternoon—the time when
you begin *broiling* things for dinner" (270). One cannot help but
be amused by the cocky certainty with which Humpty explains this

1. Carroll, *Annotated Alice,* 197. Further references to this work appear in the
text.

peculiar word. With no hesitation he simply clarifies for Alice *brillig*'s very specific meaning; understanding, his actions imply, presupposes knowing the proper sense of any and all terms of a language. Poetic words are no exception. Difficulty arises only when one is not familiar with a term's proper meaning. And so to help Alice master this poem, Humpty deems it necessary to halt the recitation and fill in the gaps in her vocabulary. In the process he becomes a translator; he clarifies the strange—*brillig*—by converting or translating it into the familiar vocabulary of everyday discourse, "four o'clock in the afternoon."

Convinced of his infallible knowledge of words, Alice ventures further and asks what the puzzling words "slithy" and "toves" might mean. With equal alacrity Humpty again elucidates proper meaning by converting these words into the familiar terms of everyday language. With "toves," however, one begins to suspect that this translation method might be a bit forced, if not ridiculous, for "toves," he professes, "are something like badgers—they're something like lizards—and they're something like corkscrews" (271). By resorting to such apparent contortions to render these words determinate, Humpty chooses three concrete object-words ("badgers," "lizards," "corkscrews") whose high referential potential might overcome the slippery nonreferentiality of those difficult poetic terms. In other words, he wants to keep its language specific and determinate so that it might effectively *narrate* information about a particular state of affairs, that is, about certain reptilian corkscrews that resemble badgers. Poetry, like everyday language, must talk about some*thing*. Reading the "hard" words in poems, he assumes, is simply a matter of decoding and converting poetically disguised expressions into recognizable referential speech in which each word contributes to the representational *narrative* import of the whole expression.

To be sure, narration is one of the basic modes of everyday

language. Speakers communicate by telling stories, by sequentially recounting information about some particular state of affairs. The narrative mode entails as such (at least) the illusion of sequential order and a cohesive message that corresponds in some fashion to the narrative intention of the speaking subject. But it also entails, as its Greek root *gnarus* implies, a form of *knowing*. In narration the speaker uses knowledge that reflects his or her particular culture or language community's shared framework of values, concepts, and ideas, in short, a shared worldview and epistemology.[2] Humpty's translation method is thus an attempt to accommodate the peculiar words of Alice's poem by bringing them within the bounds of his culture's linguistically articulated knowledge of a world inhabited by, among other things, lizards, badgers, and corkscrews. Humpty might even agree with the sentimentalist view of poetry which holds that poems elicit feelings. This would not mean, however, that poetry can do without the primary narrativity. For Humpty, like Goethe, the bottom line of poetry is the prose of a story line. "I honor rhythm as well as rhyme, through which poetry becomes poetry," Goethe wrote, "however, the really profound and thoroughly effective, the truly edifying and stimulating, is that which remains for the poet, when he translates into prose."[3] This *prose of poetry*, Goethe explains elsewhere, "is decidedly historical"; it is the foundation of *Erlebnislyrik* which is firmly grounded in the "story" of the poet's life experience.[4]

After quickly dispensing with the other difficult words of the first stanza, Humpty attempts to steer Alice away from this perplexing poem by reciting his own verse, which happens to be a

2. "To raise the question of narration," Hayden White asserts, "is to invite reflection on the very nature of culture and, possibly, even on the nature of humanity itself" ("Value of Narrativity," 1). Narration is always closely aligned with a culture's worldview and involves a translation of, in White's terms, "*knowing* into telling" (1).

3. Goethe, *Dichtung und Wahrheit*, in *Goethes Werke*, pt. 3, bk. 11.

4. See Goethe, *Weimarer Ausgabe*, 1:173.

ballad with an unmistakably clear narrative line. It is revealing that Humpty avoids Alice's "obscure" poem by diverting the discussion into the familiar territory of the traditional ballad. He, like many modern critics, is much more at home in a traditional form of poetry which does not confound his narrative expectations with the apparently indeterminate semantic possibilities of *gyring* and *gimbling slithy toves.*

"Obscure" and "unintelligible" have become in the last fifty years catchwords for describing modern poetry. Hugo Friedrich, in his epoch-making *Die Struktur der modernen Lyrik,* listed them ("Dunkelheit" and "Unverständlichkeit") among the salient characteristics of modernist (1850–1950) poetry on the first page of his work.[5] These catchwords, along with his other well-known "negative categories," derive, I would venture, from an anachronistic mismatch of values and subject matter. If one approaches, as Friedrich's analysis reveals, difficult modernist poetry with expectations and values appropriate to the canonical standard of *Goethezeit Erlebnislyrik*—expectations and values elicited by classical-romantic poetry of the early nineteenth century—the results will generally be negative: one will see how modern poetry is not *Erlebnislyrik.* Obscurity and unintelligibility are the negative signs for, among other things, the non-narrative character of much modernist poetry. It is interesting that Friedrich confesses that his sympathies lie with Goethe rather than with modern poets: "I am myself not avant-garde. I feel much more comfortable with Goethe than with T. S. Elliot."[6] The influential Swiss critic Emil Staiger also favors (like Friedrich) *Goethezeit* poetry over "modern." His preference borders on an aversion to much of the "unhumanistic" poetry of the twentieth century, "whose reason for being seems to be a wallowing in the horrible." And, Staiger contends, "that

5. Friedrich, *Struktur der modernen Lyrik,* 15.
6. Ibid., 10.

22

which is solely modern becomes quickly dated. And the kind of modernism which is most perplexing, is the quickest to become dated."[7]

In any case, the "obscurity" of Alice's poem causes Humpty to take refuge in the security of a "Goethean" model of poetic expression. The ballad, Goethe believed, was the most basic form of poetry, "the original egg" (*das Ur-Ei*) from which all other poetic genres derive.[8] In a way, Humpty's approach to Alice's "hard" words and his resorting to the narrativity of the ballad parody the narrative expectations with which many critics approach the uncompromising language of difficult poetry. Reading difficult poems such as Alice's becomes a deciphering project, a matter of decoding the author's encoded narrative. Complexities vanish as the interpretative keys are found that unlock the hidden meaning—meaning which is ultimately the product of the author's willful control and manipulation of the various semantic levels of language. Interestingly, before they had come to speak of poetry, Humpty had made it very clear to Alice that speakers must control, "master," their language. This is one reason why he is so adamant about providing Alice with such concise definitions: he must show her that he is in complete control of language. "I can manage the whole lot of them," Humpty grandiosely boasts about verbs and adjectives (267).

Let us now look at another difficult poem, one written by Georg Trakl about a decade after Lewis Carroll's death.

Gesang einer gefangenen Amsel
für Ludwig von Ficker

Dunkler Odem im grünen Gezweig.
Blaue Blümchen umschweben das Antlitz

7. Staiger, "Literatur und Öffentlichkeit," 94.
8. Goethe, *Hamburger Ausgabe,* 1:400.

Des Einsamen, den goldnen Schritt
Ersterbend unter dem Ölbaum.
Aufflattert mit trunknem Flügel die Nacht.
So leise blutet Demut,
Tau, der langsam tropft vom blühenden Dorn.
Strahlender Arme Erbarmen
Umfängt ein brechendes Herz.[9]

[Song of a Captive Blackbird // Dark breath in the green bough. /
Little blue blossoms waft around the face / Of the lonely one, the
golden footstep / Dying under the olive tree. / Night flutters up on a
drunken wing. / Humility bleeds so gently, / Dew, dripping slowly
from the blossoming thorn. / The mercy of radiant arms / Embraces a
breaking heart.]

This poem would present Humpty Dumpty with a lot of *toves* to
translate and organize into a cohesive narrative statement. He
would have to clarify for Alice the meaning of, among other
things, the night which "flutters up with a drunken wing" or
blooming thorns from which dew slowly drips. If he could accomplish this in specific and referential terms he would then have to tie
these peculiar expressions to the mercy of beaming arms, to quietly
bleeding humility, and to the golden footstep dying beneath an
olive tree. And Humpty would get little help from the syntax, the
glue of ordinary narration. This constellation of loosely connected
images seems to be somewhat randomly arranged. It appears that
one could almost rearrange the order of various lines without ap-
preciably altering the import of the poem. Certain elements, like
"the golden footstep" and the "humility," have no readily discern-
ible syntactic function. What is the subject for which "the golden
footstep" is the direct object? Is "the golden footstep" an apposi-

9. Trakl, *Dichtungen und Briefe*, 1:135. Citations hereafter in the text refer to
this edition.

tive for "the face of the lonely one"? How does the clause "Dew, dripping slowly from the blossoming thorn" connect with the bleeding humility preceding it? Are the two clauses related, or do they just happen to fall in the same sentence? This open syntactical structure cuts through another narrative principle—context determination. Each image or trope appears to stand relatively independent of the surrounding tropes and images. The contextual background in and against which images and phrases ordinarily take on significance provides no immediately apparent clues as to how things fit together. "The golden footstep" can be both a direct object and an appositive; the context does not indicate which, and so the image remains irreducibly polyfunctional.

A look at the manuscript drafts of this poem would not help Humpty unravel these "troublesome" features and, if anything, would further compound his headaches.[10] In an earlier version Trakl used, for example, "crimson wing" instead of "drunken wing," "the heart bleeds to death" instead of "humility bleeds," and alternately "the dying one's crash" and "Icarus's crash" for "a breaking heart." Words and phrases seem to be substituted, switched, and deleted at random. The semantic links that tie "crimson" to "drunken" and "breaking heart" to "Icarus's crash" are open to speculation. Icarus's complete absence in the final version is especially telltale. What might have provided some grounds for a sketchy narrative framework—Icarus's drunken flight, his befeathered arms beaming in the searing sun, his frightful crash and broken heart, and their relation to an imprisoned blackbird yearning for flight—is conspicuously missing from the final version. The absence of this mythic story figure and its ties to a long narrative tradition register this poem's difference from a kind of poetry which, in Goethe's terms, is "decidedly historical." The narrative moment, signaled by Icarus's absence, has been removed.

10. Ibid., 2:238–39.

Humpty's narrative expectations would need all the king's horses and all the king's men to put this one together again.

At this point, Humpty might, if he had his wits about him, tell Alice that these perplexing expressions are metaphors, that they are figures of speech which compare, relate, or connect conventionally disparate things. "The essence of metaphor," he could quote George Lakoff and Mark Johnson, "is understanding one kind of thing in terms of another."[11] Theories of metaphor, he might further explain to Alice, generally posit a comparison or juxtaposition of two things. He could thus argue that by bringing "humility" and "bleeds" together, Trakl seizes upon a semantic link between these words to say something that otherwise might have taken many more words. In using such metaphors, Humpty might continue by calling on the authority and wisdom of Aristotle, Trakl was able to bring to light heretofore unseen similarities, for metaphor, Aristotle believed, is a kind of name-switching which yields new perceptions of resemblances between two things.[12] Metaphor, Humpty might then conclude, is the possibility of saying, by means of a fresh comparison, *more* with *less*. It is a matter of getting language to work for its "master." (Humpty Dumpty's speech has a peculiar metaphorical quality about it, in that he often says one thing and means something else. When Alice expresses wonderment at this zany figurality, Humpty retorts, "When I make a word do a lot of work like that . . . I always pay it extra" [187]. Humpty's "metaphors" save him many words and thus deserve credit for the extra work they do.)

But what, Alice might rightfully ask, is common to "humility" and "bleeds"? What has been compared, what names have been switched, and what has been expressed? Is "bleeding humility"

11. Lakoff and Johnson, *Metaphors We Live By*, 5.

12. Aristotle defined metaphor as a process whereby one thing is "given the name that belongs to something else" (*Poetics*, 1457b), which then results in "a perception of resemblances" (*Poetics*, 1458b).

even a metaphor? These questions would be difficult for Humpty to answer; Alice's questions go to the heart of the matter, for a metaphor's success depends upon the recipient's recognition of a common link—the *tertium comparationis*. In, for instance, the metaphor "Susan is a rose," Susan is given a name that belongs to something else (a rose) to set up a comparison between these two elements. Although this metaphor is not situated in a context that would help to delimit its *tertium* (or *tertia*), it is easy to see that beauty, sweetness, and other pleasant attributes might be the *tertia* linking Susan to the rose. Though it is clearly not a textbook example of a metaphor in which one thing is given the name of another, one must say in Humpty's defense that there is nonetheless something metaphoric about ascribing to humility the ability to bleed. And though humility and bleeding may invite a productive speculation as to what features allow for such a metaphoric linking and comparison of *bluten* and *Demut,* Humpty would be hard-pressed to delineate, without resorting to his zany figurality, what *tertia* underlie this fusion of semantically disparate terms. The surrounding context provides no helpful clues, and one may even wonder whether the "dripping dew" is another metaphoric substitution for bleeding humility.

The open-ended or plural character of much of Trakl's figural language has generated a plurality of differing and often contradictory assessments. Clemens Heselhaus, for example, attributed the perplexing "kaleidoscopic" character of Trakl's imagery to his excessive use of drugs. He claims that because Trakl proceeded "more or less according to the model of drug-induced visions," he was able to break through to a "pure metaphorics" (*reine Metaphorik*) whereby "the whole poem becomes itself a metaphor."[13] This *Metaphorik* of which Heselhaus talks is pure (or absolute) because it cannot be rendered into literal language. The idea that

13. Heselhaus, "Das metaphorische Gedicht von Georg Trakl," 229, 254.

some metaphors cannot be literally paraphrased or definitively analyzed (because of the complexity of their effects or resonances) is not a new one. The issue in the absolute metaphor is, however, not directly a matter of effect but more basically the impossibility of delineating what is being compared in the first place. Because such a global and all-encompassing *reine Metaphorik* in which the whole poem becomes a metaphor seems to be more akin to allegory than metaphor, one has to wonder whether *Metaphorik* is a suitable description for Trakl's figurative expression. Moreover, does such a broad designation really help to elucidate the perplexing character of Trakl's images and phrases, of bleeding humility?

Eckhard Philipp explicitly questions the usefulness of metaphor in characterizing Trakl's figures. Although he does not abandon the traditional concept, he attempts to adjust it with his cumbersome "regressive-polyvalent metaphor" concept.[14] Walther Killy takes a different tack. Rather than stretching, as do Heselhaus and Eckhard, the definition of metaphor to accommodate the semantic peculiarities of Trakl's figural language, Killy comes to the conclusion that Trakl's most perplexing tropes are hermetic ciphers—"absolute ciphers." They are encoded messages that cannot be decoded. Such *Chiffren* arise, Killy argues, when unlikely adjective-noun combinations are made. When a noun like "wing," for example, is qualified by "drunken" "in such a way that the sense of this qualification is neither natural nor intelligible," an absolute cipher is created.[15] And Killy emphatically warns: "It would be a disastrous

14. Philipp, *Funktion des Wortes in den Gedichten Georg Trakls,* 108–23. See also Schier's lengthy discussion of metaphor and figure in *Die Sprache Georg Trakls,* 45–75. Though Schier rejects the appropriateness of metaphor for characterizing Trakl's imagery, his rather vague notion of "figural language" describes more than anything the absence in Trakl's verse of the romantic belief in an analogical relationship between mind and nature.

15. Killy, *Über Georg Trakl,* 119.

mistake to believe that this qualification can be ascertained."[16] Once again, questions arise. Does an undecipherable cipher explain any more than Heselhaus's global and indeterminate *reine Metaphorik*? Does it even make sense to talk of ciphers that *cannot* be deciphered—how are readers to know that they are dealing with a cipher in the first place? Was Trakl spinning out a secret language with an uncrackable code? Could such a hermetically sealed language, one with so little regard for readers' everyday understanding of language, continue to hold their interest for any length of time? Perhaps, but most likely not. Trakl's poetry continues to speak to its readers, not because it is impenetrable or because it is a fascinating anomaly but because it triggers responses that *begin* with our everyday understanding of language.

The contradictory nature of these respected critics' characterizations suggests that traditional categories may be unsuited and inappropriate for dealing with Trakl's more unusual or difficult figures. As early as 1948 Wolfgang Kayser chose Trakl, in his monumental work *Das sprachliche Kunstwerk,* to demonstrate the inadequacy of the traditional understanding of metaphor.[17] Some years later, Richard Brinkmann voiced a more general dissatisfaction with traditional figural classifications, writing of Trakl's "kind of imagery" (*Bildlichkeit*): "I know as yet no appropriate concept. The applicability of the various forms and distortions of metaphorical expression found in Trakl research is still far from being adequately defined."[18] This inappropriateness stems, at least in part, from the inadequacy of cipher or metaphor (or symbol) to describe Trakl's nonlinear form of expression. Cipher, on one hand, presupposes a coded message; metaphor, on the other hand, presupposes a message or idea expressed by means of comparison

16. Ibid.
17. Kayser, *Das sprachliche Kunstwerk,* 124.
18. Brinkmann, "'Abstrakte' Lyrik im Expressionismus," 101.

or substitution. All of these concepts further assume that this language is primarily representational, that it re-presents or narrates ideas that preceded the act of speaking or writing. When pushed to articulate what is re-presented, however, critics inevitably demur, claiming that its content is ineffable, *unsäglich,* that his verse points beyond the "vanishing point" (*Fluchtpunkt*) of ordinary language; or they enter into vague and (wildly varying) impressionistic speculations about this poetry's existential-metaphysical or theological implications. This problem is, to a degree, also manifest in Hans-Georg Kemper's well-received and acclaimed book *Georg Trakls Entwürfe: Aspekte zu ihrem Verständnis.* Although Kemper has done much to dispel Killy's unintelligibility thesis, his conclusion about Trakl is another variation on the *unsäglich* theme. Trakl, Kemper feels, was a mystical poet who pushed on the boundary of language. Because the "ineffable" ends up being the content of this poetry, "silence" (*Schweigen*), Kemper reasons, must be the "goal and bounds of this poetry."[19] Traditional criteria thus not only lead to contradictory characterizations but also, in the final analysis, to negative results. In recent years, however, this cul-de-sac of negative appraisals has been avoided by critics, who have largely abandoned the traditional categories of metaphor and symbol. Hildegard Steinkamp, for example, has recently elaborated the poet's "mythopoetic idiolect" by exploring, from the vantage of an everyday understanding of language, certain immanent spatiotemporal regularities in Trakl's use of landscape words.[20] Indeed, promising avenues of understanding present themselves when Trakl's writing is viewed from an epistemological standpoint germane to the modernist movement of the twentieth century.

19. Kemper, *Georg Trakls Entwürfe,* 194.
20. See Steinkamp, *Die Gedichte Georg Trakls,* and her "Trakl's Landscape Code," esp. 157–60.

CHAPTER 2

Poetry and the Mirror

The word [literature] is of a recent date, as is also, in our culture, the isolation of particular language whose peculiar mode of being is "literary."—Michel Foucault, *The Order of Things*

The Mirror of Nature

NEAR THE MIDDLE of the eighteenth century man's felicitous affiliation with a stable world at the end of his gaze began to show signs of strain. Within a rather short stretch of time the inherited notion of a secure *res cognitans*—the nonmaterial mind—whose function was constituted by its ability to *mirror*, that is, to represent to itself the material *res extensa*—became increasingly problematic; the once assumed complicity between mind and world, between man's rational vision of the world and the assumed rational order of things, could no longer be taken for granted.

In his book *Philosophy and the Mirror of Nature*, Richard Rorty argues that René Descartes was largely responsible for the "invention of the mind."[1] Descartes, Rorty believes, was the first Western philosopher to argue for a purely nonmaterial "stuff," which functioned like an internal "mirror of nature" upon which the "Eye of the Mind" gazed (39). This specular metaphor, what Rorty terms the "ocular metaphor," became deeply ingrained in Western cul-

1. Rorty, *Philosophy and the Mirror of Nature*, 17–69. Further references to this work appear in the text.

31

ture's epistemological discourse and led to the general assumption that the mind was not only subordinate to the world but also bound to it by an imitative function, that is, by its capacity to produce visual representations—internal pictures—of primary visual experiences of the world.

It is no coincidence that speculations about art in the seventeenth and eighteenth centuries should revolve around the issue of mimesis.[2] By analogy to the function of the mind, art was thought to *picture* or imitate the world—it, too, was subordinate to the epistemic priority of the material realm.[3] As this picture-mirror model of human cognition began to lose force in the mid- to late eighteenth century, so did the then prevailing mimetic theories of both art and language. A reversal was taking place: Classical[4] objectivity, which had been grounded in the priority of matter over mind (object over subject), was on the verge of being replaced by a "romantic" subjectivity of mind over matter. Though M. H. Abrams is not concerned in his seminal work, *The Mirror and the Lamp,* with exploring this epistemological-aesthetic parallel, he does remark that "the movement from eighteenth- to early nineteenth-century schemes of the mind and its place in nature is indicated by a mutation of metaphors almost exactly parallel to that in contemporary

2. Abrams points out that although reflector metaphors—including the mirror—had been used by theorists to illuminate the mimetic nature of art, it was not until the Renaissance that "reference to the looking-glass is frequent and explicit" (*The Mirror and the Lamp,* 32).

3. See Herrmann's *Naturnachahmung und Einbildungskraft* for a detailed analysis of mimesis as it was understood by German literary theorists in the seventeenth and eighteenth centuries. See also Blumenberg, "'Nachahmung der Natur,'" 265–83.

4. I use Michel Foucault's term "Classical" to refer to the period between Descartes and Kant because it does not imply any one philosophical system (as would, for example "Cartesian"), nor does it involve just one intellectual movement (such as "Enlightenment"). It designates a set of general assumptions which underlie this period. See Foucault, *Order of Things,* xxiii–xxiv, 217–50. See also note 8.

discussions of the nature of art."[5] This period's rethinking of man's relation to the world, its reevaluation of mimesis and the function of language, are all part of a general epistemological event that signals the beginning of a new era. In a way, our century is still coming to terms with this event; we are still in the process of exploring the possibilities that arise when the *mirror* is removed from the center of our conceptualization of knowledge, art, and language.

The late eighteenth century was a period of intense intellectual activity for western Europe. It was a time of rebellion, of forceful breaking with the tyrannies of the past and of forging the basis for a new society and culture. Sensing the tone and fervor of these climacteric times, Friedrich Schlegel wrote in 1815 that this period's three most important "tendencies" were the French Revolution, Goethe's *Wilhelm Meister,* and Johann Fichte's *Wissenschaftlehre:* rebellion against the tyranny of an outmoded political system parallels a subjectivistic "rebellion" in philosophy and aesthetics against the "tyranny" of the rationalistic objectivity of the eighteenth century.[6]

The abruptness and magnitude of this period's intellectual upheaval has led French philosopher of intellectual history Michel Foucault to characterize it as a "rupture" in the fabric of Western thought. He asserts that between 1775 and 1825 a cross-disciplinary mutation in scientific-philosophical thought took

5. Abrams, *The Mirror and the Lamp,* 57. Abrams also points out that though mimetic theories tended to dominate until the late eighteenth century, aesthetic theorists over the last twenty-five hundred years have also advanced "objective" and "pragmatic" theories. The objective orientation considers art (and poetry) from the standpoint of the work itself, in its parts and their internal relations, whereas the pragmatic orientation considers the work in terms of its effects on the recipient. Abrams's thorough historical research also uncovers "expressive" theories that predate romantic expressive ("poet-orientation") theories by some sixteen hundred years (59).

6. Schlegel, *Kritische Friedrich-Schlegel-Ausgabe,* 198.

place, whereby the Classical view of man and knowledge was abruptly displaced by the "modern *episteme*," which still serves as the positive ground of our knowledge.[7] The key concept in Foucault's analysis of this period of rupture is representation. He suggests that the changes that swept across a wide range of diverse fields of human research were the result of a deeper, "archaeological" shift in thinking: he argues that near the end of the eighteenth century representation lost its explanatory power; it ceased to function as an axiomatic basis for human knowledge.[8] Thinkers were no longer satisfied, as they had been in the Classical Age, with simply re-presenting the visual orders of the things. Writes Foucault: "In this way, analysis has been able to show the coherence that existed, throughout the Classical Age, between the theory of representation and the theories of language, of the natural orders, and of wealth and value. It is this configuration that, from the nineteenth century onward, changes entirely; the theory of representation disappears as the universal foundation of all possible orders." Now, rather than mechanically arranging and classifying the entire visible world into tables of representative taxonomies—which was to yield a picture of the true order of the world—effort is made to uncover and understand the *organic* functions that underlie these surface "*visibilities*."[9] The Classical studies of grammar, wealth, and natural taxonomy gave way, Foucault points out, to the organic studies of philology–language philosophy, labor analysis, and biology—new disciplines that delve beneath the classified surface orders in a search for the enabling functions and

7. Foucault, *Order of Things*, 217, 221, 245. An *episteme*, Foucault explains, is "the total set of relations that unite, at a given period, the discursive practices that give rise to epistemological figures, sciences, and possibly formalized systems. . . . It is the totality of relations that can be discovered, for a given period" (*Archaeology of Knowledge*, 191).

8. Foucault, *Archaeology of Knowledge*, 135–98.

9. Foucault, *Order of Things*, xxiii; see also 217–48.

systems that make the classification of such surface structures possible in the first place.

This reevaluation of representation and the search for underlying organic function is clearly demonstrated in Kant's critical philosophy. The acquisition of knowledge, Kant was convinced, must involve more than simply re-presenting and classifying the orders of things. He set out, consequently, to uncover the subjective (and universally valid) conditions for the possibility of representation. In place of the more static Cartesian Ego, Kant posited a new model, the transcendental subject, which, rather than passively picturing the world, actively participated in the formation—synthesis—of knowledge from a multiplicity of diffuse sensory impressions. This knowledge, Kant believed, is a function of the subject's inborn conceptual makeup; it is possible only with the help of the "reine Begriffe a priori" (pure a priori concepts) of space and time and the categories of reason, the "reine Verstandesbegriffe."[10] Understanding the world was thus always a form of projection: the subject comprehended perceptual experience by structuring sensory input according to its own innate categories and concepts.

By seeking to justify and understand man's knowledge claims— in asking for their underlying organic conditions for possibility— Kant made knowledge about the world relative to the human mind. The theory of passive mirroring gave way in his work to a complex theory of the subject in which knowledge, Rorty points out, is more the subject's "relation to propositions rather than to objects" (148). "With Kant," Rorty concludes, "the attempt to formulate a 'theory of knowledge' advanced half of the way toward a conception of knowledge as fundamentally 'knowing that' rather than 'knowing of'—halfway toward a conception of knowing

10. See Kant, *Kritik der reinen Vernunft*, in *Werke in 12 Bänden*, 3:134–48, 160–72.

which was not modeled on perception" (147). Knowledge, in other words, begins with the Kantian critique to take on a linguistic character. Words, rather than pictures—mental images—are its medium.

Before Kant, Classical thinkers had generally believed that words were derivative, being graphic and arbitrary representations of (primary) mental representations. "We are in the habit of bringing two things together in the mind . . . whereby we make the first a sign of the second," wrote Christian Wolff in 1720. "These signs," he continues, "are called arbitrary signs."[11] If one keeps in mind that mental representations had a decidedly visual character, it is easy to see how the thinkers of this period could believe that words picture the world; they were a conventional marking and articulation of man's primary visual experience and thus referential, determinate, and symmetrical with respect to the world.[12] Words were, moreover, truly meaningful and valid only when they were causally linked—when they represented—the mental images of man's primary visual encounter with the world. Taken as a whole, language was for Classical thinkers an ensemble of discrete word units, each of which stood for a particular mental representation that could be exhaustively defined by its reference to things

11. Wolff, *Vernünftige Gedanken von GOTT,* par. 294.

12. For a detailed analysis of "classical semiotic theory" as it pertains to the German Enlightenment, see Wellbery, "Aesthetics and Semiotics in the German Enlightenment," esp. 9–17, 30–53. Wellbery demonstrates how the aesthetic writings of Baumgarten, Meier, and Lessing are rooted in (and limited by) the pervasive influence of Wolffian philosophy. All of these thinkers, he argues, were linked by the "doctrine of the arbitrary sign" (30), which is based on the assumption that linguistic signs are conventional names for clear and distinct ("pre-significative") representations. "Whatever is signified or named by a sign is given in intuition [the direct perceptual apprehension of objects in the world]. The world articulates itself in the light of reflection; language merely serves to mark the already differentiated items" (33). See also Rorty, *Philosophy and the Mirror of Nature,* chap. 4. Wellbery has published a revised version of his dissertation under the title *Lessing's Laocoon: Semiotics and Aesthetics in the Age of Reason.*

(or aspects of things) in the world. This quasi-mirroring function thus served not only as an epistemological anchor but also as a guarantee for the efficacy and determinacy of language in general.

The increased interest in questions of a language-philosophical or semiotic nature in the aesthetic and philosophical tracts of the German Enlightenment is itself the product of a growing doubt about the reliability of representation. Motivated perhaps by a subliminal need to counter the incipient failure of representation, thinkers such as Georg Friedrich Meier and Christian Wolff go to great lengths to defend the assumption that human cognition is at its most fundamental level constituted by an innate representational capacity. Metaphors of visual reciprocity and reflecting surface abound in descriptions of man's cognitive faculty. Conflating representation and perception to describe the "painterly" character of the human mind, Meier wrote in 1752 that "an idea [*representatio, perceptio*] functions like a picture, which demonstrates the inherent painterly dexterity of the human psyche." Similarly, Wolff compares the impressions given to the eye of the mind (*die anschauende Erkäntnis*) to "paintings" because both are pictures of things: "We thus also call our mental representations [*Vorstellungen*] of physical things pictures [*Bilder*]," concludes Wolff. Even a term as patently abstract as "truth," Wolff believed, was grounded in the primary *anschauende Erkäntnis* and was intelligible only "insofar as it refers to certain things, whose concept is recalled in memory, that is, which is remembered by the eye of the mind [*anschauende Erkäntnis*]."[13] Truth, representation, and perception are all intertwined and united by the picturing or mirroring function of the intellect. In grounding their epistemology in the *anschauende Erkäntnis*, the philosophers of this period modeled their theory of knowing on what they believed took place in

13. Meier, *Auszug aus der Vernunftslehre*, 76; Wolff, *Vernünftige Gedanken von GOTT*, pars. 747, 751.

the act of visual perception. Knowledge, in this scheme, was a congeries of representations, of *mirrored* duplications of the seen world.

This ardent desire in the German Enlightenment to synchronize language and world in a one-to-one reciprocal relation evinces not only a quest for Cartesian certainty (and an objectively valid form of rational discourse) but also a subliminal wish to counter the incipient doubts about man's representational capacity. Such a wish surfaces in the subjunctive mood, for example, of the following excerpt from a poem published by Barthold Heinrich Brockes in 1738. Yearning for the highly desirable natural mimesis of reflecting waters, Brockes wishes that the psyche might also be a pure reflecting surface:

> Es bilden sich des Höchsten Werke,
> Luft, Erde, Wälder, Thal und Hügel,
> Gedoppelt, wie im hellen Spiegel,
> Im stillen Wasser, wenn es rein.
> Ach möcht' im steten Wiederschein
> Auch uns're Seel' ein Wasser seyn.[14]

[The works of the most exalted kind / Air, earth, forest, valley and hill, / Form doubles, like in a luminous mirror, / In quiet waters, if they're pure. / Oh, might our souls, in constant reflection / a still water also be.]

Though Brockes was one of the most accomplished poets of "beschreibende Poesie," a painstakingly detailed form of "descriptive poetry" that sought to imitate the beauty of nature, his desire for a natural mimesis of mirror reciprocity belies an underlying uneasiness or skepticism about man's representational capacity. In other words, by idealizing a form of what might be termed *absolute visual*

14. Brockes, *Auszug der vornehmsten Gedichte aus dem Irdischen Vergnügen in Gott*, 21.

mimesis, Brockes's poetic gesture reveals an awareness, subliminal at least, that the human being's representational limitations will not allow him to achieve the goal of his poetry.

Pictures and Poetry

By juxtaposing how the incipient failure of representation manifests itself in the theoretical speculations of Johann Christoph Gottsched and Gotthold Ephraim Lessing, I elaborate in the following discussion the historical context in which a modernist view of language began to take form. I explore, in particular, how a premodernist view of language operative in Gottsched's work is called into question by implications contained in Lessing's seminal *Laokoon* essay. These implications, I believe, point ahead to a modernist understanding of language which breaks the spell of representation and fills the gap between pictures and words with the evocative potential of the paradigmatic axis of language. When these implications are viewed from a psychological standpoint, however, we begin to understand how Trakl's tormented disaffection with language is to a large degree rooted in the deeper epistemological shift that transformed the intellectual horizon at the close of the eighteenth century, at the threshold of the Modern—post-Classical—Age.

Johann Christoph Gottsched (1700–1766) was a professor of logic and metaphysics at Leipzig and one of Germany's more influential proponents of the rationalistic assumptions underlying aesthetic thought in the late Classical Age. Fundamental to his theoretical writing was the assumption that poetic language is primarily representational and that it communicates by means of the pictures of real or "probable" things it engenders in the recipient's mind. His work marks the apex of the Classical coordination of *intellectus* and *res,* word and thing.

Pervading his life's work was a strong ethical concern, motivated by the profound belief that literature could and should bring about positive changes in society. "Poetry [*Poesie*]," wrote Gottsched, "is an art in the service of truth and virtue . . . in fables it becomes a pleasant teacher of morality and in drama a painter of human life." This passage announces two notions current in the early eighteenth century, namely, that poetry is a form of painting—it is a "painter"—which functioned according to timelessly enduring principles that were in no way the arbitrary creation of the human mind. They were, rather, a reflection of the preestablished harmony of nature, having "their basis in the unchanging nature of things."[15]

Gottsched devoted his theoretical work to promoting these principles. Relatively early in his career (1729) he had already written his most influential work, the *Dichtkunst,* in which he elucidated and exemplified, as the book's subtitle indicates, "the general rules of poetry [*Poesie*]." Although his was by no means the first such endeavor—Joachim Birke counts seventy *Regelkodizes* written after Martin Opitz and before Gottsched—Gottsched was the first to attempt to raise literary study to the status of a philosophical discipline.[16] By consciously grounding his approach in the conceptual matrix of Wolffian philosophy, Gottsched attempted to break with the traditional identification of poetics and rhetoric. "A critic," he wrote, "is a scholar who has grasped philo-

15. Gottsched, *Der Biedermann Zweiter Teil,* 123. In the eighteenth century the word *Poesie* was not a genre designation but a general term referring to all literary art (lyric, epic, and drama). "Literature" would be a suitable candidate for translation were it not that *Poesie* in the eighteenth century did not include prose as we understand it today (although the "less serious" novel was on the rise at this time). Accordingly, I have chosen to avoid the archaic English term "poesy" in favor of "poetry." This decision can be justified in part by the fact that the literary genres— epic and drama—of the eighteenth century were generally closer, because of their versified form, to what is understood today as poetry.

16. Birke, "Gottscheds Neuorientierung," 560.

sophically the rules of the arts, and thus is able to rationally view and correctly judge the beauty and failures of existing masterpieces and artwork."[17] Gottsched thus set the philosophical stage for the very productive literary disputes in the later eighteenth century.[18]

In the second chapter of the *Dichtkunst,* Gottsched portrays the ideal poet as a disciplined man of reason, who, when putting this reason to public use, never falls prey to the potentially dangerous *Feuer der Phantasie.* The poet, Gottsched warns, must be on constant guard lest this fire burn out of control: "An overheated imagination makes nonsensical poets [*unsinnige Dichter*], so long as the fires of fantasy are not tempered by healthy reason. Not all ideas are equal in beauty, naturalness, and probability. The dictates of rationality must be their judge" (108).

One notices here that the imagination/fantasy pair stands in opposition to and necessarily precedes the reason/rationality pair. "Ideas," the products of "imagination," are primary, that is, they are the raw material, so to speak, upon which the tempering and judging actions of reason and rationality work in the production of poetry.[19] That such an apparent priority should exist seemed to trouble Gottsched, and so to nip in the bud any valorization of imagination, he is careful to warn that an overproductive imagina-

17. Gottsched, Introduction to the *Dichtkunst.* Further references to the *Dichtkunst* are given in the text.

18. Bruno Markwardt characterizes Gottsched's philosophical turn as a transition from *Regel* to *Gesetz,* i.e., from a poetics of *prescription* to a poetics of *description* and understanding (*Geschichte der deutschen Poetik,* 34).

19. Hans Peter Herrmann points out that Gottsched's interest in the imagination can also be traced to the rhetorical tradition of the seventeenth century. Taking issue with Bruno Markwardt's contention that Gottsched's interest in the irrational evidence of the "preliminary stages of an evaluation of talent," Herrmann remarks: "What we find are not the incipient forms of modern sensibilities, but rather the remnants of notions from antiquity and the Renaissance regarding the irrational characteristics of human being and the peculiarity of the artistic creativity" (*Naturnachahmung und Einbildungskraft,* 278).

tion is the source of a destructive fire and, even worse, the cause of "nonsensical poets." Thanks to the healthy flame-retarding character of reason and rationality, however, this pernicious fire can be safely contained.

Gottsched's uneasiness with "imagination" and the "fires of fantasy" stems, at least in part, from the fact that imagination could jostle the notion that language is an objectively valid representation of the world, a challenge which, if taken seriously, could unsettle the Classical view of man and his relation to the world. Similar to Wolff, who grounded his rationalistic epistemology in the *anschauende Erkäntnis,* Gottsched also assumes the primacy of visual perception in the workings of the mind. It is for this reason that he was so wary of an overheated poetic imagination: the random and intrusive character of its "ideas" seemed to have no basis in the rational order and harmony of perceived nature. Their obtrusive character thus threatened to loosen language from its visual rootedness in the natural orders of the world, which called into question the determinacy of language. By filtering the products of the imagination through the faculties of reason, however, Gottsched keeps poetry determinately tied to the perceived world. He also diffuses the potential threat to his worldview which was implied in the apparent priority of imagination over rationality. It is also especially revealing that Gottsched believed "wit" (*Witz*) to be a quasi-perceptual capacity, which "perceives the similarities between things. . . . It entails astuteness [*Scharfsinnigkeit*], which is the capacity to perceive those things which a person of dulled senses [*stumpfen Sinn*] or impaired reason cannot" (102). This quasi-perceptual capacity, moreover, is directly related to one's ability to make sense: "The greater one's wit, the more sensible one's thoughts [*sinnreiche Gedanken*]" (102). That he capitalizes on—or perhaps is unaware of—the ambiguity of *Sinn,* the "sense" of language as well as the "sense" of perception ("Scharfsin-

nigkeit," "stumpfen Sinn," "unsinnige Dichter," "sinnreiche Gedanken") demonstrates the assumed inextricability of sense (meaning) and sense (perception).

The centrality of visual perception in cognition convinced Gottsched and other thinkers in the Classical Age that the rational mind
was best fitted, if not *only* fitted, to deal with impressions or
representations of the visible world. They thought, to speak with
Rorty, of knowledge as a relationship between persons and objects: "Given that picture . . . the notion that it [the faculty of
understanding] is fitted to deal with some sorts of objects and not
with others [makes sense]. It makes even more sense if one is convinced that this faculty is something like a wax tablet upon which
objects make impressions, and if one thinks of 'having an impression' as in itself a knowing rather than a causal antecedent of knowing" (142). If we now place Gottsched in this context of "knowing
of," where knowing is having impressions or representations of
real objects, we can see why he was so intent upon reducing imagination to a perceptual capacity. For him, the perception-oriented
faculty of understanding was predominantly vision-oriented and
hence "fitted" to understand only "some sorts of objects," that is,
possible objects of the natural world which could be seen. Consequently, those products of the imagination which stray too far
from the "natural" or "probable," that is, those that cannot pass
for visual copies of probable things, will have trouble making sense
to the vision-oriented faculties of understanding: "An overheated
imagination makes nonsensical poets. . . . Not all ideas are equal in
beauty, naturalness, and probability." By grounding the imagination in a quasi-perceptual process, Gottsched attempted to keep
the creations of poetry under the scrutiny of the inner "Eye of the
Mind." The "inner eye" was the judge presiding over the tribunal
of understanding.

Now we are in a position to understand why Gottsched, like

many literary theorists of his time, felt that poetry should follow the paradigm of its visual sister art, painting. If poetry could, like painting, imitate nature with determinate pictures, it would be able to avert the inherent dangers of overheated imaginations and abstract words. It was thus the poet's task to keep language's effect as visible as possible.[20] Linguistic imitations had foremost to elicit in the mind of the recipient a perceptual experience, that is, they had to simulate the visual experience of the *anschauende Erkäntnis* and create the illusion of being in the immediate presence of the phenomenal world. "Mimesis," Gottsched explains, functions "by creating a lively description of a thing so that it seems as if one is actually *seeing* [*als sähe man*] it in nature" (emphasis added).[21] The poet-painter painted with image-inducing words a believable scene before the eye of the recipient's mind.[22]

That poetry should create the illusion of intuitive cognition was an assumption shared by most aestheticians of the German Enlightenment. Such a goal could be achieved only by positing a transparent form of absolute visual mimesis, one which overcomes the obtrusive quality of arbitrary signs to recuperate the fullness of the world present to the *anschauende Erkäntnis* prior to the abstracting (hence reductive) grasp of words. Writes Moses Mendelssohn: "Objects are presented as if unmediated to our senses, so that the primary cognitive faculties are deceived in such a way that

20. This does not mean, however, that Gottsched wished to limit poetry to the imitation of real objects. Imaginary entities were also permissible (such as the fantastic creatures found in fables and mythology) providing they did not present a visual impossibility and did not clash with the natural order and harmony of nature. Probability and believability of Classical poetics were the criteria that governed Gottsched's rhetorical notion of mimesis.

21. Gottsched, *Handlexicon*, 67.

22. Regarding the Classical view of language in general, Wellbery writes: "In terms of both origin and end, sign-use must eventually yield to a mental act qualified as 'anschauend'" ("Aesthetics and Semiotics in the German Enlightenment," 65).

they often forget about the signs and believe to be seeing the thing itself. The value of poetic images and indeed individual poetic words, similes, and descriptions must be judged according to this maxim."[23] In other words, poetry would have to make use of signs that functioned like the naturally motivated signs of painting—signs that disappear when the recipient perceives the depicted object.

Like other thinkers of this period, Gottsched was guided by the assumption that man's rational faculty is characterized primarily by its power to represent, by its power to place before the "Eye of the Mind" visual copies of the things of the world. Therefore, he never questioned the Aristotelian equation of art and mimesis. For him and the Classical period, nothing could have been more natural than imitation. Art, as imitation, was merely one manifestation of man's copying capacity—it amounted to doing (and perfecting) that which comes naturally.[24] If one considers this era's belief that man's natural copying capacity functions according to visual principles, it is easy to understand why they should so easily align painting and poetry. Visuality lay at the heart of their conceptualization of mimesis. Because of the visual character of mental representations, "mental pictures," Classical thinkers had no reason to doubt the correspondence between the representing medium and that which was represented. Visuality guaranteed the determinacy of language and also the persuasive effect of poetry's imitations of things, people, and dramatic action.

Even more basic, perhaps, than these thinkers' assumption of the visual link between words and world was their unquestioning belief that man's mental faculty was a stable mechanism, which, at its deepest level, was constituted by the power to represent the

23. Ibid., 167; Mendelssohn quoted ibid., 250.
24. The idea that copying is a natural proclivity in man, Gottsched reports, is also found in Aristotle, who, Gottsched says, claimed that just about everything man does is learned or acquired through copying, imitation (*Dichtkunst,* 101).

fixed orders of nature. The mind of man was subordinate to the reality of the world. It is for this reason that the intrusive and seemingly arbitrary character of the imagination posed a threat to Gottsched's views, for the imagination seemed to be capable of functioning independently of the representational *anschauende Erkäntnis* and hence the sense-giving world. It was also a hazard because its "fires" could, at any time, flare up and conjure, without regard to any referential link to reality, visible improbabilities, "things" that were more the result of a random or haphazard process than the product of finely tuned cognitive faculties. If in such moments of conflagration poets were to embrace these whims of imagination, and if their poetic creations did not drift off into the netherworld of nonsense, it would be very unsettling indeed for Gottsched's representational views of man and language. It might give him pause to reconsider the Classical priority of world over subject and the corresponding complicity of word and thing. It might even lead him to the conclusion that language is more than a picture of the world, more than a representation of a representation.

Rather than questioning the premise of Classical representation (and hence, in the final analysis, the Classical priority of world over subject), he privileged a linguistic art form, drama, in which the challenge was least threatening. The visual and iconic character of performed drama minimized the potential free play of arbitrary linguistic signs; its impact was much more effective because "the *visible* presentation of people is much more moving than the best description."[25] The visual character of performed drama compensated for the inadequacies of language and approached a transparent "natural" aesthetic representation akin to the absolute visual mimesis posited by Meier and other late eighteenth-century theorists.

25. Ibid., 91.

In his well-known *Laokoon* essay (1776), Lessing undertakes a careful examination of the concept of poetic imitation as it was understood in the mid-eighteenth century. Although his sentiments were outspokenly anti-Gottschedian, Lessing's work did not favor Gottsched's Swiss opponents either. His polemics, rather, were aimed at the *ut pictura poesis*[26] doctrine, which had underwritten the work of both factions in the so-called Leipzig-Zurich "literary war" (*Literaturkrieg*).[27] To believe, as these theorists did, that poetry follows the model of painting, revealed, in Lessing's view, a fundamental misunderstanding of the temporal nature of language. The question is no longer, for example, to what extent *das Wunderbare* (the fantastic) is permissible in literary depiction, but rather to what extent literary depiction—"picturing"—is even possible.

26. This short simile, *ut pictura poesie*, taken from Horace's *Ars Poetica*, gave rise to an inordinate amount of debate and theoretical speculation in the seventeenth and eighteenth centuries; it became, in J. Hugo Blümner's words, the "battle cry" for literary critics who debated the syncretism of the arts (*Lessings Laokoon*, 16). Ironically, it seems that Horace wanted to warn against rather than advocate the identification of painting and poetry. See Buch, *Ut Pictura Poesis*, esp. 20–22, and Abrams, *The Mirror and the Lamp*, 33.

27. Bodmer and Breitinger, like their opponent in Leipzig, also believed that poetry, like painting, was concerned with visual imagery. "Both [the painter and the poet] have the same intention, that is, to place absent things before our eyes; or rather, so that I express myself more philosophically: so that we have the sensation of experiencing these objects" (*Vom Einfluß und Gebrauche der Einbildungs-krafft*, 11). Herrmann revises the standard view of the Zurich-Leipzig controversies by pointing out that it was not a difference in attitude toward *das Wunderbare* and the imaginative element of poetry that separated these camps, but rather a more fundamental difference in their understanding of mimesis. For Gottsched's tradition, poetry was primarily didactic and only indirectly concerned with nature. Mimesis was their means to an end: it was a normative principle that assured (and governed) the persuasive effect of poetry. Their theoretical orientation was thus, in Abrams's terms, "pragmatic." For the Swiss, however, poetry was more directly about nature; it was a quasi-cognitive act, an *Erkenntnisakt* that went hand in hand with man's exploration of nature (Herrmann, *Naturnachahmung und Einbildungskraft*, 276). Their orientation was, in Abrams's terms, more purely "mimetic."

47

The prevailing alignment of painting and poetry in the German Enlightenment was motivated, at least in part, by a subliminal desire to keep language determinate. To assure this determinacy, these aestheticians made use of three interrelated assumptions—that art is primarily mimetic, that the intellect is a visual-perceptual faculty, and that language has a quasi-perceptual character. Because of the visual effect of the painted canvas, it is easy to see why painting was generally privileged over poetry. Its copies of the world were more effective because the painter was able to use naturally motivated signs—colors and shapes—which were natural (nonarbitrary) in that they visually corresponded to the colors and shapes of the natural world they were to represent. Like these thinkers, Lessing wished to overcome the obtrusive quality of signs, and so he also speculated about naturally motivated signs. But making the effect of poetic language purely visual to achieve the status of natural signs was, in Lessing's mind, a misguided tactic.[28] While accepting the Classical premise that all art is mimetic, Lessing is quick to point out that painting and poetry entailed "different kinds of mimesis and different kinds of objects to be imitated."[29] Imitation entails different things for different arts; it is, in fact, the difference between these two arts, painting and poetry, rather than their similarity, that leads Lessing to some far-reaching insights into the nature of poetic language.

Lessing's analysis of painting's and poetry's differing modes of imitation focuses on these art forms' respective media. He finds that poetry's medium, language, is essentially temporal, consisting of "articulated tones in time," whereas the plastic arts are essentially spatial, consisting of "figures and colors in space" (102). This

28. See Buch, *Ut Pictura Poesis*, 41–46, and Wellbery, "Aesthetics and Semiotics in the German Enlightenment," 395–408.

29. Lessing, "Laokoon: Oder über die Grenzen der Malerei und Poesie," in *Gotthold Ephraim Lessings Werke*, 10. Subsequent references in the text are to this edition.

fundamental temporal-spatial difference in medium necessitates, in Lessing's view, a corresponding difference in subject matter, that is, the object of imitation: "Consequently," sums up Lessing, "physical things and their *visible* qualities are the appropriate objects of painting . . . actions are the appropriate objects of poetry" (emphasis added; 103). The primary concern of painting, owing to the visual (*sichtbar*) nature of its medium, is with visual things. Poetry, by contrast, must devote itself to action and performance (*Handlung*) and should not, in fact cannot, dally with the detailed description of things because language is not suited for such a task. Poetry should not describe "a physical thing in all of its detail . . . because the coexisting aspects of the thing will come into conflict with the consecutive aspect of speech" (112–13): medium and subject matter will clash whenever poetry attempts to paint, that is, present a detailed depiction of physical things.

Lessing's analysis of the temporal structure of language may have been motivated by an incipient awareness that language, especially poetic language, cannot be satisfactorily characterized in terms of the "pictures" it engenders in the recipient's mind. Lessing was also openly skeptical of this widespread notion, as can be seen from his remarks about Brockes's "descriptive poetry": "The learned poet has painted herbs and flowers with great skill and very true to nature. Painted, however, without creating any illusion. . . . I hear in each and every word the travailing poet, but I am far from seeing the thing itself" (111–12). Though Lessing, like other critics of his era, felt poetry's mimesis elicited the illusion of immediate intuitional experience, he clearly did not feel that this experience was purely visual. His *Laokoon* essay is to a large degree a reaction to his predecessor's preoccupation with visual detail. For him, the most important part of the poetic experience was not so much the images as the ideas the poem elicits. This "ideal" effect constitutes one of poetry's major advantages over painting.[30] Whereas painting can depict only that which is visual, poetry can elicit ideas that have no visual component. The incomparable, ideal, beauty of Helen of Troy, Lessing argued, cannot be painted: "Indeed the poet [Homer] knows . . . how to convey beauty which far surpasses anything painting can do in this regard. . . . Paint for us, poet, the pleasure, the dedication, the love, the delight that [Helen] . . . causes, and you have painted beauty itself" (138–39). The painter would be hard-pressed, Lessing points out, to depict invisible entities. This capacity to depict the invisible, Lessing comments in reference to the invisible "presence" of gods in the poetry of antiquity, "allows one to expand imaginatively upon the scene by providing the imagination with a certain free play to conjure how great and elevated above the common man the gods' personalities and actions might be" (90). Not being limited to the visible thus gives freedom to the imagination, "free play" to soar beyond the perceptual limitations of worldly painting.

Poetry also had, Lessing believed, the further advantage of being able to call up very specific ideas: "Language provides the poet with abstract concepts which are independent entities and any particular word never ceases to conjure the very same idea" (446). Lessing, like his contemporaries, was convinced that words were incisively specific; they were markers for specific ideas/representations and thus had no surplus of meaning. The signs of painting, by contrast, he found less specific because they were, by and large, incapable of designating specific ideas. Painting was, somewhat paradoxically, less specific in that it was overdetermined by necessary but peripheral visual details. David Wellbery sums up Lessing's point as follows: "The word . . . delivers directly to the imagination the ideal entities, the meanings, which in the plastic arts are

---

30. See Wellbery, "Aesthetics and Semiotics in the German Enlightenment," 358, and Buch, *Ut Pictura Poesis,* 40.

encumbered and occluded by a host of other features. The reader's imagination is granted the freedom to fill in the linguistic scheme as it pleases, without being limited by the full determinateness of things. . . . Poetry . . . is therefore the sphere in which the imagination exercises itself with optimal freedom, in total independence from actual sense experience."[31] Although Lessing was far from abandoning altogether the prevailing representational model of language, he was, to a certain degree, aware that the inherent power of language could be tapped by the poet whenever his creations went beyond a mere picturing function. By pulling pictures and poetry apart, Lessing began to open an autonomous space for readers and poets in which imagination could play. Not being limited to pictures provided the possibility of saying more, the possibility of freeing language from the strictures of the empirical experience.

In conclusion, I would like to look at a passage in Lessing's *Laokoon,* which is clearly at odds with his (basically) Classical view of a controllable and completely determinate language. In discussing the inclusion of things in poetry, Lessing states: "Actions cannot stand alone, but rather are connected to certain entities. Only insofar as these entities are physical objects, or are considered to be physical objects, does poetry also describe objects, but only through allusion by means of actions" (103). Action, Lessing reasons, necessarily involves objects that act and/or are acted upon. But because these objects cannot be effectively depicted, they must be alluded to by other actions. What ensues is a loop or "action regress" in which actions depend on actions which depend on yet further actions. In his polemics against the purveyors of the endemic "descriptive poetry" of the mid-eighteenth century, Lessing, it seems, has unwittingly discovered in poetic language a self-sufficiency or immanent reflexivity. The interdependency of action

31. Wellbery, "Aesthetics and Semiotics in the German Enlightenment," 394.

and allusion suggests a potentially infinite concatenation of linguistic allusions, a system of references whereby language makes
constant reference to itself. Lessing's statement would seem to
imply that the interconnectedness of language's constituent parts
(words) is at least as important as their representational power. It
also runs counter to his (defensive?) claim that "any particular
word never ceases to conjure the very same idea," for potentially
unending chains of allusions can never be halted to yield finite and
determinate ideas.

By pushing the Classical view of language to the point of contradiction, Lessing's work threatens to break the complicity of
word and thing. In retrospect we see that his thinking is on the
verge of breaking away from a conception of language grounded
in visual representation. Though he was convinced of the determinacy of words, his analysis of the limitations of linguistic depiction begins to undercut such determinacy. What we see forming in
his thought is a view of language which would embrace language's
inherent reflexivity as well as its independence from the world of
perception.

Psychological Perspectives

The desire of Classical aestheticians to counter the abstract and
alienating effects of language by means of an absolute visual mimesis reveals not only an uncertainty about representation but also a
growing concern about language itself. Ordinary words—nonpoetic words—these thinkers felt, were obtrusive because they
wedged in between the subject and its primary visual encounter
with the world. Being ultimately a representation of a representation, these words tended to put their speakers and listeners at an
abstract remove from the privileged (and desired) realm of visual
experience. Absolute visual mimesis begins to register a subliminal
uneasiness about man's position vis-à-vis the world; it is a dis-

content that found a poignant expression in Rousseau's back-to-nature idylls and the romantic generation's lament about the alienating effects of human rationality. But there is another side to this uneasiness with the obtrusive and rationalizing effects of ordinary words. In speculating about a poetry whose idealized form of mimesis surpasses the efficacy of the painted canvas, thinkers of the late Enlightenment privileged the (written) word over sensory experience and, in effect, upheld the deep-seated metaphysical prejudice of the Judeo-Christian tradition, which insists, as Françoise Meltzer has argued, "upon the meaning as against the sensory." It is, Meltzer claims, a particular manifestation of a Western ideology, of a (subliminal) "logocentric" strategy which protects and preserves the word as the vehicle of divine truth and ensures "a metaphysics of divine presence and, therefore, of transcendental meaning, as over sensory representation."[32] In her discussion of this prejudice against visual representation, Meltzer quotes the following observation from Sigmund Freud's *Moses and Monotheism:* "This is the prohibition against making an image of God—the compulsion to worship a God whom one cannot see. . . . But if this prohibition were accepted, it must have a profound effect. For it means that sensory perception was given second place to what may be called an abstract idea—a triumph of intellectuality over sensuality or, strictly speaking, an instinctual renunciation with all its necessary psychological consequences."[33]

There are clearly "psychological consequences" to the "triumph of intellectuality over sensuality"—of elevating the abstract over sensory perception—which entails not only the rational estrangement from nature lamented by the romantic generation but also an instinctual renunciation. The power of an ideology that privileges the word over the image is derived from the instincts and paid for

32. Meltzer, *Salome and the Dance of Writing,* 39, 89.
33. Freud, *Standard Edition,* 23:112–13.

in the psychological malaise that contributed to the search in the German Enlightenment for a poetry of absolute visual mimesis. Such poetry would compensate for both the denigration of sensory perception and the incipient failure of representation by reforging an unmediated and visual link to the world of experience without disrupting the "logocentric" metaphysics of the Judeo-Christian tradition.

If one can talk of an epistemic psychological need or perhaps obsession, unmediated and pure visual experience would certainly figure prominently for the late Classical period. In his discussion of the German *Anakreontik* poetry of this period, Rainer Nägele takes such a macroscopic view, writing: "In its preference for vision, the Anacreontic participated in an obsession of the Enlightment which privileged the eye as the exemplary organ through which one hoped to gain certainty, and above all overview."[34] This obsession, motivated at least in part by anxiety about the alienating effects of language, bears a striking similarity to the "paranoid alienation" Jacques Lacan discusses in his seminal "Mirror Stage" essay.[35] Lacan argues that although the preverbal human child—the "mirror-stage" infant—exists in a somewhat undifferentiated visual symbiosis with its mother and its environment just before the acquisition of language, it senses nonetheless a vague "organic insufficiency" or "primordial discord" because of the *"specific prematurity of [human] birth"* (4). The infant's psyche attempts to compensate for its physiological immaturity by identifying, aided by its innate "mirror apparatus" (3), with certain reassuring visual images of others and, most important, of the unified image of itself seen in mirror reflections. A vague sense of fragmentation is thus answered by identifying with fixed visual images, which, Lacan believes, become the foundational base for the future development

34. Nägele, "Das Imaginäre und das Symbolische," 54.
35. Lacan, *Ecrits,* 1–7. Further references to this work appear in the text.

of a stable, unified, and rigidly structured ego. The happiness of the mirror stage, however, comes to a traumatic end with the "paranoid alienation, which dates from the deflection of the specular I into the social I" (5), with, in other words, the acquisition of the naming, abstracting, and objectifying social structures of language. The child must renounce an existence dominated by sensory perception and physical contact with the actual world (which typically centers around maternal nurturing) and enter into the constructed world predetermined by the social and cultural relationships of language. In submitting to the inherited coordinates of language and society, the child begins to function as the subject in an impersonal, symbolic system through which it will learn to talk about itself as something opposed to the world presented in visual experience. Language marks and articulates the psyche's inexorable separation from the world of visual perception. From Descartes to Gottsched, from the mental mirror of nature and the *anschauende Erkäntnis* to an aesthetics of absolute visual mimesis of unmediated visual plenitude, one senses a growing uneasiness—a psychological malaise—about the abstract and devisualizing effects of language and a corresponding desire to overcome this anxiety and loss by returning to what might be characterized, in contemporary terms, as a fantasized, regressive, narcissistic prelinguistic state in which reality mirrors back to the subject a reassuring similarity—an identity of self and other.

"And as I bent over the silent waters, I saw that my face had left me" (1:169), writes Georg Trakl some two hundred years later in his thinly veiled autobiographical prose poem "Offenbarung und Untergang" (Dream and Derangement). Trakl's poetic subject seems to have fused in fantasy with the mythological figure of Narcissus, who was pathologically mesmerized by his own reflected image in a pool of water. The Trakl subject, by contrast, gazes at the beckoningly silent reflecting waters only to discover the horrifying absence of a reassuring self-reflection. This absence, I discuss in the final chapters of this book, is directly linked to his own disaffection with language. It is as if Trakl's psyche creates the narcissistic security of a prelinguistic mirror-stage link to its environment, only to recognize this as a wishful projection, a beautiful myth engendered by a linguistically alienated psyche that was forced to renounce a visual identification and unity with that which is other. Trakl thus parts ways with the narcissistic fantasy of a "golden age" childhood of innocence and perceptual unity. This means, however, that he must also part ways with Rousseau's dream-wish fantasy of humanity's lost state of uncivilized innocence, for Rousseau's utopic longings were themselves a fanciful product, a wishful retroprojection that might reverse or compensate for the linguistic alienation of civilization and its discontents. Unlike the Rousseau of the eighteenth century, Trakl is wary of the narcissistic dreams of what Françoise Meltzer calls "mimetic desire": "When Rousseau claims . . . to be at odds with his century, he is tacitly placing himself in harmony with the lost Eden he so compellingly paints in his *Discours*. And when he insists on seeing that utopian landscape as being more 'real,' more 'true' than his own, he is attempting to bring back to life . . . the Rousseau who never was. All the more reason, then, for the author of the preface to *Narcisse* to claim that his youth was even more corrupt than his more mature years: the time of innocence does not lie in childhood, it lies in fantasy; it does not lie in intellect, it lies in mimetic desire."[36]

36. Meltzer, *Salome and the Dance of Writing*, 155.

CHAPTER 3

Romantic Optimism and the Philosophy of Language

Das Äußre ist ein in Geheimniszustand erhobnes Innre.

So kann auch eine Unabhängigkeit von der wirklichen Sin-
nenwelt entstehen, indem man sich an die Zeichenwelt . . .
gewöhnt.—Novalis[1]

Transcendental Subjectivity

THE RETHINKING OF man's relation to the world begun in the eighteenth century became a motivating force in the romantic era—roughly 1790 to 1825—as thinkers programmatically addressed the issue of what art, language, and knowledge might be without the cornerstone concept of representation. Put in epistemological terms, romantic thought can be viewed as a response to an epistemic reversal of the Classical privileging of *res* over *intellectus*, that is, matter (subject) over mind (object). Reflecting on this dramatic change, Kant speaks in the "Preface to the Second Edition" of his *Critique of Pure Reason* (1787) of a second "Copernican" revolution, pointing out that, whereas one had previously

1. "The external is the internal elevated into a secret form." "And thus an independence from the real sensory world can also arise when one becomes accustomed to the world of signs" (Novalis, *Schriften*, 3:103, 2:339).

57

assumed "that all knowledge and cognition must conform to objects," one must now assume the opposite, that "the objects must conform to our cognition."[2]

Although the Kantian critique of reason ultimately opened the door for a romantic glorification of subjectivity, it was a door to a Pandoran box of troubling philosophical implications which undercut the naively optimistic assumption of the Enlightenment that human beings could apprehend with their rational intellect the true essence of nature. Objective, eternally valid knowledge about the world proved to be an impossible dream, for the human subject's apprehension of the world will always be limited by its mode of access, by its innate subjective conditions for cognition. The supreme faculty in the thought of the Enlightenment, rationality, becomes a liability because the human subject can never get beyond its structuring faculties to uncover the ultimate nature of things. In elucidating the necessary subjective conditions whereby nature can become an object of cognition, the Kantian critique in effect cut off access to absolute knowledge of the world and thus poignantly formalized the problematic man-nature split forming in the late Classical Age.

The romantic solution to this dilemma was to totalize the projecting character of the human mind by making nature the product of the transcendental subject: the objective realm became derivative of the subjective and thereby kept alive the possibility of the unity of the two. Fichte, for instance, argued in his *Wissenschaftslehre* (Science of knowledge) that the subject (*das Ich*) could become conscious of itself only by positing (*setzen*) something against which it could define itself—a *Nicht-Ich*.[3] Without a *Nicht-Ich,* the *Ich* is undifferentiated, mere potential. Such a positing, he argued, was the primary and unconscious activity of the *Ich;* it was

2. Kant, *Kritik der reinen Vernunft*, in *Werke*, 1:25.
3. See Fichte, *Wissenschaftslehre*, esp. 73–75.

the first reflexive step whereby the subject defines itself and moves toward fuller self-consciousness. Viewed from a psychological standpoint, one can see that Fichte's philosophical system is motivated by the same subliminal problematic that gave rise in the aesthetic tracts of the German Enlightenment to the concept of absolute visual mimesis. In that he wished to prove that man is able to perceive nature only as a reflection or part of his own ego, Fichte attempted, like his early eighteenth-century predecessors, to keep man and reality united through perceptual reflection. This *Ich/Nicht-Ich* reciprocity is a variation of the earlier eighteenth-century aesthetic-philosophic gestures to fancifully counter man's estrangement from nature with a compensatory, narcissistic unity of self and other.

One of the first romantic writers to put Fichte's egocentristic philosophy into the service of aesthetic theory was Friedrich Freiherr von Hardenberg—better known by his pseudonym of Novalis. In his *Philosophische Studien, 1795–1796,* Novalis sums up the Fichtean lesson in the following disjunctive fragment: "The subject [*das Ich*] must posit itself as creatively projective [*darstellend*]. . . . There is a special creatively projective force—which in order to create, creates; creating in order to create, is free creation. This indicates that it is not the object (as such) but rather the subject [*das Ich*], which is the basis of this process, that which determines the process. The work of art takes on as such its free, independent, idealistic character—its impressive spirit—because the work of art is a visible product of the subject."[4] The activity of the *Ich* was for Novalis a self-contained creative—"projective"—process, which is, as intimated here, ultimately the same force behind art. Freed by the transcendental philosophy of Kant and Fichte from a representational tie to the empirical world and from the logical strictures of rationality, the poetic subject becomes the

4. Novalis, *Schriften,* 2:193. Further references to this edition appear in the text.

supreme principle unto itself in romantic thought. It is thus understandable that their speculations revolved around an exploration of subjective "transcendental" conditions for poetry which were far removed from the mimetic theories prevailing only a few decades earlier. Whereas Lessing questioned language's capacity to imitate in the fashion of the graphic arts, the romantics flatly rejected any notion of mimesis, of *ars imitatur naturam:* "No imitation of nature," writes Novalis, "poetry is precisely the opposite" (4:336). Poetic words, Novalis proclaimed, do not refer to a world on the other side of language; they point, rather, to the mysteries of their own being within the subject. Novalis believed that only after we have grasped that language is "a world unto itself" and is like a set of mathematical formulas which "are self-contained and express nothing but their own fantastic nature" (2:431) can we begin to comprehend the nature of poetry. For Novalis, poetic language represented the ultimate in emancipated language—it was "mere wordplay" par excellence (2:430).

By breaking language away from the representational discourse of ideas and determinate content, in short, from any mimetic function, the early romantic theorists felt that they were freeing language to speak its own essence, an essence that linked the individual to the all-encompassing world spirit (*Weltseele*). Through words the subject was put in touch with the spiritual sense of things, or, in borrowed Kantian terminology, with the "transcendental" conditions for empirical experience. Language was thus never a product of nature but rather a medium of inward reflection and revelation (*Offenbarung*). In poetry, language achieved its highest reflexive potential, as A. W. Schlegel's truly modern remarks indicate: "The medium of poetry is the same as that medium through which the human intellect achieves consciousness . . . language. Poetry is thus not bound to objects, it creates rather its own. . . . Language is not a product of nature but rather an im-

print of the human intellect in which the origin, interconnectedness of ideas, and the whole mechanism of its operations are set
down. In poetry, that which has been created is created again; the
malleability of poetry is just as limitless as the mind's ability to
return to itself through ever higher potentializing reflections."[5]
"Language is not a product of nature"—language is not episte-
mically subordinate to or derivative of the empirical. It is not a
form of signed perception or a picture of the world but rather a
subjective medium of self-realization that achieves its highest potential in poetry. Poetry is reflexive language, language that "po-
tentializes" its own inherent reflexivity.

Of equal importance in the early romantics' exploration of subjectivity were their rather explicit speculations about certain unconscious forces operative in the human psyche. Not surprisingly,
the German word for "unconscious" (*das Unbewußte*) figures
prominently in the aesthetic writings of Novalis and the Schlegel
brothers. These speculations were lent credence by the work of
Gotthilf Heinrich von Schubert, a theology student who turned
to the study of medicine and was eventually appointed professor
of natural sciences at the University of Erlangen. Influenced by
Fichte's *Wissenschaftslehre* and the nature philosophy of Schelling,
most notably his *Ideen zur Philosophie der Natur*, Schubert wrote
a number of widely read "scientific" works on the subconscious
workings of the mind and their relation to man's apprehension
of reality. His *Ansichten von der Nachtseite der Naturwissenschaft*
(Views on the nightside of the natural sciences 1808) and *Die
Symbolik des Traumes* (Symbolism of dreams, 1814) nurtured the
romantics' interest in the unconscious and pointed ahead to the
writing of a later nineteenth-century medical doctor, Sigmund
Freud. The notion that, as one critic recently put it, "the structure

5. A. W. Schlegel, "Vorlesungen über schöne Literatur und Kunst," 261.

of literature *is* in some sense the structure of the mind"[6] is not exactly new. It has its roots in the aesthetic speculations of the romantic era, speculations which explicitly formulate the inseparability of literature and mind, and, ultimately, the union of literary analysis and psychology.

The Crisis of Representation Forestalled

Though he was aware of the negative implications of the Kantian critique, Novalis's youthful exuberance seemed to save him from the despair suffered by Heinrich von Kleist.[7] He saw, rather, other, positive implications contained in Kant's transcendental philosophy which he then melded with Fichte's "transcendental physics" to produce an optimistic form of aesthetic philosophy, what he called "magical idealism" (3:66–67). This magical idealism was grounded in the Fichtean *Ich/Nicht-Ich* unity—the unity of *Geist* and *Natur*—and had as its purpose bringing their "magical" inseparability to light. This was to be accomplished through the magical powers of poetry (*Poesie*), more specifically, through the magical power of words. The poetic word, Novalis postulated, transforms the reified world back into spirit by conjuring for the recipient the indubitable consciousness of unity of the two. Poetry's magic words (2:325) thus did not *re*-present or picture nature; they, rather, *pre*-sented the synthesis of the two, of *Geist* and *Natur:* "The poet is truly robbed of his senses—thus everything happens within him. He imagines, quite literally, both subject and object—mind and world. Thus the infinity of a good poem, eternity" (3:349). After Kant there opened up a problematic gap between thing and

6. Brooks, "The Idea of a Psychoanalytic Literary Criticism," 148.

7. Convinced, after reading Kant's first *Critique,* of the possibility of attaining meaningful knowledge about nature, Heinrich von Kleist experienced in 1801 a serious emotional crisis, his so-called *Kant-Krise.*

representing faculty, sign and referent, man and nature. Without a representational foundation, language ultimately loses the possibility of a natural (visual) grounding in the empirical and becomes more purely "linguistic," that is, more a function of propositional content which is embedded in the systemic relations of language's constituent parts. For Novalis this could not be a problem because, although sign (*Zeichen*) and signified (*Bezeichnetes*) are "totally disparate," "in different spheres," they are nonetheless identical in the speaking subject's mind—"identical in the mind of the person who signifies" (2:165). Sign and referent are unified in the mysterious inner realm of the subject where spirit/mind and nature are one. This mysterious or magical union is also the necessary condition for intersubjective understanding: "If sign and signified, as we have seen, are totally separated, and if they are only connected in the mind of the person who signifies, then it can only be by coincidence or miracle that a sign can communicate its signified to a second person" (2:165). In any case, by linking *Ich* and *Nicht-Ich* Novalis was able to forestall the upcoming crisis of linguistic representation which followed in the wake of the Kantian critique. In analogy to Kant's "Copernican" revolution, he shrewdly reversed the epistemological priority of representing faculty over thing represented and redefined the problematics of representation with his concept of magical "mutual representation" (*Wechselrepräsentation*): "Thus, one can only understand the subject [*das Ich*] in that it is represented in the object [*Nicht-Ich*]. The *Nicht-Ich* is symbol of the *Ich* and serves the self-understanding of the *Ich*" (3:66). Similar to Fichte, Novalis compensates for the incipient problem of arbitrary and abstract signs by resorting to a quasi-mystical, narcissistic reflexivity of self and other.

Coincidence and miracle hold language together. "Words are miraculous," Novalis writes, "they are the synthesis of the arbitrary and the nonarbitrary" (3:168). With the wave of a magic wand Novalis closes the schism between man and nature, sign and signified, representation and that which is represented. Elliptically, he writes: "Magic (mystical doctrine of language), the affinity of the sign and the signifier (one of the basic ideas of cabalism)" (3:85). The sweep of his magic wand likewise resolves the late Classical problem of the arbitrary and alienating sign, viz., "The so-called arbitrary signs are ultimately not as arbitrary as they seem—but rather connected to the signified through a certain real nexus" (3:114).

Novalis's semiological deliberations, albeit a somewhat confused and at times contradictory mixture of mysticism, semiological analysis, and idealistic philosophy, nonetheless portend a profoundly modern understanding of poetic language. Although in retrospect many of his explanations seem dubious, his insights do not. Most significant, perhaps, is his refusal—like A. W. Schlegel's—to ground even nonpoetic language in a representational relation to the empirical world. Novalis makes this point emphatically in his "Monologue on Language": "Authentic speech is pure word play. It is an amazing mistake that people make when they believe that they speak about things. No one seems to know that in reality language is only concerned with itself . . . and whenever a speaker wants to talk about something determinate, the capricious nature of language will have him say the most ridiculous and incorrect things" (2:430). Language, not just poetic language, is ill-suited to talk about anything determinate—determinacy in reference to things is not the way of words. Language does not mirror the world; it is a word play that plays itself as well as its speakers—"whenever a speaker wants to talk about something determinate, the capricious nature of language will have him say the most ridiculous and incorrect things." The uncontrollable nature of words will always resist and subvert the speaker's intentions because they (words) are "preoccupied" with expressing the magical-spiritual essence of the *Nicht-Ich*. In successful poetry, Novalis expounds, the poet is consumed by his language "and becomes the unconscious organ and property of a higher power. The artist belongs to the work of art, not the other way around" (3:141). Further, "The poet orders, brings together, and invents—though it is incomprehensible to him why he should choose to do so" (3:349). The poet's words are magically related to the essence of nature, which is always striving through him toward a fuller and more self-conscious form of expression. Each word points within, to the secrets contained in the *Gemüth,* where "everything is united in the most intimate, pleasing, and lively fashion. . . . And so it is that the most amazing unities and strange connections come into being—here everything alludes to everything else; everything becomes the sign of many other things and is in turn signified and conjured by many other signs" (3:318).

It is through the "mind and spirit" (*Gemüth*) of the poet, more specifically, through his words, that the "spirit of the cosmos" (*Weltgemüth*) speaks. The poet is thus transformed into a reflexive medium whereby the cosmic spirit turns back upon itself in its striving for self-consciousness. "Art" in general, and poetry in particular, were, in Novalis's words, "the conscious part of nature" (3:326), striving for yet further self-consciousness. It is the reflexivity and eternally self-referential character of nature—"the self-viewing, self-imitating, self-creating nature" (3:246)—that is graphically expressed in the words of poetry. Poetic language was thus more than personal expression, more than a medium for the re-presentation of ideas and intentions; it should be, Novalis urged, a pure form of speaking, "language to the second power . . . expression . . . for the sake of expression . . . the complete production of a higher power of language" (2:373). Poetic language is only transitive, referential, in that it always and only takes itself, language, as its object or referent. "Poetry refers directly to language" (3:240). In this reflexive play, language becomes both subject and object and leaves behind the concerns and intentions of the poet's empirical self. Poetic language is not a medium of self-expression nor is it the countersign of thought: it is emancipated both from the conscious control of its speakers and from the empirical world of things.

It should come as no surprise that the romantics should so highly prize music, perhaps the most nonrepresentational of all art forms. It was art in its purest form, autonomous, self-contained, pure production—never a sign of something else. "The musician draws the essence of his art from within—and here there is not the slightest suspicion of mimesis" (2:360). Yet the romantics' interest in music ran deeper; as a spontaneous expression of the soul, untainted by the intellect and untrammeled by worldly concerns, music represented the purest expression of the creative spirit of all things. It was the purest manifestation of what Schopenhauer called a few decades later the *Wille*—an amorphous and anonymous drive that brings about all appearance.

Behind all appearance, Novalis also believed, were the mysterious "musical relations of the soul" (3:291), "the primordial relations of nature" (3:473). Novalis was thus convinced that poetry, like other art forms, should follow the paradigm of music; music is where poetry begins,[8] and poetry is where music takes on another form, the more self-conscious form of words. The words of the

8. Nietzsche takes a similar position in *The Birth of Tragedy* and credits a poet of the romantic era, Friedrich Schiller, as the source of the idea. Nietzsche quotes a letter from Schiller to emphasize his point: "'The sentiment is in the beginning without any definite object; this only takes form later. For me a certain *musical mood* always precedes the poetic idea'" (emphasis added; Nietzsche, *Werke*, 1:37). On lyrical poetry, Nietzsche writes: "This whole treatise is based upon the insight that lyrical poetry is just as dependent upon the spirit of music as music itself" (43).

poet, Novalis proclaims, "are the musical instrument of ideas" (3:206), the tones of resonating ideas—"not common signs—but tones—magic words, which vibrate through beautifully enveloping groups of words" (2:325). It is, thus, in and through these resonating words that the "musical relations of the soul" and, ultimately, the transcendental essence of all things sound. To be sure, the transcendental meaning of such poetic words has little to do with the discourse of determinate ideas and daily concerns. The "beautiful pure sound" of poetry is thus "without sense and coherence, at most intelligible in single verses, with associations, however, akin to dreams" (3:323).

Yet, very importantly, language, especially poetic language, is more than the sensual play with the phonic qualities of words; its tones are also associated with meaning, ideas, and feelings. It is through these associations that the "musical relations of the soul" of the cosmos achieve a higher level of self-consciousness. By allowing the language in poetry to play itself like an instrument, by setting into motion in the sound chamber of the *Gemüth* the harmonic resonances between words, ideas, and feelings, Novalis believed that the poetic subject—be it writer or sympathetic recipient—would be cast back upon its transcendental self to catch a glimmer of the mysterious play of the cosmos.

The governing principles of this "self-generating" play, we can now say with the hindsight of two hundred years, was not the linearity of narrative representation or authorial intention but rather the paradigmatic relations between words: "The poet uses things and words like the keys of a piano; poetry is based upon an active association of ideas, a self-generating, intentional, idealistic process of coincidence (coincidental, free concatenation) (casuistry) . . . (play)" (3:249). The poet's role in this reflexive word play is that of a catalyst; he or she only sets the self-acting and coincidental production into play. Such words were like keys of the piano, which, when "struck," resound in the recipient's prerational/transcendental *Gemüth,* conjuring other words and ideas.

Novalis's speculations about the free play of resonating words, which takes precedence over conceptual clarity and determinate mimetic or narrative content, bears, to be sure, a more than coincidental similarity to Kant's frequently quoted "Analysis of the Beautiful" found in his *Critique of Aesthetic Judgment.* There Kant had explained that the response to the aesthetic object is a psychological state (*Gemüthszustand*) whereby the reason and imagination engage in "free play": "The faculties of cognition . . . are engaged in free play because they cannot be limited by any definite concept or cognitive principle [*weil kein bestimmter Begriff sie auf eine besondere Erkenntnisregel einschränkt*]."[9] Indeed, romantic poetic theory appears to owe much to Kant's general, nonutilitarian views on art. Though Kant did not propose a unified theory for any particular art form—least of all for poetry—his definition of the aesthetic (beauty) as a kind of "purposiveness without purpose" (*Zweckmäßigkeit ohne Zweck*) adumbrates the aestheticist tradition and points, as one recent literary critic put it, to a "road [which] leads to the very heart of modernism."[10] For Kant, the aesthetic was an end in itself, subservient to no extrinsic doctrine and indifferent to reality; it did not seek commensurability with anything beyond its own form and could not be reduced to explicit concepts or determinate ideas, for its effects, what Kant termed "aesthetic ideas," were the result of an "arbitrary play" of the categories of reason without regard for empirical necessity. The aesthetic idea, Kant wrote, was a logically autonomous idea whose sole purpose was to "induce much thought yet without there being any thought, i.e., concept, whatever which could be adequate to it

9. See Kant, *Kritik der Urteilskraft,* in *Werke,* 10:bk. 1, par. 9.
10. Sokel, *Writer in Extremis,* 12.

[the aesthetic idea]; consequently, language can never come to terms with it, nor render it completely intelligible."[11]

Transcendental Poetry

Poetic reflexivity assumes another form in the theoretical work of Friedrich Schlegel. Poets, he argued, should be highly conscious of their creative activity; they should not simply write but continuously reflect upon the act of writing and integrate this reflection into the work itself. In analogy to Kant's *Transzendentalphilosophie,* Schlegel termed such "modern" poetry, *Transzendentalpoesie:* "Since one would not lay much stock in a transcendental philosophy which is not self-critical, that is, which did not contain a transcendental reflection upon the nature and function of the subject, there should likewise be a kind of poetry in which modern poets combine transcendental materials—preliminary exercises for a theory of poetic productivity—with beautiful self-reflection . . . this poetry would be both poetry and poetry of poetry [*Poesie der Poesie*], since all of its creations would contain a reflection both of itself and of poetry in general."[12] Modern poetry, Schlegel muses, was to combine theory and practice. It should do so by being programmatically reflexive, by always turning back upon itself to consider, in Kantian terms, its own "transcendental conditions of possibility."

By weaving self-referential "transcendental" observations into the fabric of the text, in other words, by reflecting in the process of creation upon the very process of creation, the poet would call attention to the fictionality of the work and, in effect, break the illusion that was so important in preromantic poetics. The self-

11. Kant, *Kritik der Urteilskraft,* in *Werke,* 10:bk. 2, par. 49.

12. Schlegel, *Kritische Friedrich-Schlegel-Ausgabe,* 2:204; hereafter cited in the text.

consciousness of *Transzendentalpoesie* thus turns the Classical mirror of nature around, inward.[13] The result is not crystalline reflections—pictures—of things, but rather a reflection of the transcendental (linguistic) conditions of poetry, the poet's (and reader's) psyche.[14]

Friedrich Schlegel begins his well-known fragment on *Transzendentalpoesie* with the following description: "There is a kind of poetry whose everything is the relationship between the real and the ideal. It begins as satire about the absolute difference between the ideal and real, floats in the middle as elegy, and ends as idyll with the absolute identity of the two" (2:204). Transcendental poetry is, ultimately, about the relationship between the ideal and the real; it is neither purely idealistic, like philosophy, nor realistic in the sense of *imitatio naturae* and begins by satirizing the (apparent) absolute difference between the two. Its satire points out that the difference between real and ideal, between the physical and the mental, the empirical and the transcendental is not absolute but only appears to be. Still, appearances are hard to deny, hence the elegy in the middle—an elegy or lament about the empirically

13. Schlegel uses this mirror image to describe the effect of such reflexive "universal poetry" (*Universalpoesie*), suggesting perhaps even a subliminal tie to the egocentristic mirror reciprocity underlying so much of the aesthetic-philosophic writing of the eighteenth and early nineteenth centuries: "And thus universal poetry, freed from all real and ideal concerns, can suspend itself upon the wings of poetic reflection between that which is portrayed and the one who does the portraying to realize again and again a potential which is like an endless series of mirrors multiplying a reflection" (2:182).

14. The concept of transcendental poetry is also closely connected with Schlegel's notion of romantic irony. Through an ironic stance, or what Schlegel once termed "transcendental buffoonery" (2:152), poets distance themselves from their creations, escaping, among other things, the work's finite scope and linguistic limitations. Irony is as such an awareness of limitations, of the impossibility of "complete communication": "Irony contains and induces a sense of the irresolvable conflict between the determinate and indeterminate, between the impossibility and necessity of complete communication" (2:160).

undeniable real/ideal dichotomy. Were it not for the early romantics' unflagging optimism, their belief that the whole world could be "poeticized," that the elegy will in the end give way to the idyll, we might be left in a profoundly modern predicament where real and ideal gape at each other from opposite sides of an unbridgeable schism. For the early romantics, however, the elegy is only transitional and will, in some hopefully not so distant, spiritually enlightened future, give way to the idyll (untainted by satire) of the unity of real and ideal, the "absolute identity of the two."

In the space that had opened during the late eighteenth century between words and things, the early romantics began to articulate a new and modern view of poetic language which willfully subverts the representational logic and discourse of ideas, determinate content, and authorial intentions. By leaving the visually defined course of mimetic pictures, these proto-modernists were able to explore the possibilities of a poetic creativity more closely aligned with the *Nachtseite* of the human spirit than with the luminous daylight world of vision—more closely aligned with the linguistic structures of the psyche than with the objective structures of the world. For them, the way of poetic language was no longer the linearity of narrative, syntagmatic discourse, but rather the more diffuse psycholinguistic tracks of paradigmatic play—of "association" and "self-generating" "word play," which is "without sense and coherence" and "akin to dreams." In recording their search to understand the underlying subjective conditions of poetic creativity, the early German romantics began to articulate, and, in a sense, invent the modern discourse of the unconscious. Their speculations about a poetry which, like dreams, issues from a powerful, unknowable, and mysterious area of the human psyche registers an early awareness, to put it in Julia Kristeva's psychoanalytic terms, of an impersonal (preconscious) "semiotic" dimension of language which is opposed to the "symbolic" language of the conscious, socialized ego.[15]

The early romantics looked upon language, especially poetic language, with great optimism. It held the key both to unlock the slumbering spirit of man and compensate for man's intellectual disconnection with nature. Such faith, however, waned as the nineteenth century progressed; by the close of the century it had been almost totally eclipsed by a cultural pessimism and skepticism. Whereas the romantics viewed language's emancipation from things, pictures, and intentions as the necessary and positive condition for the magic of poetic creativity, later thinkers began to view this free play—not unlike their late Classical predecessors—as symptomatic of the alienating effects of human rationality.

Modernism and the Crisis

The term "modernism," as it is used in this and the following chapters, is a cultural concept which, as its more literal sense suggests, entails an arbitrary juxtaposition of two segments of time: the modern and the premodern. Implied also in this division, which derives from the etymology of the word "modern" (from Latin *modo,* meaning lately, just now) is the sense that "modern" is closely related to the present, the new, and, by extension, to that which is up-to-date, not obsolete. Used as an aesthetic concept, the term "modernism" characterizes a general development in the arts in the last 150 years which has made the primary, descriptive sense of modern—up-to-date, new, present—into an aesthetic value. Modernism is thus programmatically modern: it stresses an acute awareness of the present to the point of a historical relativity that

15. Kristeva, *Desire in Language,* 133. Using the Lacanian distinction between "semiotic" and "symbolic," Kristeva opposes the "semiotic" language of the unconscious, which is sensuous and "heterogeneous" to meaning, to the "symbolic" language of the conscious ego. Poetry, she argues, relies heavily on the "semiotic."

opposes the authority of the tradition and becomes, in its more militant moments, a willful and self-conscious revolt of the present against the normative past. Though a questioning of the authorities of the past began in such eighteenth-century movements as the German Storm and Stress, it was not until the mid-nineteenth century, especially in France, that a major "modernist" break from the Classical aesthetic values of permanence and beauty was definitively made. "What we have," writes Matei Calinescu in his *Five Faces of Modernity*, "is a major cultural shift from a time-honored aesthetics of permanence, based on the belief in an unchanging and transcendent ideal of beauty, to an aesthetics of transitoriness and immanence, whose central values are change and novelty."[16] By the early twentieth century, this adversarial tendency was sharpened to the point that, in movements such as expressionism, crisis and revolt became both an aesthetic value and a source of creative energy—as clearly was the case with Georg Trakl. When taken to an extreme in the rebellions of the avant-garde, this flirtation with crisis took on the nihilistic dimension of self-negation: here modernism victimized itself in "a deliberate and self-conscious *parody of modernity* itself" (141).

From a sociological standpoint, modernism is also a response to the dehumanizing effects of the modern, technological world. Regarding the irony of modernism's antimodern stance, Calinescu writes that there are "two conflicting and interdependent modernities—one socially progressive, rationalistic, competitive, technological; the other culturally critical and self-critical, bent on demystifying the basic values of the first." As an adversary to technological modernism, aesthetic modernism rejects the "dogma of progress, in its critique of rationality, in its sense that modern civilization has brought about the loss of something precious"

16. Calinescu, *Five Faces of Modernity*, 5. Further references to this work are in the text.

(265). Though clearly connected to romantic ideology, this critique of rationality and civilization became especially acute by the beginning of the twentieth century.[17]

I use the terms "modernist" and "modernism" in a third and final sense to designate a kind of writing—literary modernism—in which meaning achieves a decided autonomy from empirical reference, authorial intention, and the linear discourse of communication. Though the early romantics of Germany speculated about such a literary discourse, they were largely incapable of putting this theory into poetic practice; they were, nonetheless, the first theorists of modernism, the first theorists of what Foucault calls the "literary," an explicitly anti-Classical concept which began to form in the nineteenth century,

> at a time when language was . . . reconstituting itself elsewhere [in the "literary"], in an independent form, difficult of access, folded back upon the enigma of its own origin and existing wholly in reference to the pure act of writing. . . . Literature becomes progressively more differentiated from the discourse of ideas, and encloses itself within a radical intransitivity; it becomes detached from the values that were able to keep it in gen-

17. There is a growing consensus that the international movement of modernism reached its zenith between 1910 and 1940 and is now either "dead" or going through a period of crisis or reorganization. This has led many to characterize the present era as "postmodern"; indeed, many of the aesthetic values esteemed by artists of "high modernism" are often rejected, parodied, or inverted by practitioners of contemporary art. I am not concerned with speculating whether these recent trends are either a continuation, perhaps mutation, of modernist assumptions, or the indexes or beginnings of a new "postmodern" aesthetic. One thing, however, is clear: the recent modernism-postmodernism debate has helped in hindsight to clarify many of the assumptions and motivations shared by artists in the modernist era. For an interesting view on modernism, see the following: Calinescu, *Five Faces of Modernity;* Foster, *The Anti-Aesthetic;* Hassan, *The Postmodern Turn;* Huyssen, *After the Great Divide;* Hoesterey, "Review Essay"; and the special issue "Modernity and Postmodernity" in *New German Critique* 33 (Fall 1984).

eral circulation during the Classical age . . . and creates within its own space everything that will ensure a ludic denial of them . . . it breaks with the . . . order of representations and becomes merely a manifestation of a language which has no other law than that of affirming . . . its own precipitous existence . . . where it has nothing to say but itself, nothing to do but shine in the brightness of its being.[18]

If the German early romantics were the first modernist theorists, then the nineteenth-century French symbolists must be considered the first group of decidedly self-conscious modernist poets. Baudelaire was the first to use the term "modern" in the literary sense to designate his depersonalized and abstract verse, described by Hugo Friedrich: "With Baudelaire 'abstract' means primarily 'intellectual' in the sense of 'not natural' . . . taking the heart out of the subject of poetry . . . de-thingifying and drawing upon the magical powers of language . . . nurtured by the abstractions of mathematics" (37–38). Baudelaire's poetry was, in other words, the form of poetry which the early German romantics had envisioned but were largely incapable of writing. There is, however, no evidence that the French symbolists ever concerned themselves directly with German romantic theory.[19] A more direct theoretical influence on them were two remarkably modern essays by Edgar Allan Poe, "A Philosophy of Composition" (1846) and "The Poetic Principle" (1848), both translated by Baudelaire. Building upon Poe's speculations about the autonomy of the pure "poem per se," which is "quite independent of . . . the intoxication of the

18. Foucault, *Order of Things,* 300. See Friedrich, *Die Struktur der modernen Lyrik,* 27–28 (English: *The Structure of Modern Poetry,* trans. Joachim Neugroschel [Evanston: Northwestern University Press, 1974]). Subsequent parenthetical citations in the text refer to the German edition.

19. Vordtriede has traced a number of paths over which the ideas of German romantic thought made their way to the French symbolists in his *Novalis und die französischen Symbolisten.*

heart,"[20] the French began to elaborate and also put into practice their aestheticist *l'art pour l'art* theory of poetic creativity.

Although theoretical affinities existed between the French symbolists and the work of Novalis and Schlegel, there were also major differences. Clearly, the symbolists did not share in the early German romantics' messianic fervor and optimistic self-confidence. For their generation, faith in the inherent goodness of man and nature had been broken by the inhumanity of the new technological ethos. The filthy sterility of a burgeoning industrial era cast a dark cloud of doubt over the idealism of romantic humanism. The problems of the quickly expanding industrial city were felt earlier in Paris (Baudelaire's residence) than in other Continental cities. While Berlin had fewer than five hundred thousand inhabitants in 1850, Paris was already approaching two million. It was in this alienating labyrinth of streets, factories, and faceless people that Baudelaire's malformed *fleurs du mal* were nurtured. In a negative sense, his concept of modernity points, as Hugo Friedrich aptly puts it, "to the world of large cities devoid of plants, to the ugliness of cities with their asphalt, their artificial light, their canyons of stone, their sins, their masses of lonely people" (42). For Baudelaire's generation, the (early romantic) divine chaos and pure productivity of nature had turned demonic and was now figured in the monstrosities of the modern metropolis.

Understandably, Baudelaire and his compatriots could not share the early romantics' faith in the complicity of art, culture, and the divine. Faced with a growing spiritual-cultural void, the symbolists were cast back upon themselves. Their aesthetic survival, it seems, depended on the cultivation of a more self-sufficient *l'art pour l'art* order. "The wretched, the decaying, the dark and evil, the artificial become stimulating irritants," Hugo Friedrich remarks, "that demand to be poetically apprehended. They contain

20. See Poe, "The Poetic Principle," in *Complete Works,* 14:271, 290.

secrets, which steer poetry in new directions" (43). Perhaps the most important of these "new directions" was the one that led to a new examination of and experimentation with the medium of poetry, language. Not only did the symbolists reflect on the status of poetry in the new technological age, they also took a hard look at the inherent power of words themselves. What they found was a new chaos of creative inspiration and poetic expression which could both withstand and capture the intensity of the new world of steel, machines, and slums. "In the dregs of the metropolis," Friedrich concludes, "Baudelaire sensed a mystery" (43), the "last mystery," Gottfried Benn seems to rejoin, in which the "latent existence" of words and psyche are one.[21]

Developing parallel to the spiritual-cultural crisis underwriting the symbolists' experimentation with the "poem per se" was the crisis of linguistic representation which followed on the heels of the Kantian critique. Foucault's oxymoronic description of the modern era's "discovery of the word in its *impotent* power" points to the source of the trouble: impotence. The inadequacies of language that the thinkers of the late Classical period tried to overcome with a natural and transparent form of absolute visual mimesis, that Novalis tried to sweep away with his wand of magical idealism, returned with a vengeance at the close of the nineteenth century. If one couples this with the gradual demise of the divine—the ultimate romantic ground for language—then one can begin to talk of a full-blown crisis: the negative side of romantic emancipation of language from representation. Without the divine guarantee of meaningfulness and the mystical union of word and *Weltseele,* language becomes a thorny epistemological problem in itself. "Those abstract words, which roll so naturally from the tongue," Hugo von Hofmannsthal lamented at the turn of century, "disintegrated in my mouth like so many moldy mush-

21. Benn, *Das Hauptwerk,* 2:336–37.

rooms."[22] The words that were once so easy to use had lost their substance and failed their speaker. Under the guise of a writer explaining his creative silence, Hofmannsthal relates, in his landmark *Lord Chandos Brief* (1902), how he seems to have fallen out of grace with the cosmos; he feels isolated, alone and, most important, forsaken by words that have become miserably insufficient for expressing that which we see and sense: "a watering can . . . a dog in the sun, a run-down churchyard, a cripple, a small farmhouse. . . . Each of them . . . which the eye glides over with understandable indifference . . . can assume an aspect sublime and moving: but words are inadequate for expressing this" (2:343–44). A gaping cleft had opened between words and world: "Disjointed words swam about me. . . . They are a vortex and I could not look into them without becoming dizzy, and their incessant spinning only drew me down into emptiness" (2:343). These troublesome vertiginous effects are related, furthermore, to the autonomy and self-referentiality of language so esteemed by Novalis and the early romantics: "I understood these concepts all too well: I saw their wonderful play of interrelations rising up in front of me like glorious fountains of water tossing golden balls into the air. I could see them swirling around playing with one another; but they were only related to each other" (2:343). Hofmannsthal's writer has been excluded from the wonderful self-referential play of words. Fascinating but foreign, language has become an epistemological liability, not the key to understanding and higher self-realization.

With the passing of romantic optimism also passed the possibility of an idyll of the "absolute identity of the ideal and real," language and world theorized by Friedrich Schlegel in his *Universalpoesie* fragment; the satire of the "absolute difference between

22. Hofmannsthal, *Ausgewählte Werke*, 2:342. Further references to this edition appear in the text.

the real and ideal" cannot be overcome: what remains is the elegy of emancipated language forever suspended in the space between ideal and real, man and world.

The Philosophy of Language

In his recent book on Gottlob Frege, Hans Sluga remarks: "First philosophers thought about the world. Next, they reflected on the way the world is organized. Finally, they turned their attention to the medium in which such recognition is expressed. There seems to be a natural progression in philosophy from metaphysics through epistemology to the philosophy of language."[23] Although the epistemological philosophy of the late eighteenth and nineteenth centuries did not move the study of language per se to the center of its deliberations, thought about language was nevertheless on the increase. Johann Gottfried Herder, remarks Sluga, can be seen as one of the important founding fathers of what has come to be known as the analytic tradition of philosophy. This tradition, whose thin thread stretches from Herder across the nineteenth century (Wilhelm von Humboldt, Otto Friedrich Gruppe, Adolf Trendelenberg, Heinrich Czolbe) to Frege, became in the twentieth century with Wittgenstein and the Anglo-American thinkers a prominent intellectual force.

After 1830, idealistic philosophy began to decline; its quasi-mystical form of speculation seemed ineffectual in the face of the social and political transformations of the times and the practical gains made by the empirical sciences. Philosophy thus retrenched and became self-critical, defensive, or positivistic. Among those who turned their pens critically against the philosophical tradition can be counted Karl Marx, Ludwig Feuerbach, David Friedrich Strauss, and Gruppe. All assailed Georg Hegel's antimaterial ideal-

23. Sluga, *Gottlob Frege*, 1.

ism. Otto Friedrich Gruppe, for one, took him to task for his un-critical use of language. Hegel's philosophy, he maintained, did not sufficiently take into account the relationship between thought and language. Concepts, he felt, were hypostatized in the Hegelian system and not recognized for what they are: constructs of natural language. "Truth" was a prime example. Predating Friedrich Nietzsche's critique of the Western valorization of truth by some fifty years, Gruppe wrote in 1831: "Truth, universality, necessity, the absolute etc. these are in reality the disastrous words, the culprits . . . which we wanted to control. . . . It was, however, the philosophers who fell upon the word truth and ripped it up by the roots—roots firmly implanted in the ground of language through which the word had received its vital and healthy meaning."[24] Nietzsche, another late nineteenth-century philosopher of the critical ilk, aimed his criticism at Western culture and its implicit metaphysics of power. He was also one of the first modern philosophers to undertake a critique of linguistic representation. His discussions of the Western concept of truth in the articles "On the Pathos of Truth" and "On Truth and Lying in an Extra-Moral Sense"[25] present a serious indictment of language and representation in general. Truth, he argued, is a mystification, a potent concept that had evolved to facilitate man's acquisition of power. Its mystifying power lies in the fact that it is not recognized as a human construct, but rather taken as an absolute, ahistorical value which is invoked to adjudicate the veracity of man's assertions about, among other things, the world. Nietzsche thus hoped to expose the implicit assumption underlying Western culture that truth is an absolute value which stands above and prior to language. For Nietzsche, truth is one linguistic concept among many others. "Truth," he exclaimed, is "a movable army of metaphors, metonomies, and an-

24. Gruppe, *Philosophische Werke*, 12:352.
25. Nietzsche, *Werke*, 3:265–71, 309–22.

thropomorphisms, in short the totality of human relations, which has been poetically and rhetorically intensified, embellished, figuralized, and, after long use, appears to a people to be canonical and binding: truths are illusions—we have just forgotten that they are such."[26] Nietzsche did not wish to eliminate the concept of truth but rather relativize it to language and thereby deny it any absolute status. Such a relativization means, ultimately, that there can be no standard outside of language to justify or secure its representations. Man is like an island, always at a remove from the mainland of the world, adrift in an endless sea of signs. Truth, being part of a metaphoric-metonymical figural practice, cannot be employed to characterize or ground man's assertions about the world. Friedrich Schlegel's *Elegie* minus a *deus ex machina* "Idylle" resurfaces once again.

What Nietzsche and Hofmannsthal expressed at the close of the nineteenth century became an intellectual epidemic in the early twentieth century. Writers, philosophers, and theologians experienced more poignantly than ever before a debilitating insufficiency of words. Language turned perplexingly opaque; its words ceased to be a transparent medium for expression and representation. Reflecting back on the early days of his career at the beginning of this century, Bertrand Russell remarked that language at that time ceased to be for him and generally for his generation a transparent medium that could be used without paying particular attention to it.[27]

Russell introduced the work of the German logician and mathematician Gottlob Frege to the philosophers at Cambridge. Frege, troubled by the insufficiency of natural languages, set forth in the last decade of the nineteenth century to remedy the situation by developing a coherent semantic theory for formalized languages

26. Ibid., 314.
27. See Magee, *Men of Ideas,* esp. 182.

which then could be used as a model for understanding natural language. Believing that language functions at its deepest levels according to principles of logic (as do formalized languages), Frege worked to uncover these principles and provide an abstract and formal account of meaning. Frege thus inveighed against the prevailing late nineteenth-century psychologism and positivism, which held that words stand for ideas or mental concepts. Each word, he believed, when stripped of its subjective coloring (*Färbung*), bore a logical, semantic core.[28] This core he called sense (*Sinn*); it was neither an idea nor a mental image but an invariable and transcultural semantic unit that governed a word's logical function. Most important, *Sinn* is distinct from the word's reference (*Bedeutung*), as can be seen in the following excerpt from his well-known essay "On Sense and Reference": "The reference of a name is the object which is signified; the corresponding mental representation which we then have, is totally subjective; between this representation and referent lies the sense, which is no longer subjective, like the mental representation, but also not the object itself. . . . Sense is the common property of many . . . it is not part of or a mode of the individual psyche."[29]

Frege illustrates the all-important distinction between sense and reference with the following example: the terms "Morningstar" and "Eveningstar" have two distinct senses, sociocultural values within the semantic field of English (which happen to parallel *Morgenstern* and *Abendstern* in German). Roughly, the first star to appear in the evening is known as the "Eveningstar," whereas the last star to vanish with the coming day is the "Morningstar." Two terms, two senses. Their reference, however, as astronomers tell us, is the same: both terms have the same referent, the planet Venus (144). It is easy to see that the sense of a term cannot be

---

28. See Hacking, *Why Does Language Matter to Philosophy?* esp. 49–53, 70–92.
29. Frege, "Über Sinn und Bedeutung," in *Kleine Schriften*, 146. Further references to this essay appear in the text.

equated with its referent. Yet they are related: "A proper name (word, sign, sign combination, expression) expresses a sense, and signifies a referent. The sense of a sign is expressed in order to signify its reference" (148). Frege continues, stating that it is our striving for truth which compels us to advance from sense to referent (from *Sinn* to *Bedeutung*): "The striving for truth is that which always drives us to advance from sense to reference" (149). The implication is clear; although the sense and referent are associated in normal speech, sense does not depend upon the referent, truth does.

With Frege's analysis of sense and reference, the dawning awareness of the independence of meaning and world which began in the Classical Age was finally philosophically formalized. Words mean more than the things they may name. Not necessarily tied to the world, sense (or meaning) is now understood as an intersubjective, transcultural semantic force that binds the speakers of a particular speech community together. By isolating the *Sinn* from all other elements of subjective *Färbung*, Frege attempted to make natural language better suited for logical analysis. Once the *Sinn* is properly delineated, he felt, one can begin to analyze the basic units of communication: sentences. This is where the referent or potential referent comes into play, for the "truth value of a sentence," Frege believed, is its "referent" (149).[30] Without referents, sentences are incomplete assertions, in a way, a play with sense without commit-

30. Although Frege's conceptualization of truth is too complex to discuss here, it is not to be understood in terms of a correspondence between word and thing or language and world. Truth, for Frege, is more a cultural norm, an agreement between sentences and what a culture holds to be true about the world. Answering the skeptic's question: "How do you even know that there is such a thing as a referent?" Frege retorts: "We assume that there is a referent . . . of course we can be mistaken in this assumption. . . . The question whether we are always wrong in this assumption cannot be answered. Suffice it to say—in order to justify our intentions when talking or thinking about the referent of a sign—that we must make one qualification: that there is a referent" (ibid., 147–48).

ment to their truth or falsity. Poetry, it seems, has long exhibited this fact, as reflected in Frege's remark: "When listening to an epic, for example, that which fascinates, above and beyond the sensuous quality of the words, is simply the sense of the sentences and the ideas and sentiments which this sense induces. We would, however, leave the realm of the aesthetic if we were to ask about the truth [of these utterances]" (149). In a footnote, Frege adds: "It would be desirable to have a special expression for [such] signs which only have sense. Let us call them images [*Bilder*]" (149). Sense without reference is an image, *ein Bild*. That Frege should use a word with such strong visual connotations—"Bild" (image, picture, figure)—to describe the referentless, evocative signs of poetry, even though the effects ("ideas and sentiments") of these poetic signs are admittedly not purely visual, exemplifies the modern difficulty of breaking away from a long aesthetic-philosophic tradition of visual metaphorics. The later Wittgenstein, when alluding to Western philosophy—including Frege's work—before the definitive twentieth-century break with representation, speaks to a captivation by such visual metaphorics, writing: "A *picture* held us captive. And we could not get outside it, for it lay in our language and language seemed to repeat it to us inexorably."[31] One might also argue that this "inexorable repeating" of "picture" in our language registers the lingering vestiges of Western culture's deep-seated desire to keep man and his language visually connected to the world. It is a desire that gave rise to an aesthetics of absolute visual mimesis in the German Enlightenment, as well as, perhaps, the more recent "mythology" of a mirror stage as it is elaborated in the discourse of (Lacanian) psychoanalysis.

Late in Frege's life, Ludwig Wittgenstein, then a student of philosophy, approached the aging philosopher for academic advice. The counsel he received was that he should go to Cambridge,

31. Wittgenstein, *Philosophical Investigations*, par. 115.

where Bertrand Russell and others were continuing his pioneering work on the logical analysis of language. Like Frege, Russell approached the analysis of language from the standpoint of logic. He also agreed with Frege that a semantic theory must proceed not from the analysis of individual words but from the logical analysis of sentences. Russell, however, differed with Frege in an important way. He privileged reference over sense. He believed, by contrast to Frege, that it is a term's reference—not some unquantifiable transcultural semantic core such as sense—which forms the meaningful link between speakers of a language: meaning, he advocated, was a function of reference. This view, of course, puts Russell in a "referential theory of meaning" camp, yet it must be stressed that his construal of reference was wide in scope and includes much more than a simple designation of objects of the physical world. Actually, that sort of naming, thought for so long to be the basic function of language from Plato through the late eighteenth century, is to Russell but a very small portion of language. The vast majority of linguistic references, in his view, is to abstracted generalities—concepts, aspects, properties, and universals. An assertion such as "This rose is red," Russell would argue, when uttered seriously in an appropriate context, denotes a unique flower by reference to generalities—roughly, "redness" and "the class of flowers called roses." The word "this," albeit an incomplete description, is the word that points out the rose, which led Russell to assert that the only true names (proper names) in English are "this" and "that." They are the only words capable of denoting unique things in the world. With the preponderance of reference being involved with abstract qualities and generalities, however, it would seem that Russell really has not avoided the Fregian notion of *Sinn*. In retrospect we can see that Russell's tenacious adherence to a referential theory of meaning reveals the lingering effects of the late nineteenth-century quest for unqualified objectivity. Russell had been convinced that it was the logical-referential structure of language (not its misleading grammatical structure) that held the key to understanding language and the possibility of solving the endemic crisis of linguistic representation. To accommodate this belief, he was forced to posit a world of atomistic simples—objects, things—to which a logically ordered language could unproblematically refer and represent.

The significance of Russell's work lies not so much in his referential theory of meaning as in the theoretical response that ensued from his pioneering work in linguistic philosophy. Probably no other philosopher in the first decades of this century had as much influence on the outcome of Anglo-American philosophy as Bertrand Russell. Both the culmination and ultimately the rejection of Russell's referential analysis of language can be found in the work of Ludwig Wittgenstein. In his early work, the *Logisch-philosophische Abhandlung* (the *Tractatus*), published in 1922, Wittgenstein continued Russell's logical analysis of language.[32] After years of reflection upon the problems and assumptions of the *Tractatus,* however, Wittgenstein came to the conclusion that his approach to language had been misguided. In the *Tractatus,* Wittgenstein had held that language corresponds one-to-one with reality. Determinate meaning was the product or result of this correspondence. Understanding language was knowing to what the names of sentences refer. This was accomplished, he argued, by recognizing that which is common to both language and reality: their shared "logical form": "That which any *picture* [*Bild*] . . . must have in common with reality, in order to *depict* it—whether correctly or not—is the logical form, that is, the form of reality." Language is like a replica of reality—each proposition "is a model

32. The Chaucer Press (1974) edition of Wittgenstein's *Tractatus* contains the original German text with its translation on facing pages and the original (1922) introduction by Bertrand Russell.

of reality as we believe it to be." The elements of the "sentence-picture" stand in the same relationship to one another as do the discrete objects of reality. And so, Wittgenstein concluded, "To elucidate the essence of a sentence entails elucidating the essence of all description, that is, the essence of the world."[33] Language, he proffered, has a determinate content because it re-presents objectively a determinate reality of discretely articulated elements.

In his later work, Wittgenstein spurns basing the understanding of language on a referential model of objective representation. Now, rather than trying to conceptualize language in terms of a representative or "picturing" function, Wittgenstein turns, in the *Philosophical Investigations*, to an almost behavioralistic form of descriptive analysis. Language, he finds, is not, as he previously thought, primarily a collection of names which can be arranged in order to represent the "facts" of the world. It is, rather, a flexible "form of life," a multiplicity of *Sprachspiele* (language games) whose rules are determined not by a referential relation to the world but by the play itself.[34]

The *Sprachspiel* metaphor underscores the fact that language is not meaningful solely by virtue of its relation to the world. It becomes meaningful only in the larger context of the role it plays in human interaction, which can, of course, include dealing with the world. The point is that words and concepts do not have an essence or absolute meaning in isolation from their use in any number of "forms of life." "*By itself*, every sign is dead. *What* gives it its life? In use it is *alive*." The *what* of language is its use, not named things. "Consider the sentence an instrument," Wittgenstein suggests, "and its sense as its use."[35]

In rejecting his own Tractarian language-as-picture theory,

33. Wittgenstein, *Tractatus*, pars. 2.18, 4.01, 5.4711.
34. Wittgenstein, *Philosophical Investigations*, pars. 7, 23. See also Wittgenstein, *On Certainty*, 359.
35. Wittgenstein, *Philosophical Investigations*, pars. 432, 421.

Wittgenstein also abandons the quest for a neutral set of representations that stands independent of speakers in a nonintentional
relation to what is supposed to be represented. The late nineteenth-
century scientific ideal of objectively valid knowledge (and its neutral presentation in language) fades into the obscurity of a dream.
Later, Wittgenstein formed a "new" philosophy that no longer
privileges representation as the basis for man's linguistic encounter
with the world; it is also a "devisualized" philosophy in that the
definitive break is made from visual metaphorics and a deep-seated
desire to keep man and his language perceptually bound to the
world.[36] It is, in Richard Rorty's terms, a "post-Kantian philosophy" in that transcendental conditions of possibility for representation in general are no longer sought.

Post-Kantian philosophy does not attempt to ground words in
a true correspondence between the world and a nonempirical
"transcendental" subjectivity. Words and things, philosopher Willard van Orman Quine shows, never unproblematically correspond. Furthermore, it is a mistake to suppose, Quine urges, "that
the truth of a statement is somehow analyzable into a linguistic
component and a factual component."[37] Quine argues that single
utterances seldom correspond to a "unique range of events, such
that the occurrence of any of them would add to the likelihood of
truth of the statement" (77). Our knowledge about the world is
not a one-to-one correspondence of propositions to facts, but
rather a dense web of interwoven theories, beliefs, and schemes
which are only *theoretically* related to actual experience. Writes
Quine: "The totality of our so-called knowledge or beliefs . . . is a
man-made fabric which impinges on experience only along the

36. See Rorty, *Philosophy and the Mirror of Nature,* chap. 6. Rorty views current
Anglo-American philosophy, Quine, and especially Davidson, as well as the Continental hermeneutic tradition, as post-Kantian philosophies.

37. Quine, "Two Dogmas of Empiricism," 77. Subsequent citations are in the
text.

edges . . . total science is like a *field of force* whose boundary conditions are experience" (78).

Even "occasion sentences," those few sentences at the very periphery of the web of beliefs which are used to refer to particular things or events, are plagued, Quine asserts, by a certain "indeterminacy of reference." Extralinguistic reference, Quine illustrates in his "indeterminacy of reference" thesis, is not a simple matter of hooking words up to things because "things" are not preorganized prior to man's concept-laden gaze.[38] Quine argues that divergent referential schemes may be compatible with the dispositions of a community even though they are incompatible with each other. Little, insignificant details of reference that rarely affect communication may vary between speakers. That which is referred to can never be made absolutely explicit, and so reference will always remain, in principle, indeterminate and theoretical.

Quine's post-Kantian holism, which posits language as a whole meeting the world, reinforces the Wittgensteinian break with referential theories of meaning. "Once the theory of meaning is sharply separated from the theory of reference," he writes, "meanings themselves, as obscure intermediary entities, may well be abandoned" (64). Trying, as did Humpty Dumpty, to hook meaning onto some definitive, clearly delineated referent has, in Quine's view, caused people to think of meanings as a set of discrete mental entities. Once meaning and reference are "sharply separated," meanings as mental entities preceding speech begin to look impossible. Understanding language is thus not recognizing some inner state or meaning "behind" the expression, but rather relating any expression to the whole of the speaker's and the language community's fabric of beliefs and behavioral dispositions, to, in short, a multiplicity of language games.

Quine's and Wittgenstein's campaign against reification of

38. Quine, *Word and Object*, chap. 2.

meaning extends to concepts as well. Concepts, as part of the ever-flexible cultural-linguistic web of beliefs and dispositions, are likewise denied the certainty they enjoyed in the Kantian transcendental subject, itself a misleading reification. Concepts must be seen for what they are—variable sociocultural abstractions, which at any time can be adjusted by new information at the "edge of experience." Truth must also be seen as variable and depends as much on "intralinguistic" reference as on extralinguistic facts. It could be said that language represents more its own structures—the weave of beliefs, dispositions, and concepts—than the structure of the world. The structure of the world is itself one among many "cultural posits." "Physical objects," Quine reports, "are conceptually imported into the situation as convenient intermediaries, not by definition in terms of experience, but simply as irreducible posits, comparable epistemologically to the gods of Homer. Gods and objects differ only in degree and not in kind" (79). The physical objects we talk about are an effective way of *coping* with the world, not *copying* it. They are one part of one language game, a game whose rules can be altered, changed, and transformed—and, in poetry, broken.

The turn away from representation that first emerged in the late eighteenth century came full swing in the work of Wittgenstein and Quine. In giving up the notion that language is a neutral schema for depicting the world and by locating meaning or sense in games and behavioral dispositions, there is no longer a need for a Kantian transcendental subject that must stand outside of language to judge the (referential) validity of its speech acts. Words and sentences take on significance and value by virtue of their position in a textual field, by "reference" to one another, rather than by reference to specific facts of the world. "Statements about the external world," Quine writes, "face the tribunal of sense experience not individually but only as a corporate body" (46).

CHAPTER 4

Modernism and the Proliferation of Literary Theory

And we all, with unveiled face, reflecting the glory of the Lord, are being changed into his likeness.—2 Corinthians 3:18

Je commence à entrevoir ce que j'appellerais le "sujet profond" de mon livre. C'est, ce sera sans doute la rivalité du mond réel et de la représentation que nous nous ens faisons.—André Gide[1]

Relativity

THE FIRST DECADE and a half of the twentieth century was an explosive period marked by revolutionary changes in art, literature, and science. These few years witnessed the dramatic culmination of intellectual developments whose roots reached back to the epistemological transformations of the closing years of the eighteenth century and produced such revolutionary movements as cubism and surrealism in painting and futurism and expressionism in literature. It also produced the influential work of such luminaries as Igor Stravinsky, James Joyce, Sigmund Freud, and Albert

1. "I'm beginning to glimpse that which I would call the 'deep subject' of my book. It is and will be without doubt the rivalry between the real world and the representation which we have fashioned of it" (André Gide, *Les Faux-Monnayeurs* [Paris: Gallimard, 1925], 261).

Einstein. "These men and others like them," remarks Walter Sokel, "have revolutionized our world and changed our concepts of the universe and of the self."[2] It was also—not coincidentally—during the first decade and a half of this century that Georg Trakl succeeded in breaking away from the linearity of classical-romantic confessional poetry to explore the expressive potential of an axis of language which does not heed the logic of representation.

Paradigmatic of this revolutionary juncture in Western intellectual history is Albert Einstein's theory of relativity, published in 1905. Einstein's early work brought traditional physics to an abrupt turnaround by demonstrating that space and time, matter and energy—the axiomatic givens underwriting Newtonian physics—were not the absolute invariants of reality but, rather, relative not only to one another but also to the standpoint of the perceiving subject. The traditional givens of material substance, three-dimensional space and linear time, the necessary conditions for objectively valid knowledge, began to look like the mythic artifacts of an older epistemological model. Space was now relative to time, whereas matter lost its axiomatic status, becoming, in the final analysis—and depending on the perceiving subject's relative vantage point—a manifestation of energy. Reality in a sense loses its reality; what we perceive is only a surface manifestation engendered by our relative position and not by some static noumenal (Kantian) *Ding an sich*.

The objectivity undermined by Einsteinian relativity and quantum mechanics found a parallel and related development in the new field of psychology. The work of Sigmund Freud, for example, unsettled the belief in the stable and unified conscious individual and suggested that the self might also be another illusory surface manifestation. In Freudian theory the human subject is relative to the unknown labyrinth of the unconscious. What we

2. Sokel, *Writer in Extremis*, 1.

think, say, dream, or joke about, Freud theorized, is not what it seems to be but, rather, a distorted manifestation of the deeper "truth" of the human psyche—a manifestation whose hidden (and unknowable) agenda is always relative to the subject's unconscious fears, desires, repressions, and psychic history.

The bond between man and world—words and things—that had been loosened by the incipient failure of representation in the eighteenth century was rendered in Einsteinian and Freudian theory doubly problematic by a modern relativity that destabilizes both subject and object. This chapter brings the foregoing analysis of intellectual history to a conclusion by relating trends in twentieth-century literary theory to the modernist movement and the emergence of this modern relativity. Though marked by a proliferation of often diverse approaches and goals, nearly all literary theory from 1920 on shares an increased concern for the nature and function of language and is thus related to the destabilizing effects of the modern relativity that emerged in the first decade of this century. Literary theorists have been forced to define a new ground for the "literary" that could answer the unsettling relativism of the era and also justify and legitimate its existence in general. It is perhaps ironic that many theoretical movements of the twentieth century have in one form or another made the problematic split between words and world into the virtue of autonomy. It is precisely this detachment of intellect and nature which has been used to guarantee the freedom and validity of the literary-textual universe. The "textuality" of the work has become almost sacrosanct, a value in itself. In valorizing the complex self-sufficiency and autonomy of the textual system, theoreticians satisfied a deep desire to establish a noncontingent refuge for the free-floating human subject—and, ultimately, the human sciences. Northrop Frye's speculations, for instance, about a mythic unconscious that is forever repeated in the various mythic structures of the closed circuitry of the literary universe shelters the literary from the disintegrating effects of the groundless contingencies of modern existence. His project and its motivations are, further, related not only to the structuralist search for collective psychic universals, which, at a deep and intersubjective level, objectively constitute all human behavior, but also to Lacanian speculations about an imaginary, prelinguistic mirror stage that retroactively escapes the relativizing forces of social discourse.

Though in part defensive in nature, this abounding valorization of autonomy in the twentieth-century aesthetics of modernism is, as Jürgen Habermas has argued, also the product of a larger cultural phenomenon which he calls the "project of the Enlightenment."[3] As the unity of religion and philosophy fell apart under the weight of the Enlightenment's quest for verifiable truth unencumbered by myth and prejudice, the fields of science, morality, and art became increasingly differentiated and separated autonomous spheres. The "project of modernity," Habermas believes, was developed in the eighteenth century by the philosophers of the Enlightenment and "consisted in their effort to develop objective science, universal morality and law, and autonomous art according to their *inner logic* (emphasis added; 9). The result was a professional specialization, which originally was to serve the common good by releasing "the cognitive potentials of each of these domains from their esoteric forms" (9). The idealism of the early German romantics was thus the first blush of such a specialization and autonomy that was to serve—"poeticize"—society and culture and not isolate the artist. As the humanistic promise of romantic autonomy went sour in the increasingly rationalized world of the industrial revolution, however, so too did the promise of a

3. Habermas, "Modernity—An Incomplete Project," 8. Further references to this essay appear in the text. Habermas's essay was published originally in *New German Critique* 22 (Winter 1981).

utopic reconciliation of art and society. In the work of early modernist poets such as Baudelaire and other nineteenth-century symbolists, the irreconcilability of art and society became increasingly the oppositionality of the two. By the twentieth century this oppositional stance becomes programmatic as modernism—almost synonymous with the scandalous, profane, and revolutionary— takes flight from the leveling, trivializing, and defusing effects of bourgeois culture by withdrawing into a stronghold of complete autonomy.[4]

The Proliferation of Theory

In Chapter 3 we saw how the epistemological problematics of representation dating to the mid-eighteenth century found a modern articulation and elaboration in Quine's technical "indeterminacy of reference thesis." Representational-referential indeterminacy— or relativity—is not limited to certain enigmatic poetic texts, it is a fact of all natural language; the representational hookup between language and world is, as Quine has demonstrated, always a theoretical event that can neither ground language nor constitute its meaningfulness.

The linguistic turn in twentieth-century philosophy and the corresponding analysis of reference and representation find an analogous development in the field of literary criticism. As early as 1924 I. A. Richards, in his *Principles of Literary Criticism,* noted a certain nonreferential character of literary language and opposed this "emotive" language to the scientific or referential language of

4. See Dowden, *Sympathy for the Abyss,* esp. chap.1, for a good general discussion of literary modernism. Though Dowden's study focuses on the German modernist novel, the four salient features of modernism which he enumerates in the first chapter (*Wirklichkeitsverlust, Verinnerlichung, Sprachkrise,* and self-consciousness) are generally applicable to the modernist movement as a whole. For a nearly exhaustive catalog of discussions of literary modernism, see esp. n. 8, pp. 11–12.

everyday discourse. "Emotive" language, as he understood it, is not characterized by its reference but by the effect it elicits in the reader: "As a rule, a statement in poetry arouses attitudes much more wide and general in direction than the references of the statement."[5] The Slavic formalists, however, were the first to pursue in detail this referential aberration to which Richards alludes. In their attempt to isolate the distinguishing features common to all literary expression, what they called "literariness," they developed the notion of the autotelic or self-referential. The fundamental difference between literary expression and other speech acts was, in their opinion, to be found in the medium itself, not in its message. Verbal art, they claimed, is not primarily characterized by its content, its mode of potential reflection on the world, or the ideas it represents, but by its form, in particular the conspicuous form of its language. The study of literature, Roman Jakobson would argue, should not concern itself with "literature in its totality" but with "those formal characteristics which make a given work a work of literature."[6] In their most extreme moments, the formalists' analysis of "literariness" brought them hyperbolically to deny relevant ties between literary language and anything extraliterary. They argued that literary words attract so much attention to themselves—they foreground the "texture" of their codes, rhetorical devices, structuring principles, formal attributes, and the like—that they become autonomous objects in their own right.[7] Literature, Jan Mukarovskí wrote, "concentrates attention on the linguistic sign itself—hence it is exactly the opposite of real orientation toward a goal which in language is a message."[8] The experi-

5. Richards, *Principles of Literary Criticism*, 273.
6. Jakobson, "Linguistics and Poetics," 350–57.
7. Rhythm, rhyme, meter, and euphony are a few of the more obvious ways in which poetic words foreground their own texture.
8. Mukarovskí, *The Word and Verbal Art*, 9. It is such hyperbolic formulations that motivated Fredric Jameson in his *Prisonhouse of Language* perhaps too hastily to

ence of verbal art becomes, in varying degrees, the apprehension of this self-referential effect whereby the text "bares its devices" and "speaks" of its own coming into being.[9] Literary texts only appear to have extraliterary referents or an intended real-world orientation.

In view of these early explorations of the referential aberration of the literary text, it is easy to see, on one hand, that the formalist project is not only an analogous development to linguistic philosophy of the early twentieth century but also a theoretical response to the modernist movement of the nineteenth and early twentieth centuries. Indeed, the formalists' doctrine of the autonomous literary text or even I. A. Richards's deliberations on the emotive, nonreferential use of language are almost unthinkable without the precursor developments in the theoretical writings of the early German romantics and the poetry of the French symbolists. Viewed, on the other hand, from a more purely epistemological standpoint, one may also discern a general uneasiness or dissatisfaction with ordinary (nonpoetic) language, a sentiment that moves these theorists to valorize and totalize the nonreferential character of literary language. It is a compensatory gesture whose motivations are not much different from those that gave rise to the absolute visual mimesis speculations of the eighteenth century.

By 1930 the formalist movement was all but extinct in the Soviet Union, where it had begun, having been condemned by orthodox Marxists as an effete form of bourgeois escapism. The movement nonetheless continued to flourish elsewhere, most notably in Prague, where Roman Jakobson had resided since 1920.

dismiss the formalists' project. Robert Scholes counters Jameson's "formal prison" thesis by showing that the Russian school was in fact concerned with cultural and historical (diachronic) aspects, in short, the extraliterary implications, of literary discourse (*Structuralism in Literature*), 74–91.

9. Jameson, *Prisonhouse of Language*, 50.

Here, under the influence of the Wittgensteinian Prague School of linguistic philosophy, Jakobson further elaborated his analysis of the literary. Language, he postulated, can be broken down into six functions, one of which is the aesthetic or poetic function. In literature, the poetic function predominates. Characterized by its self-referential effects, this function thus promotes the "palpability" of signs: "The poetic function is not the sole function of verbal art but only its dominant, determining function, whereas in all other verbal activities, it acts as a subsidiary, accessory constituent. This function, by promoting the palpability of signs, deepens the fundamental dichotomy of signs and objects."[10] Jakobson also pursued another very productive line of thought. Using Ferdinand de Saussure's syntagmatic/paradigmatic distinction, he urged that literature, and especially poetry, opposes the horizontal and linear syntagmatic organization of content, favoring the vertical (and more diffuse) paradigmatic parameter. Syntagmatic, as the word's root suggests, involves a syntactical description of language. It covers the possibilities of linear and contiguous combinations of words or strings of semantic units within a given text and is, as such, the sine qua non principle of narrativity. Paradigmatic, by contrast, involves the relation any syntagmatic element may have to other elements and words (or discourses) not contained in the given sentence or text. Such relations may be morphological in nature—prefixes and suffixes, for example—or they may be semantic and involve such relations as connotation, association, or opposition. The word "sun" is, for example, paradigmatically related to its celestial counterpart "moon" as well as any number of other semantic elements such as "warmth," "life," "Apollo," and so on. "Sun" could conjure via Apollo, and, of course, depending on other contextual elements, the rich cultural heritage of classical mythology. The paradigmatic axis of language thus can and will

10. Jakobson, "Linguistics and Poetics," 356.

always reach beyond the bounds of any single text and relate not only whole classes of potentially interchangeable units but various cultural discourses as well. Moreover, an emphasis on the paradigmatic axis characteristic of modernist poetry serves further to foreground the "palpability of signs" and consequently downplay the linear "message" coordinate of language—an effect which, as we saw in Chapter 1, is accentuated by the conspicuous "hard" words in Lewis Carroll's "Jabberwocky." Those words depended more on the associative paradigmatic (or vertical) relations between words and consequently confounded Humpty Dumpty's narrative, syntagmatic (or horizontal) expectations.

By 1940 interest in the nonreferential aspect of poetic language had become a crucial concept in the fledgling New Critical movement. In 1941 John Crowe Ransom published a book, entitled *The New Criticism,* in which he reviewed the then new trends in literary criticism. Although he had not intended to found a new school of literary criticism, his book marks the point in Anglo-American critical history when structural-linguistic analysis of literature was on the verge of becoming the dominant critical approach. Reacting to the increasing rationalization of culture and society by the modern technological ethos of the rapidly advancing empirical sciences—and to the reductive positivism of certain of their predecessors—the New Critics attempted, in their decidedly modernist stance, to "justify poetry by securing for it a unique function for which modern scientism cannot find a surrogate." This unique function was to be found in poetry's autonomous form of discourse, a discourse which was a "self-contained and self-sustaining world of linguistic interrelationships."[11] The trend was thus to purify approaches to poetry from "scientific" studies of biography, sources, history of ideas, or social and political influences. In their emphasis on the autonomous linguistic structure of

11. Krieger, *New Apologists for Poetry,* 19, 20.

the literary text, the New Critics focused attention on the unquantifiable plurality or ambiguity of poetic idiom. Literature, they argued, will always resist determinate, and hence reductive, readings because of its purposely plural mode of expression. "Conflict structures," which frustrate determinate interpretation, will always arise upon closer examination of any text.[12] Plurality and indeterminacy thus prove to be the modernist poem's defense against reading that seeks to ground, determine, and understand it in terms other than its own. Atop the list of the New Critics' forbidden extrapoetic determinations was authorial intention. Far from denying the significance of the author's intentions and desires in the creation of the work—be they conscious, preconscious, or unconscious—the New Critics showed that meaning cannot be reduced to or derived from these desires and intentions. "Good" poetry, they argued, almost necessarily outstrips the intentions of its writer.[13] Expounds Murray Krieger: "It is language that has created the poetic idea, as this idea comes to be the complex of words that constitutes the completed poem. . . . The poet's original idea for his work . . . undergoes such radical transformations as language goes creatively to work . . . that the finished poem, in its

12. See Cleanth Brooks, *Well-Wrought Urn*.

13. The notion that meaning and authorial intention do not coincide is not new. The romantic *Besserverstehen* principle is a case in point: "Literary criticism," wrote Friedrich Schlegel, "means understanding an author better than he understood himself" (*Literary Notebooks*, 111). Friedrich Schleiermacher refined the dictum by shifting emphasis to the linguistic parameter. The task of interpretation, he wrote, "is understanding an author's speech at first as well as and then better than its creator" (Schleiermacher, *Hermeneutik*, 87). Kant also mused about the possibilities of understanding individuals' expressions "better" than they themselves do: "Let me remark that it is not unusual, both in speech and writing . . . to understand someone better than he understood himself" (*Werke*, 1:322). For a good discussion of the New Critical "Intentional Fallacy," see Beardsley and Wimmsatt, "Intentional Fallacy," 468–88. See Juhl, "Intention and Literary Interpretation," for a critical analysis of Beardsley's and Wimmsatt's thesis.

full internal relations, is far removed from what the author thought he had when he began."[14]

Rather than investigating the personality of the writer or the relation of the text to something extraliterary, the New Critics thus followed their romantic (and formalist) precursors and argued that the literary text was an organic whole that could never be articulated in determinate assertions. By organic they meant a verbal structure whose "meanings" issue from that work's particular configuration of component parts, its organic structure. The sense of a word, a phrase, or an image derives, they advanced, from its contextual value and is not a function of extratextual determination. "To allow the poem to function referentially," wrote Krieger, "is to break the context. It is to allow the poem to point outside itself and thus lead . . . into the uninspiring familiarities of the workaday world."[15] There is, as one might suspect from the defensive tone of the New Critics' "apologies" for poetic language, more at stake than their glorification of the poem's emancipated gestures. By protecting poetry from the mundane and uninspired modern "workaday world," these neo-Kantian critics hoped to provide man's endangered spirituality with a secure ontological mooring. For them, poetry (and art) held out the last possibility of keeping Western man's spirituality alive; the quasi-religious sanctuary of the aesthetic thus filled the void created by the modern "death of God" allowing man "to partake of being as it closes the distance between our consciousness and the ultimate origin of things."[16] More urgently than ever, the New Critics give expression to a deep-seated need to counter the inexorable effects of man's ra-

14. Krieger, *New Apologists for Poetry*, 21. The postwar intrinsic *Werkimmanent* approach in German was a closely related formalistic movement and followed the lead of the Anglo-American New Criticism and its *explication du texte* counterpart in France. See Hermand, *Synthetisches Interpretieren*, 143–47.

15. Krieger, *New Apologists for Poetry*, 20.

16. Lentricchia, *After the New Criticism*, 6.

tionalized estrangement from nature. By closing the gap between subject and object in the autonomous language of poetry, they were in effect trying both to legitimate the modernist poem's oppositional and autonomous stance and to compensate for the relativity of language and a modern crisis of representation. They were, in Jungian terms, seeking in poetry a prerational synchronicity of psyche and matter, a "meaningful coincidence"[17] that would compensate for the dehumanized (demythologized) modern, post-Enlightenment world of rationality.

In the 1960s another critical movement with a decidedly formalistic bent began to make an impact on the theoretical scene. Known as structuralism, this movement first emerged in France after the publication of Claude Lévi-Strauss's anthropological work *Tristes Tropiques*. Drawing upon his 1938 fieldwork study of the social codes, language, and dietary habits of the Nambikwara Indians of Brazil, Lévi-Strauss published this work in 1955 after returning to France from the United States, where he had resided for nearly ten years as a Jewish refugee during World War II. It was in New York at the New School for Social Research that he met Roman Jakobson, who introduced him to the work of de Saussure and the Russian formalists. Using the formalistic-Saussurian axiom of linguistic relativity—that meaning is a product of the inherent relational structures of language—Lévi-Strauss began a fruitful avenue of research that bridged the fields of anthropology and linguistic analysis. Similar to the formalists, who had studied language irrespective of extralinguistic determinants as an autonomous system that "presupposes the exclusion of everything that is outside its organism or system,"[18] Lévi-Strauss now worked to elaborate a methodology for studying culture that did not posit

17. Jung, *Man and His Symbols*, 41–42, 226–27.
18. Saussure, *Course in General Linguistics*, 20.

or assume an idealistic reciprocity between man and world. The model he strove to articulate would also overcome the opposition between the individual and the collective nature of culture by demonstrating that both individual and culture are constituted by deeper, largely unconscious structural codes. Lévi-Strauss's work on myths is exemplary of his "linguistic" approach.[19] By applying the semiotic conceptualization of meaning (as the product of differential structure), Lévi-Strauss broke down the "surface" content of myths into component parts or "mythemes," which, like the words of language, acquire significance only when combined according to the systems' governing codes and rules. These mythemic relations, Lévi-Strauss believed, were—like Jungian archetypes—inherent to the human mind: they were the universal mental determinants for the plethora of myths which human cultures have and will continue to generate. This means that in exploring the deep mythic structure, or ultimately language, as the spin-off field of literary structuralism would hold, the anthropologist-linguist is investigating not the manifest content but the objective mental processes that precede the creation of the myth and enable an individual (or culture) to classify and organize its phenomenal experience. The human being, its thought, behavior, and also its language, is actually a function of a deeper structural system. Our behavior is governed, Lévi-Strauss irreverently argued, not by conscious intention and ethical principle but by the "deeper level" determinism of the collective mind itself. Myths are thus paradigmatic of such a determinism, as he muses: "If it were possible to show . . . that the apparent arbitrariness of myths, the supposed freedom of inspiration, the seemingly uncontrolled process of invention, implied the existence of laws operating at a deeper level, then the conclusion would be inescapable. . . . If the human

19. Lévi-Strauss, "Structural Study of Myth," 428–44.

mind is determined even in its creation of myths, *a fortiori* it is determined in other spheres as well."[20]

This is Lévi-Strauss's ultimate anti-Cartesian conclusion. Because both the individual and culture are subsumed under the "laws operating at a deeper level," Lévi-Strauss could argue that man is the product of unconscious structure, of an objective system he does not control. Myth and language predate the individual; they are not the product of consciousness; consciousness is, rather, the product of them: man is spoken by his myth and language. "I therefore claim to show, not how men think in myths but how myths operate in men's minds without their being aware of the fact. . . . It would perhaps be better to go still further and, disregarding the thinking subject completely, proceed as if the thinking process were taking place in myths."[21]

Applied to literature, structuralism thus presents a radical demystification of the New Critical literary religiosity: the literary is not a unique form of discourse originating in the inspired poet but a plurality of voices, the product of a set of impersonal systems or discourses—be they social, aesthetic, philosophic, political, or other—that have converged in the text. The author—the "writer"—is a medium who is spoken, manipulated by these independent and impersonal "intertextual" cultural forces. Incapable of controlling these forces, the writer can no longer be viewed as an inspired conveyor of individual experience, for meaning proves to be a complexly overdetermined and entangled tissue of traces from various preformed, prearticulated, "already written" texts. Meaning is not identical with itself; it is through and through differential and can never be controlled by its speakers. Structuralist meaning, as Terry Eagleton puts it, "is a matter of what the sign is *not*, its meaning . . . is scattered or dispersed along the whole chain of

20. Quoted by Culler from *Le Cru et le cuit*, in *Structuralist Poetics*, 45.
21. Lévi-Strauss, *The Raw and the Cooked*, 12.

signifiers: it cannot be easily nailed down, it is never fully present in any one sign alone, but is rather a kind of constant flickering of presence and absence together."[22]

Structuralism thus suggests a new antihumanistic model that displaces—decenters—the individual as the locus of meaning into the structure of the system. It decries the "death of the subject" and the "death of the author."[23] As one likely senses, not only does the work of de Saussure and Jakobson figure prominently in the structuralist reevaluation of the author—writing subject—but also the work of Marx, Freud, and Nietzsche, who are hailed by the second-generation structuralist (poststructuralist) critics as the precursor fathers of the postmodernist "deconstruction" of the concept of an autonomous and self-possessed individual in control of its destiny.

One of the most important figures in the dissemination of structuralism in France, the United States, and also to a certain extent Britain and West Germany was Roland Barthes, who was the editor of the influential journal *Tel Quel* in France in the 1950s and 1960s. Barthes's developing career, as reflected in four of his widely read books, *Writing Degree Zero* (1953), *A Theory of Semiotics* (1964), *S/Z* (1970), and *The Pleasure of the Text* (1973), charts the evolution of structuralist literary criticism from its beginnings in postwar Heideggerian existentialism to its appropriation of Lévi-Straussian deep-structure analysis, and, finally, to its psychoanalytic variant in the deconstructive analysis of Derridean poststructuralism. It must be said that even though the structuralist project tends to become idealistic and respond to the modern ontological relativity of language by deferring, ultimately, to the invariant deep structures of the system—be they mythic, psychological, cultural, or purely textual—the structuralist movement has

22. Eagleton, *Literary Theory*, 128.
23. See Barthes, "Death of the Author," and Foucault "What Is an Author?"

generated a productive interdisciplinary discussion that has helped to overcome the modernist–New Critical opposition of intrinsic and extrinsic approaches by reading any text, literary or other, as a convergence of forces from disparate textual or cultural sources, be they unconscious or conscious in origin or nature.

This analysis of deep structure and intertextual forces operating in language, literature, and culture was not an isolated event that took place only in France. Noam Chomsky's work in the 1960s and 1970s, for example, on the deep universal structures of a transformational grammar—with its bow to Roman Jakobson—or Northrop Frye's work in the 1950s on a mythic unconscious-preconscious archetypal structure passed on by a poetic society—a literary universe that "shapes itself and is not shaped externally"[24]—both register a similar response to the modern relativity which poignantly undermined in the first decades of this century the vestiges of the Enlightenment's quest for reciprocity of subject and object.

The implicit idealism of universal deep-structure analysis is seized upon by Jacques Derrida in his postmodern strategy of dismantling and neutralizing idealized concepts such as structure, presence, self, spirit, or even God. Derrida's "phonocentric" critique of the three-thousand-year history of the Western metaphysical tradition links the privileging of certain supersensible, idealistic concepts to a cultural repression of the material basis "upon which all spirituality and all dignified superstructures depend."[25] Various idealistic concepts have been engendered, Derrida argues, by the "logocentristic" "debasement" of writing as an inferior derivative of "full" (phonic) speech. Derrida argues: "The system of 'hearing (understanding) oneself speak' through the phonic substance— which *presents itself* as a nonexterior, nonmundane, therefore non-

24. Frye, *Anatomy of Criticism,* 97.
25. Latimer, *Contemporary Critical Theory,* 165.

empirical or noncontingent signifier—has necessarily dominated the history of the world . . . and has even produced the idea of the world, the idea of world-origin, that arises from the difference between the worldly and the nonworldly, the outside and the inside, ideality and nonideality, universal and nonuniversal, transcendental and empirical, etc."[26] This phonocentristic privileging of sound has led us to believe, Derrida claims, that the sound of the voice or spoken word is immediately connected to the mind and full meaning whereas the written word is a derivative, fallen exteriority that can only represent (not express) the full meaning residing in the mind. Once we have recognized that the supposed phonetic basis of primary language is itself material (in that it is composed of physical units of sound) and thus also the product of differential structurations, all of our culture's privileged spiritual, supersensible, nonempirical concepts—including structure itself—will prove to be idealistic projections that rest on the systematic repression of the undesirable material basis of things. Our culture has valorized the spoken over the written, Derrida argues, "because the voice, producer of the *first symbols,* has a relationship of essential and immediate proximity with the mind. . . . It signifies 'mental experiences' which themselves reflect or mirror things by natural resemblance." As one immediately notices in the phrase " 'mental experiences' which themselves reflect or mirror things by natural resemblance," Derrida is debunking an eighteenth-century representational conceptualization of meaning which posits a natural form of mirroring discourse—an absolute visual mimesis that links mental experience to reality by means of natural resemblances and correspondences. Derrida, however, claims to be running out the implications of de Saussure's structural insights into signification, namely, "in language there are only differences with no positive terms." Meaning, he feels, can never be a "positive term," a stable

26. Derrida, *Of Grammatology,* 7–8.

and "fully present" sense, because of the endlessly relational, differential structure of language. Once the lessons of the differential structure of language have been grasped, Derrida claims, everything becomes "discourse . . . a system where the central signified, the original or transcendental signified, is never absolutely present outside a system of differences. The absence of the transcendental signified extends the domain and the interplay of signification *ad infinitum*."[27] "Words, even if we take them as magic," expounds Harold Bloom in a Derridean moment, "refer *only* to other words, to the end of it."[28] There is thus no sign, or signified, which stands above this infinite play of differences: "The sign and divinity," Derrida suggestively concludes, "have the same place and time of birth."[29] Our beliefs, our ideal concepts, and our longings for a noncontingent transcendent realm prior to the graphic signification of language are at once the product of the differential structure of language, what he calls writing (*écriture*) and a massive cultural repression. The nonprivileged, negative side of any binary pair, however, always leaves traces on the surfaces, in the repressed margins or unconscious (of the text), and can return from this state of repression at any time to disturb the stability of language, expression, or the self-presence of the speaking subject.

Although Derrida never openly admits the impact of the seminars of Jacques Lacan on his writing—Derrida, like Roland Barthes, attended Lacan's influential seminars at the University of Paris—it is clear that the psychoanalytic aspect of his work bears the stamp of the Lacanian enterprise. Indeed, Lacan can be seen as a forerunner of the poststructuralist movement; his writings in the 1930s and lectures in the 1950s, 1960s, and 1970s take up many of the poststructuralist concerns in a germinal form. Lacan, like

27. Derrida, "Structure, Sign and Play," 249.
28. Bloom, "Breaking of Form," 9.
29. Derrida, *Grammatology*, 14.

Lévi-Strauss, made use of de Saussure's linguistic theory to reinterpret the basic Freudian texts. This was accomplished by running out certain implications which Freud could not explore because he did not have at his disposal the structural linguistic principles for articulating the supposed semiotic nature of the unconscious. The unconscious, Freud had suggested, operates at its basic level according to the principles of condensation and displacement (*Verdichtung* and *Verschiebung*), which neatly correspond to the linguistic concepts of metaphor and metonymy. Lacan worked to elaborate how the insight that the unconscious functions like a language leads to a radical rethinking of the Freudian concept of self or ego. Lacan thus rejects the concept of the ego, arguing that Freud had unwittingly reified a fictional concept (the ego, *Ich* or self) that arises, he feels, when the human subject leaves the Imaginary (capitalized to distinguish the Lacanian concept from the ordinary; nonpsychoanalytic term) by acquiring language and objectifying itself in the inherited social structure of the symbolic order. Language not only shapes the unconscious, it shapes the conscious as well and creates such (indispensable) but purely structural concepts as an ego, or self. Because of the uncontrollable expansiveness of language's differential structure, the linguistic subject can repress, displace, and condense its desire along the unconscious tracks of the linguistic other—the inherited, impersonal linguistic discourse of culture and society. Language thus always expresses unconscious desire and need which issues from, Lacan hastens to point out, the human subject's inexorable existential estrangement. Every surface statement thus carries the shadow of an unconscious desire or "hidden meaning." In that this shadowy discourse of the "Other" accompanies each and every utterance— whose alternative meaning may undermine, contradict, or militate against the surface meaning of the utterance—one can see that Lacan's work does indeed point the way to a postmodern "deconstructive" criticism that keys upon the unconscious, relational, and indeterminate plurality of all language.

In any case, the radical indeterminacy posited by the poststructuralists is thus a fact of natural language and is especially apparent, they argue, in literary texts—above all in modernist texts. Such indeterminacy is operative at two levels, that of the individual word (signifier) and that of the text itself. Being the point of convergence for the "always already written," or the "already read," any text is just the tip of an intertextual iceberg, the product of a vast history of texts and discourses that are always working in and through the author. According to Bloom, "The truest sources . . . are in the powers of poems *already written,* or rather, *already read.*"[30] Such an influence is pervasive; authors can no sooner control these textual forces than they can control the endlessly relational play of signifiers. Words and texts cannot be grounded—"Il n'y a pas de hors-texte," Derrida is often quoted as saying, there is not an outside text, no referent, no transcendental signified, no subject or center that can limit or govern language's "chain of differential references." Because words in themselves, the poststructuralists argue, have no stable value and because they gain significance only through their ever-flexible relations to and differences from other words—through a seemingly infinite regress of linguistic references—nothing can arrest this movement to produce determinate meaning. "Writing," they claim, is a never-ending process, an "aphoristic energy,"[31] which always undermines the writer's undertaking and demonstrates the writing subject's lack of self-possession.

One of the important lessons to be learned from the radical indeterminacy of language, the poststructuralists believe, is that

30. Bloom, "Breaking of Form," 3.
31. Derrida, *Grammatology,* 158–59, 18.

an ungrounded language cannot avoid internal contradictions.[32] Writing, they feel, always rides upon a repression of troubling marginal principles, which surface in the form of, among other things, radically undecidable "aporias" or contradictions. Derrida tries to show that without the guardian notion of unqualified pre-differential (prestructural) truth and a solid centering in a stable and self-possessed speaking subject, language and thought become a relativistic entanglement of endlessly proliferating intertextual forces. Language thus bears within itself the seeds of its own critique, its own "deconstruction"—a cornerstone principle of post-structuralist literary criticism. Writes Paul de Man: "The deconstruction is not something we have added to the text, it has constituted the text in the first place. A literary text simultaneously asserts and denies the authority of its own rhetorical mode, and by reading the text [a passage from Proust] as we did we were only trying to come closer to being as rigorous a reader as the author had to be in order to write the sentence in the first place. Poetic writing is the most advanced and refined mode of deconstruction; it may differ from critical or discursive writing in the economy of its articulation, but not in kind."[33] Literature, poststructural critics demur, always exhibits in one form or another this critique; it plays off and exaggerates the fundamental and problematic free play thought to be constitutive of language in general. "Literary language," Geoffrey Hartman contends, "foregrounds language itself as something not reducible to meaning: it opens as well as closes the disparity between symbol and idea, between written sign and assigned meaning."[34] Not unlike the Slavic formalists, then, the poststructuralists feel that the literary text always displays its own form and in so doing thematizes the dichotomy of signs and refer-

32. The deconstructionist fondness for aporia and indeterminacy is reminiscent of the New Critical concern with "conflict structures" and plurality.

33. Man, *Allegories of Reading*, 17.

34. Hartman, "Preface," viii.

ents. Thus poems are really about poetry and poetic invention: "All that a poem can be about," Harold Bloom decrees, "or what in a poem *is* other than trope, is the skill or faculty of invention or discovery." Bloom continues, "A trope is troped whenever there is a movement from sign to intentionality, whenever the transformation from signification to meaning is made."[35] Interpreting is thus always a form of misreading—"misprision" (Paul de Man)— where one metaphorical chain is substituted, somewhat illegitimately, for another.

To the awareness of linguistic plurality and the rigors of close reading, the poststructuralists have added a commitment to the historicity and intertextuality of literary discourse. Their attacks, however, against eighteenth-century realistic notions of truth, determinate and easy referentiality, and representation were, as we have seen, all contained in the work done in the 1930s, 1940s, and 1950s by Anglo-American philosophers, most notably Wittgenstein and Quine. For these philosophers, language is neither a picture of the world nor a one-to-one match-up of words with ideas, intentions, or things. Rather than despairing about the indeterminacy of language, as do so many poststructuralist critics— "every poem becomes as unreadable as every other, and every intertextual confrontation seems as much an abyssing as any other"[36]—Wittgenstein and Quine were able to situate this indeterminacy in a sociocultural context that does indeed impinge "on experience along the edges."[37]

On the positive side, it is precisely this lack of direct connection with the world, this referential free play, that gives language its great flexibility—its Wittgensteinian play. Language is a flexible, ever-malleable "form of life," not a picture of the world—"words,"

35. Bloom, "Breaking of Form," 10–11.
36. Ibid., 9.
37. Quine, "Two Dogmas of Empiricism," 78.

Donald Davidson quips, "are the wrong currency to exchange for a picture."[38] The expressions of language become meaningful not by virtue of referential values but in their *useful* play, played out by speakers and hearers, or, in the case of literary criticism, by texts and critics. Referential free play, or radical indeterminacy, as Derrida would have it, is the condition for the possibility of not being limited to a mirroring, representational function, which ultimately would spell the end of what can be said. Not being limited to referential representation thus creates a field of tension which empowers, at least in part, the poet's compulsion to speak. It is the possibility of evoking new responses, which in turn lead to new interpretations and articulations of our dual existence in language and world.

Free play, or whateverr term one wishes to use, is an *Appell*,[39] the call of language which the modernist poets answered in their search for new ways of saying, showing, illustrating that which seems to be always on the horizon of language and consciousness. "The indolent word is always grasping / In vain at the ineffable / Which rests in dark silence at the last bounds of the spirit" (1:149), wrote the somewhat pessimistic young Trakl, who, in the following years, continued to push hard and not without results upon those "last bounds" of the spirit. Meaning is the product of language and speakers—and the goal of poetry. It is never completely present before or after the event of speaking or writing; it takes form, so to speak, somewhere between reader and text. Critics do not capture, recognize, or recover meaning; reading generates it.

38. Davidson, "What Metaphors Mean," 263.

39. Reception theory, an important hermeneutic movement with adherents in both Continental and Anglo-American camps, addresses the *Appell* (invitation, call) structure of the literary text's *Leerstellen* (empty spaces, gaps) that invite the reader to participate actively in the production of meaning—meaning which is actualized by the reader and not dependent on or derivative of representation or reference. See Iser's *Implied Reader* and *Act of Reading* or Jauss, *Toward an Aesthetic of Reception.*

Meaning is thus not hidden in the text, nor is it shrouded in more originary authorial intentions or transcendental subjects. Reading is the production of meaning; it plays or performs the text as the musician does a musical score. And like the musical score—a set of black marks on the white page—the text is without life before it is played, or produced by its various readers. Each performance, to extend the music analogy, will be slightly different, and as times, performers, and contexts change, so too will the resonances of each and every performance.

The Impossibility of a Negative "Modernist" Poetics

In 1960 Hans Magnus Enzensberger edited an anthology, in his words a *Museum*, of modern poetry. In his preface he makes a plea to the reader to avoid typecasting poetry as either *poèsie pure* or *poèsie engagée*. The whole question of formalism in modernist poetics is, in his eyes, an invention—the result of an overreaction on the part of some literary critics to the symbolist movement; it is a pseudo-problem (*Scheinproblem*) and confounds more than it illuminates. It is unthinkable, Enzensberger believes, to talk of poetry that bears no relation—no matter how indirect, tenuous, or "negative"—to the socioeconomic (and other) forces of its particular time.

In Enzensberger's view, poetry, especially modernist poetry since Baudelaire and Mallarmé, is an "anticommodity" (*Antiware*), which is always a contrary response to "the powers that be" (*zum Bestehenden*). The relationship, however, is neither simple nor direct, as orthodox Marxists often hold: "Modern poetry is done an injustice by the those Marxists who say superstructure [*Überbau*] and mean precisely economic determination. To be sure, modern poetry keeps pace with the prevailing means of production, but only as one keeps pace with an enemy."[40] Modern poetry, Enzensberger adamantly concludes, has been "from its very beginnings . . . intent upon eluding the law of the marketplace" (15). Enzensberger generally accepts placing Baudelaire's *Fleurs du Mal* or Walt Whitman's *Leaves of Grass* at the beginning of the modernist period; as its end point he sets the year 1945: "Its world language has shown since 1945 the signs of exhaustion, aging" (14). "The great historical ruptures also reach verse. Fascism and war, the breakdown of the world into hostile blocs . . . has deeply shaken the [international] consensus of poetry" (15).[41]

In response to the often negative appraisals of a scandalous, opaque, or antihumanistic modernism, Enzensberger retorts, " 'negative' behavior, is poetically impossible; the reverse side of any literary destruction is the construction of a new poetics" (11). To the "sweeping indictment" that modern poetry is unintelligible, Enzensberger has a ready answer: it just isn't so. Such a recrimination, owing to the vast range covered by modernist poetry, could hardly be the case and signals general resentment, rooted, Enzensberger charges, in modern society's alienated condition. "The accusation that they are unintelligible, makes poets into scapegoats for alienation" (10, 16). Difficulties (*Schwierigkeiten*) are indeed encountered, Enzensberger admits, but unintelligibility is not one of them. Such difficulties, he posits, are largely the result of the modernist poem's pronounced *Antiware* character, for its contrary resistance to the leveling, defusing, and neutralizing tyrannies of the marketplace and the prized status quo. Modern poetry, Enzensberger reminds the reader, does not have a corner

40. Enzensberger, *Museum der modernen Poesie,* 15. Subsequent references are in the text.

41. Enzensberger claims that between 1910 and 1945, poets achieved an "Einverständnis [. . .] das wie nie zuvor die nationalen Grenzen der Dichtung aufgehoben [hat]" (13) ("mutual understanding that as never before transcended national boundaries").

on the difficulty or "obscurity" market; it is just less "forgotten" and "repressed" than the "obscurity" of Goethe or even Pindar's lyrics (16). His essay closes with a rejection of the debate centering around the issue of form and content. When Mallarmé exhorted the poet to exclude the real from his work, or when Gottfried Benn exclaimed, "there is only one object of poetry: the poet himself," Enzensberger points out that such pronouncements were polemical in nature, reactions to nineteenth-century attitudes, "reactions to a preoccupation with content, to the narrow minded question, 'what is the poet telling us'—reactions to attitudes, which prevailed in the nineteenth century. . . . Like any poetry, modern poetry also speaks about *something*, it speaks out about that which concerns us" (19, 20). It seems, however—Enzensberger's arguments notwithstanding—that the formalist controversy cannot be so easily dismissed. Maybe it is because there is something else at stake in modern poetry, something at least as urgent as the contradictions of the *Antiware;* the poem, Paul Celan tells us, speaks on one hand "always of and in its own and quintessentially unique matters," yet, on the other hand, "the poem wants to approach an other, it needs this other, it needs something juxtaposed. It seeks it out, it speaks to it. Each thing, each human being is for the poem, which is headed for the other, the *Gestalt* of this other."[42]

42. Celan, "Der Meridian," 142, 144.

PART TWO

Georg Trakl and the Mirror

CHAPTER 5

Georg Trakl's Broken Mirrors

Ach daß das Schicksal der edelsten Seelen ist,
nach einem Spiegel ihres selbst vergebens zu
seufzen.—Goethe, letter of November, 1772[1]

> In meiner Seele dunklem Spiegel
> Sind Bilder nie geseh'ner Meere
> —Georg Trakl, "Drei Träume"[2]

The Psychological Dimension

SIGMUND FREUD, Harold Bloom has recently claimed, "is at once the principal writer and the principal thinker of our century,"[3] a bold statement befitting the "postmodern" desire to break down barriers between disciplines and expose philosophy, psychoanalysis, literature, and literary criticism as different names for the same thing, namely, *writing*. By affording Freud the privileged position as the "principal writer" of our century, Bloom points to that (now) mythic writer whose work began to make such postmodern thinking (writing) possible in the first place. It was, after all, Sigmund Freud, the medical doctor, who used the authority of science to legitimize the writing of his romantic precursors. Ad-

1. "Alas, it is the fate of the most noble of spirits to sigh in vain for the mirror of themselves" (quoted by Pietzcker in *Trauma, Wunsch und Abwehr*, 29).
2. "In the dark mirror of my soul / Are images of never-seen seas" (1:215).
3. Bloom, ed., *Sigmund Freud*, 1.

dressing the far-reaching impact of the Freudian enterprise alluded to in Bloom's rhetoric, Jeffrey Adams writes:

Although this [Bloom's] statement many seem extravagant to many, few of us would be willing to dispute its essential validity: Father Freud has shaped the ways in which we now think about the psychic world as much as Einstein shaped the ways in which we now think about the world external to the mind. *Freud is a Homer* of the twentieth century. He has created a "*mythic*" language without which we would not know how to talk about our inner reality. Certainly, no other thinker/writer outside the sphere of literature (except perhaps Nietzsche or Marx) has had a greater impact on recent trends in literary criticism. . . . Since Freud's analytical focus concerns the products of the human imagination . . . it is not difficult to grasp the relationship which unavoidably obtains between psychoanalytical thought and the study of literature. Even though Freud's model for psychoanalysis drew heavily on biological metaphors and despite Freud's wish that psychoanalysis become a natural science, the fact remains that Freudianism is essentially a theory of meaning . . . and interpretation its central enterprise. Given the further fact that Freud himself *defers to the creative writer as his guide* . . . it seems inevitable that the eye of literary studies should eventually fix itself on the body of writings assembled under the aspect of Freudian theory. (Emphasis added.)[4]

Whereas Freud's theories once deferred to the poet, from Homer and Sophocles to the German romantics, literary theory must now, whether happily or not, defer to the Freudian presence in the various "mythologies"—psychological and epistemological models—which attempt to understand the human condition in the modern world of Einsteinian relativity. Though various aspects

4. Adams, "*Literaturpsychologie* Today," 540–41.

of Freud's scientific explorations of the *Nachtseite* of the human psyche seem dated, epistemologically naive, or limited by certain assumptions rooted in the cultural milieu of his *fin-de-siècle* Vienna, one would be hard-pressed to deny its seminal position in the intellectual panorama of the language-conscious twentieth century.

This chapter turns directly to Georg Trakl's poetry, which will be treated as an exemplary convergence of intellectual and personal histories. The readings are suggestive and not meant to present a new or in any way comprehensive interpretation of his work. My goal is, rather, to provide a perspective that relates Trakl's writing to the crisis of representation of the early twentieth century. In exploring this poetic-epistemological mutuality, this and the following chapters will not only complement recent critical approaches to Trakl's enigmatically "obscure" verse but also show how this poetry can shed light on the epistemological transformations of the past 250 years.[5] The complex character of Trakl's verse—with its frequent allusions to Narcissus, manifest in images and figures of mirrors, vision, and visual reciprocity—registers an aesthetic response to the modern relativity which derives in part from the post-Enlightenment's unpacking of what I have called the epistemology

5. Eckhard Philipp also views Trakl's work as a reflection of intellectual history, relating it to the increased language consciousness of the twentieth century. See his book *Die Funktion des Wortes in den Gedichten Georg Trakls*, esp. 23. Hans Esselborn, similarly, relates Trakl's work to the "language crisis at the beginning of the century" (*Georg Trakl*, 2). Esselborn argues that the difficulty of Trakl's work is the product of a clash or discrepancy between content and medium (or form) that arose when Trakl attempted to express in the traditional medium and mode of nineteenth-century *Erlebnislyrik* a new (psychological) experience for which the language of *Erlebnislyrik* was largely unsuited. Esselborn's book is the first attempt to understand Trakl's work as a manifestation of a deep problematic relation to language, though his analysis of Trakl's particular "language crisis" emphasizes more the aesthetic manifestations of this crisis than its deeper epistemological/psychological determinants.

of pictures and mirrors. Though Trakl's work is, perhaps, an extreme response to this modern problematic, its aesthetic of mirrors nonetheless presents a striking psychological perspective whose implications cast light on other modern and postmodern views of culture and civilization.

There is, however, a significant psychological dimension to Trakl's poetic achievement, which, though related to the deeper epistemological determinants and intertextually mediated cultural currents of his era, was shaped by personal factors unique to his life and work. It is—especially in Trakl's case—a naive and limiting mistake, I believe, to valorize the aesthetic autonomy of this seemingly self-contained verse by interpreting it in total (New-Critical, formalist) isolation of the poet's trauma-filled existence of clinically diagnosed schizophrenia, drug addiction, alcoholism, and, ultimately, suicide, for certain crucial events and personal problems not only repeatedly found their way, albeit highly aestheticized, into the form and content of his poetic language but also directed the course of his development as a poet. Indeed, recent criticism has brought into clearer focus how Trakl used his writing as a "poetic self-understanding,"[6] "literary self-analysis,"[7] or a form of poetic "act of penance" for deep-seated psychological trauma.[8] I thus fully concur with Hilde Domin, who challenged the Trakl establishment in 1977 at the Salzburg Trakl Symposium by insisting that along with the consideration of influence, "we have to

6. Pfisterer-Burger, *Zeichen und Sterne,* 133. Further references appear in the text.

7. Esselborn argues that Trakl's mature work (from 1912 on) was made possible by his bohemian "substitute life [*Ersatzleben*] . . . into which he poured all his energies." This "bohemian life-style" allowed him "to concentrate totally upon his poetry," which becomes more and more a form of "literary self-analysis" (*Georg Trakl,* 238, 239; see also 237–50).

8. See Kleefeld, *Das Gedicht als Sühne,* esp. 97–103, 117. Further references appear in the text.

include Trakl's extremely labile personality and the extreme situation in general in which poems come about."[9]

This analysis of Trakl's work is thus, in the widest sense, psychological. There are, I believe, in addition to the "extreme situation" of Trakl's troubled existence, other compelling reasons for approaching his work from a psychological standpoint. Trakl was in an important sense a psychological writer: he was interested in psychological issues and, as his letters often clearly evince, gifted at observing and expressing in figural language the exigencies of his own inner states. And though he may not have deliberately set out to write psychological poetry, he possessed not only a keen sensitivity to psychic process and its relationship to poetic creativity but also an uncanny ability to allow his own psychic process to surface in and through the act of creative writing.

In a letter written in June 1909 (which accompanied his first collection of poems, *Aus goldenem Kelch*) Trakl alludes to the psychic forces that motivated his writing. Here he explains to his friend Erhard Buschbeck, who was acting as his unofficial literary agent: "You can hardly imagine what a delight it is when everything that has plagued one for a year and torturously demanded release, suddenly and unexpectedly storms into the light and is released" (1:475). Trakl was, moreover, a compulsive poet who lived for his art, and it drove him "into delirium," he lamented in another letter to Buschbeck, that he did not have enough time "to in some small measure" give "form to an infernal chaos of rhythms and images" (1:479). It is also significant that Trakl showed early on an explicit interest in the relation between art and psychology—a fact often overlooked by Trakl scholars. In a short review

9. Quoted by Sharp, *Poet's Madness,* 10. Sharp points out that the "unspoken taboo" of Trakl's schizophrenia served to squelch the "short-lived revolt" at the 1977 Trakl Symposium in Salzburg, when one participant "noted the absence of reference to Trakl's 'incredible sensitiveness in psychological matters'" (10). Further references to Sharp's book appear in the text.

essay—one of the three extant literary reviews he wrote—Trakl comments on the psychological implications of several works by the Austrian dramatist Gustav Streicher. Here Trakl praises one of Streicher's earlier works because it "seeks to solve a psychological problem of the most subtle kind by means of modern psychoanalysis [*Seelenanalyse*]" (1:207).[10]

In a way, Trakl's poetry is the result of a derangement of the senses that Rimbaud—whose presence can be felt in almost every line of Trakl's mature verse—believed to be the necessary condition for authentic poetic creativity. The poet, Rimbaud was convinced, must induce *drunken boat* chaos and break from habitual thought patterns to reach a prepersonal level of objectivity, a "universal language."[11] In his recent study on Georg Trakl, Michael Francis Sharp argues that this Rimbaudian "disarray of sensory experience" and "induced changes of mind" are closely related to R. D. Laing's central concept of *metanoia*. Free of the pejorative overtones of "schizophrenia," *metanoia*, Sharp contends, "denotes a fundamental change of mind, a shift in an ontological center of the self" away from the "lingua franca of sanity" in the direction of an ontologically desirable "lyric consciousness" (46). Although Sharp makes the problematic claim that this lyric consciousness or "mind space" is ultimately "anterior to language" (45), his readings produce some helpful insights into "Trakl's attempts to chart

10. Though Trakl uses the (somewhat archaic) term "Seelenanalyse" ("psychoanalysis"), there is no evidence that he was familiar with Freud's early work. It is possible that he came into contact with Freudian ideas through his association with Karl Kraus. Trakl once wrote to Kraus to thank him for a "moment of the most painful lucidity" after he had read one of Kraus's aphorisms, which ends with the following Freudian cliché: "They come into this world with a cry of shame, a world which leaves with them the first and last sentiment: Back to the womb, oh mother, where things were good!" (quoted in Doppler, "Die Stufe der Präexistenz," 280). Interestingly, Kraus wrote this aphorism as a way of thanking the poet for dedicating a poem, "Psalm," to him.

11. See Friedrich, *Die Struktur der modernen Lyrik*, 63.

unique experiential patterns in a recalcitrant language" (45). In any case, I think one can safely say—and the following readings are intended to bear this out—that the process of writing brought Trakl's labile psyche into contact with a dimension of language which was only tangentially connected to the desires and intentions of his conscious self. It was a dimension, one could argue, that simulates the psychoanalytic experience in which, as Jacques Lacan puts it, the subject (patient) is introduced "into the language of his desire, that is to say, into the *primary language* in which, beyond what he tells us of himself, he is already talking to us unknown to himself."[12] Trakl's psychoaesthetic explorations, it would seem, enabled him—his writing subject or lyrical I[13]—to reach a primary level of language, which, to a large degree, outstripped both the intentions and comprehension of his empirical self. These explorations did not lead to lucidity of rational expression but rather to a poetic "lunacy" that manifested itself in evocative images, rich rhythms, and resonating sounds. Trakl's resonating "lunacy" operated, in Julia Kristeva's postmodern terminology, in a preconscious "semiotic" language whose "heterogeneousness to meaning" is always at odds with the "symbolic" language of the conscious, social ego. Such language, she believes,

12. Lacan, *Ecrits*, 81. Further references appear in the text.

13. I use "writing subject" to denote a subjectivity or altered state of consciousness engendered in the act of creative—imaginative—writing. In that this subjective state is often only indirectly related to the conscious wants, needs, and intentions of the empirical person of the author, the notion of a "writing subject" is also closely related to the subjective state traditionally attributed to the "lyrical I" (*lyrisches Ich*). (See Pestalozzi, *Die Entstehung des lyrischen Ich*; Spinner, *Zur Struktur des lyrischen Ich*; and Sorg, *Das lyrische Ich*; see also Esselborn, *Georg Trakl*, 145–52). The notion of a writing subject, which includes a linguistic-intertextual pre- or subconscious dimension, is similar to the Pfisterer-Burger's concept of "lyrical existence" and that developed by Esselborn to describe the end point in the evolution of the "lyrical I" in Trakl's writing, though these critics do not consider the intertextual-linguistic moment of lyrical consciousness. See Pfisterer-Burger, *Zeichen und Sterne*, 8–9, and Esselborn, *Georg Trakl*, 251–52, 211–26.

functions on the level of primary process and is closely connected to what she calls the poetic function.[14]

The readings of Trakl's work in this and the following chapters present a psychological perspective that, very generally, uses some basic tenets of Lacanian psychoanalysis. This does not mean I believe that a Lacanian theory provides an interpretative key or model that can unlock once and for all the mystery of Trakl's "obscure" verse. In viewing Trakl from such a vantage point, I work to complement other recent psychological approaches by situating my approach in a common intellectual/epistemological context of which both Lacan's and Trakl's works are related manifestations. There are, in other words, points of coincidence between Trakl's poetry and Lacan's psychoanalytic project, which in turn complement other twentieth-century psychological speculations. It is my intention to explore the ways in which Trakl's enigmatic poetry and personal trauma are linked to a more general psychological discourse that issues from the alienating "triumph of intellectuality over sensuality"[15] in the post-Enlightenment world.

The idea of a Lacanian psychoanalysis is itself highly problematic. Indeed, Lacan is often criticized and rebuffed for his opaque and inaccessible style, which he ironically defends as a "kind of tightening up . . . in order to leave the reader no other way out than the way in, which I prefer to be difficult" (146). One often gets the feeling when working through the maze of his dense and willfully unaccommodating writing that there is truly "no way out" of this cerebral labyrinth, which seems to be a complex metacommentary on the impossibility of grounding psychoanalytic dis-

14. Kristeva, *Desire in Language*, 133. Kristeva goes on to say that this heterogeneousness to meaning "operates through, despite, and in excess of it [the signifying function of the speaking, empirical subject] and produces in poetic language 'musical' but also nonsense effects" (133).

15. Freud, *Standard Edition*, 23:112–13. See the section "Psychological Perspectives" in Chapter 2.

course in the clarity and coherence of rational thought. To be sure, the slipperiness of his arcane and "poetic" style—likely a carry-over from his earlier alignment with the surrealist movement—precludes any systematic explication or appropriation of his work. Lacan devotees claim that his "celebrated" obscurity protects his work from easy appropriation, on one hand, while, on the other, it emulates the irrational workings of psychic process (the "shifting signifiers" of the linguistic unconscious). Though these rationales may help us to understand why he may have chosen to write so obscurely, I am inclined to agree with Catherine Clément, who writes in her book on Lacan that he "has perhaps never *thought* anything else besides the mirror stage. . . . It is the germ containing everything,"[16] that is, the concept of the mirror stage and its subsequent articulation in his later work represents his most significant—perhaps even his only major—contribution to the reevaluation of Freudian psychoanalysis. Be that as it may, Lacan's work has nevertheless managed to spawn a new school of psychoanalytic thought which has, in Jane Gallop's words, "had a tremendous and unsettling effect . . . on both what we call the humanities and . . . the social sciences."[17]

In that the Lacanian structural project moves psychoanalysis away from a preoccupation with the individual subject—the Freudian ego—to a more general sociolinguistic plane, it can also serve as an antidote to the genetic preoccupation of orthodox psychoanalytic criticism, which focuses on the author and his or her psychobiography as the source or origin of the poetic impulse. It thus provides a dynamic model of intersubjectivity which over-comes the rigid nineteenth-century dualism of an autonomous subject who stands opposed to and passively perceives a suppos-edly invariant objective reality. In Lacanian theory, both subject

16. Quoted by Gallop, "Lacan's 'Mirror Stage,'" 119.
17. Ibid., 118.

and object are relativized by the mutuality of language, which mediates between them without prioritizing the ontological status of one over the other. Moreover, in placing the individual subject within a cultural-psychological context constitutive of both individual and collective, a Lacanian approach also moves literary psychology away from narrowly biographic speculations about infantile-childhood maladjustment. It also provides a corrective of sorts to the cultural relativity of classical Freudian psychoanalysis that sprang from the Victorian familial values of late nineteenth-century Vienna.

The fundamental Freudian principle of Oedipal conflict is in Lacanian psychoanalytic theory not so much an empirical familial crisis (between child and parent) as a psychic conflict between subject and society; it is a conflict in and through which the subject must come to terms with denial, prohibition, and deferred desire. The Oedipal juncture is thus transposed onto the sociocultural plane and is linked to the acquisition of language, that is, to the subject's subjugation to the alienating mediations and anxiety-inducing patrocentric orders of society. These orders, embedded and transmitted within the intertextual fabric of social discourse, are patrocentric in that they represent not only a socially mediated paternal disruption of the mother-child dyadic duality but also because they embody an implicitly hegemonic and paternally genderized form of social law. This social hegemony, as Lacan argues, is linked to the "appearance of the *signifier* of the Father, as author of the Law" (emphasis added; 199). The transition from the dualistic world of the Imaginary order (of the prelinguistic mirror-stage world of visual images) to the Symbolic order (of language and society)—"the deflection of the Specular I to the Social I"[18]—thus

18. See the section "Psychological Perspectives" in Chapter 2. In characterizing mirror-stage consciousness as "Imaginary" (as opposed to the "Symbolic" mode of post-mirror-stage existence), Lacan plays off the polyfunctionality of the word

involves accepting the law of the father, which underwrites and dominates, in Lacan's view, all of society and culture. The signifier "father" (*le nom du père*) can in this sense be seen as the visible portion of a vast, pervasive, and largely subliminal matrix of sociocultural imperatives and ordering principles. It (the name of the father) is also the specific marker of the original prohibition whereby the human subject was forced to renounce its access to the mother and, consequently, its primitive desire to maintain the primary union with her. Its needs and demands become thereby largely unfulfillable desires that are channeled and displaced through the quickly developing symbolic system. Lacan thus writes that "the moment in which desire becomes human is also that in which the child is born into language" (103). It is, furthermore, this being born into the Symbolic order of language and the corresponding subjugation to the law of the father that opens up and, in a sense, creates the unconscious, for the resulting humanization and articulation of desire is based on the subject's primary repression of its Imaginary unity with the mother. Desire is henceforth mediated through language and pushed underground in this period of denial and *Urverdrängung*.[19] Regarding this intertwining of language and desire in the formation of the unconscious, Toril Moi writes: "In one sense the unconscious *is* desire. . . . Desire 'behaves' in

---

"imaginary" (*imaginaire*), which in addition to the sense of "visual image" also can denote something unreal but imagined. The mirror stage is thus not strictly a chronological phase but an imagined mode whose psychic effects are retroactively constructed or imagined. Writes Jane Gallop in this regard: "It [the mirror stage] produces the future through anticipation and the past through retroaction. . . . It is the founding moment of the imaginary mode, the *belief* in a projected image" ("Lacan's 'Mirror Stage,'" 121). I capitalize the terms "Imaginary" and "Symbolic" to distinguish them from their nonpsychoanalytic use.

19. Freud likewise believed that the unconscious was formed by a process of "Urverdrängung" (primal repression), which he described as a "Niederschrift" (writing down) whereby libidinal energies and instincts are fixed onto ideas. See Freud, *Standard Edition*, 14:148.

precisely the same ways as language: it moves ceaselessly on from object to object or from signifier to signifier, and will never find full and present satisfaction just as meaning can never be seized as full presence. . . . There can be no final satisfaction of our desire since there is no final signifier or object that can *be* that which has been lost forever (the Imaginary harmony with the mother and the world)."[20]

The human psyche's desire, its endless quest for that which is lacking, follows a paradigmatic course through the unconscious, where it is channeled "like an underground river through the subterranean passageways of the symbolic order, which makes possible that things be present in their absence in some way through words."[21] "The unconscious," as Lacan himself puts it, "is neither primordial, nor instinctual; what it knows about the elementary is no more than the elements of the signifier [language]" (170). In other words, "what the psychoanalytic experience discovers in the unconscious is the whole structure of language. . . . The notion that the unconscious is merely the seat of the instincts will have to be rethought" (147). It also follows that there is no unconscious in the Imaginary because the unconscious comes into being as the result of the repression of the Imaginary.

Crucial to the Lacanian linguistic recasting of the Oedipal crisis is the controversial "phallocentricism" (Lacan's term) of the Symbolic order of language.[22] Language, as Lacan contends, builds from a (metaphoric) displacement and (metonymic) rechanneling of denied and prohibited desire for the mother. It is a desire which he characterizes in an essay on the treatment of psychosis as "the desire for her desire" whereby the subject "identifies himself with the imaginary object of this desire insofar as the mother herself

20. Moi, *Sexual/Textual Politics*, 101.
21. John Muller and William Richardson, *Lacan and Language*, 23.
22. See Lacan, *Ecrits*, 197–202.

symbolizes it in the phallus" (198). The phallus represents not only the law of the father but also a primal desire for an Imaginary unity and comes to signify the separation from, and loss of, the mother. The term "phallus" is a quintessential symbol, which, as Serge Leclaire states, becomes (retroactively) "the signifier of the impossible identity"[23] of mother and child, subject and object. It is a central but problematic signifier in what Lacan calls the "paternal metaphor," which, similar to *le nom du père,* issues from the primordial suppression of desire for the mother and which, in turn, gives rise to the need for the other metaphoric/metonymic substitutions of language.

By focusing on this sociolinguistic dynamic and its relation to a pre-Oedipal vision-dominated mirror stage, a "Lacanian" approach to Trakl's work can help to mediate between individual aesthetic (poetic) productions and larger cultural (linguistic) manifestations. It will, ultimately, allow us to view Trakl's ambivalent fantasizing about a quasi-mythic, prelinguistic realm of luminous visual reciprocity and *melo*dious or musical effects as related culturally, epistemologically, and psychologically to what could be called the Lacanian mythology of the mirror stage.

Psychobiography

Classical Freudian psychobiography has generally fallen into discredit in literary scholarship and is, not without good reason, rejected for its reductive narrowness because it tends to treat literature as a document of psychological study. In treating the "literary text as clothing which masks naked psychoanalytic truth,"[24] orthodox psychoanalysis tends to disregard the "literariness" of the work—the formal, textual, and aesthetic features that distinguish it

23. Quoted by Muller and Richardson, *Lacan and Language,* 23.
24. Meltzer, "Reiter- (Writer- Reader-) Geschichte," 39.

from other forms of language. In focusing, moreover, on the work as an outgrowth of hidden and suppressed desires that issue from early mental development and are able, by virtue of their disguised aesthetic form, to bypass the censoring function of the conscious (adult) ego, "depth psychology reduces individual life history . . . to typical psycho-sexual symptoms and to the ever recurring wishes and clichés . . . which [the poet] more or less shares with *Jedermann*."[25] These reservations notwithstanding, one should be careful not to reject such approaches out of hand. Though their results may be limited in interpretive value, they do shed light on certain aspects of the genesis and nature of poetic creativity and present one perspective, which, when complemented by other approaches and methods, contributes to the larger picture of a poet and his or her work.

Though critics have always known about Georg Trakl's precarious psychological state, it was not until the new critical edition to his complete works appeared in 1969 that a number of scholars began to consider seriously the relationship between Trakl's mental disorder and his poetic creativity.[26] That edition presented for the first time in a lengthy critical apparatus an extensive collection of the manuscript draft versions which Trakl had scribbled on anything from a scrap of paper to a napkin or menu. Exhibiting what at first glance seems to be an illogical or even random process of creation, these series of revisions—the so-called variant versions—reveal a strangely compulsive method of revising in which Trakl repeatedly switched, added, or deleted in line after line of composition often apparently unrelated—even contradictory— strings of words and phrases. The troubling question of insanity, which had been almost disregarded or suppressed by generations

25. Kemper, "Georg Trakl and His Poetic Persona," 24.

26. See Kleefeld, *Das Gedicht als Sühne*, 1–22, for a survey of psychological studies on Trakl written before and after the publication of the 1969 *Historisch-Kritische-Textausgabe* edition.

of Trakl critics and admirers alike, thus arose more poignantly than ever. Does it make sense to try to "make sense" of Trakl's reputed "unintelligibility"? Is this seemingly illogical process of creation and compulsive revision the aesthetically controlled and modulated work of a literary artist or the product of a deranged mind in which, as one recent critic characterized his mature work, "there is no longer any directing idea to control the play of involuntary pathological associations and complexes"?[27]

Post-1969 research seems to bear out that, though his poetry and mental maladjustment may be as inseparable as two sides of a coin, his creative process was most certainly far from random. Gunther Klcefeld counters the not infrequent claim that his writing evinces the classic symptoms of schizophrenic speech—association disorders—by shrewdly pointing out that his letters are devoid of such telltale signs.

Kleefeld, like Francis Michael Sharp, works to overcome the prejudices against psychopathology to explore the psychological determinants of Trakl's work. Writing poetry, he claims, was for Trakl an all-consuming preoccupation of crucial existential importance, "an attempt to maintain a sense of self in the face of psychological collapse. . . . Trakl opposed a threatening chaos with creativity" (9). The classical Freudian instinct theory that Kleefeld expertly puts to use—in exploring how Trakl's poetry arises from a desire to appease the castigations of the Oedipal *Über-Ich*—produces undeniably convincing readings of a psychic dimension to Trakl's poetic creativity. The persuasiveness of his detailed analyses, I believe, is possible, in a way, because Trakl was such a gifted psychological poet. Indeed, one comes away from Kleefeld's book with the sense that it is almost as if Freud had read Trakl's poetry—had "deferred" to this "creative writer as his guide"[28]—and then

27. Kurrik, *Georg Trakl*, 3.
28. Adams, "*Literaturpsychologie* Today," 541.

133

set out to articulate in scientific discourse what he found there. The neatness of the Freud-Trakl fit, however, leads Kleefeld optimistically to overestimate the interpretive value of his genetic research, and he thus tends to close off the possibility that other nongenetic investigations may produce equally convincing results. He suggests that the Freudian model is the long-awaited interpretive key: "His poetic images point beyond the poem itself to a reality which only psychoanalysis is able to describe: the world of the unconscious" (129). If one considers, however, that both Freud and Trakl were working in the same sociocultural milieu of Austria— and all that this may entail—one might be inclined to view the correspondence elaborated in Kleefeld's book as just as much a result of their common ground as the appropriateness of classical psychoanalysis for the interpretation of this *fin-de-siècle* poetry. Trakl and Freud were mythographers who responded to the commonality of their Austrian heritage and the psychoepistemological determinants of the post-Enlightenment era, but they happened to be on opposite sides of the scientific fence.[29] It should also be kept in mind that Trakl was working in an era when the articulation of decadent themes of psychological exigency and extreme introspection, which bordered on the pathological, were in vogue.[30]

Other critics of late have suggested a correlation between the disintegrating effects of his progressively deteriorating psychological state and the increasing abstractness and self-contained density of Trakl's mature work. Shortly before he died at age twenty-seven

29. "Trakl's greatest achievement in the history of lyrical poetry," Esselborn claims, "is his poetic discovery of the unconscious, which took place at the same time and in the same social milieu as Freud's scientific discovery" (*Georg Trakl*, 144).

30. Alfred Doppler points out that Trakl possessed Otto Weininger's *Sex and Character*, a book which expresses similar ideas to Freud's "that all intellectual drives have their roots in sexuality" ("Georg Trakl und Otto Weininger," 43–44).

134

of a self-administered overdose of cocaine—as a trained phar-
macist and frequent user of cocaine, it seems unlikely that this
overdose was a mistake—Trakl was clinically diagnosed as suffering from dementia praecox, schizophrenia in today's psychiatric
terms. Reports from Trakl's friends and acquaintances about his
behavior from his childhood days on abound with signs of a seriously maladjusted personality. Trakl himself claims to have first
attempted suicide at age five; once as a young boy he tried to throw
himself in front of an onrushing train. His adulthood was marked
by increasingly severe depressions and drug addiction; he was
given to radical fluctuations in mood and could lapse from gar-
rulousness into protracted introversion and silence; he had a narcissistic aversion to being touched and would pace in the corridors
on long train rides because he could not tolerate the gazes of the
other passengers in the seating compartments.[31]

Faced with these facts alone, it is difficult to approach Trakl's
poetry without wondering at least what relation his bizarre imagery might have to his psychological infirmity. Whether addressed
as such or not, the question of schizophrenia and poetic creativity,
of madness and poetry, will always figure in studies that attempt to
grasp the fascinating allure of this strange and often inhospitable
verse. Perhaps an even more compelling reason for pondering the
relation between his imagery and psychological state is that he is
said to have been critical of poets such as Goethe because they did
not write "neurasthenically."[32] Moreover, in the last months of his

31. See Spoerri, *Georg Trakl*, 31–42.

32. Szklenar, "Beiträge zur Chronologie und Anordnung von Georg Trakls
Gedichten," 227. Though undoubtedly affected by turn-of-the-century decadent
speculations about the correlation between insanity and artistic creativity, Trakl
seems to have been especially receptive to such a notion. His letters occasionally
imply that his poetic creativity is related to his melancholy disposition (e.g., 1:500–
501), whereas his work abounds with words denoting insanity, many of which
figure in images that thematize artistic and poetic creativity.

life he once referred to his poetry as an "incomplete atonement" for "unresolved guilt" (1:463). Indeed, Trakl's compulsive poetic production, as Kleefeld's work would seem to show, was motivated to a large degree by a desire to resolve this deep and for him inexplicably intense feeling of inadequacy and personal guilt.

Recent psychological profiles of Trakl's upbringing indicate that his earliest childhood was not normal or healthy.[33] He was born in Salzburg on February 3, 1887, and though raised in the affluent ambience of an upwardly mobile middle-class family, he and his five siblings appear to have suffered from their depressive mother's chronic lack of warmth and concern for her children. Trakl's younger brother Fritz described their reclusive mother: "Mother was more concerned with her antique collections than with us. She was a cool, reserved woman: she provided for us well, but there was no warmth. She felt misunderstood by her husband, by her children, by the whole world. She was only really happy when she was alone with her collections—and then she sometimes would lock herself up for days in her rooms."[34] The psychiatrist Theodor Spoerri reports that Trakl's mother, like the poet himself, showed clear signs of schizophrenia and was addicted to drugs. Though Spoerri does not document the claim, he suggests that four of her six children also "tended toward drug addiction" (42). It is, however, well documented that both Georg and his younger sister Grete used drugs frequently from their adolescent years on; two years after her brother's drug-induced death, Grete likewise took her own life. Such facts would add credence to the psychoanalytic claim that "the emotional frigidity of Maria Trakl" (Kleefeld 33) crippled the Trakl children, especially the sensitive and artistically inclined Georg and Grete. Arguing that the "disrupted

33. See Kleefeld's chapter section "Der Mythos von der 'glücklichen Kindheit' Trakls," in *Das Gedicht als Sühne*, 39–48.

34. Quoted by Basil in *Georg Trakl*, 17. Further references are in the text.

mother-child dyad" of Trakl's early childhood led to retardation in his psychological development, to a "narcissistic fixation," Kleefeld demonstrates how this fixation could be responsible for many of his later symptoms: his dependency on drugs, introversion, paranoia, trenchant self-reproach, debilitating feelings of guilt, and chronic social ineptness (39–48).

Trakl's pre-Oedipal "narcissistic fixation" and psychological retardation, Kleefeld believes, were compounded by an unsatisfactory resolution of psychodrama associated with the Oedipal stage of child development. This does not mean, Kleefeld points out, that there was any direct confrontation between the elder Trakl and the son, if anything, it was more the absence of his father during this crucial period which exacerbated the problems rooted in the "failed synthesis of mother and child." Trakl's father, Tobias, who was fifteen years his wife's senior, devoted himself to his expanding hardware business and appeared to have had little time or understanding for either his wife or his children.[35] What seems to have been missing, Kleefeld contends, was a supportive and congenial family, which under normal circumstances would have allowed the young child to pass through this critical Oedipal stage. Without the necessary warm and supportive familial environment, Trakl's already precarious state worsened. Kleefeld argues that if "the disintegration of the triad [mother-father-child] is not corrected; aggression and fears . . . are not reduced but rather intensified. This leads to the formation of a pathologically strong superego. . . . The father image which develops in Trakl takes on gruesome traits and forms a superego with a sadistic-punishing character . . . because the pre-Oedipal destructivity of the child could not be controlled" (55).

Trakl's familial situation was further complicated when Trakl was three years old and his parents hired a French governess

35. See Kleefeld, *Das Gedicht als Sühne*, 50–52.

named Marie Boring to care for the children. Although she supplied the children with a care and warmth not provided by the natural parents, this solicitude was likely sensed as compensation for the lack of parental care. Her presence and influence, nonetheless, were far from unproblematic. She was a devout Catholic and apparently tried strenuously to win the Protestant Trakl children over to her faith. Another potentially problematic influence was the French language. Because of the major role she played in their upbringing, the young Trakl children are said to have spoken only French among themselves, reserving their native tongue for communication with the German-speaking domestic help and their distant parents. The children were thus not only further estranged from their parents but from their mother tongue as well. German, for young Georg, became doubly authoritarian, being primarily the language through which his initial socialization was articulated and secondarily—from age three on—associated with the authority of his distanced and uncaring father. The voice of German is the voice of authority, conscience, and estrangement—all of which figure importantly in Georg Trakl's poetic struggle with language some twenty years later.

Trakl's school years were marked by failure, disinterest, and frustration. Described as introverted and passively rebellious, Trakl appears to have had trouble with the rigors of a tightly structured and performance-oriented humanistic *Gymnasium*. Because of unsatisfactory marks in Greek, Latin, and mathematics, he was required to repeat the *vierte Klasse*. When he then failed to pass a general examination necessary for advancing from the *siebte Klasse,* Trakl was forced in 1905 to leave the *Gymnasium* for good. Failure in school, however, does not mean that his intellectual growth was "regressively fixated." In 1904, while still in school, Trakl helped to found a literary circle called the Apollo and became one of its most prolific writers, producing mostly short prose pieces and poetry.[36] Friends reported that he was an avid reader and that he devoted himself with passion to the writings of Dostoyevsky and Nietzsche. Basil writes: "We learned from Buschbeck that Trakl 'began to read very early and with great intensity Dostoyevsky,' and that soon he knew him quite thoroughly" (45). Basil also contends that Dostoyevsky's "strong religiosity and mystical-national revolutionary antibourgeois attitude must have made an indelible impression on Trakl. . . . With equal 'intensity' Trakl read Nietzsche at about the same time or even earlier" (45–46). "In views on the world and intellectual development," a fellow *Gymnasiast* stated, "Trakl was superior to his contemporaries, something which was universally respected. He was much brighter than us and far ahead" (45). Trakl's youthful exuberance for Nietzsche was more than a personal interest in philosophy per se and was rooted, it would seem, in the pervasive sociocultural transformations that swept through rapidly industrializing Germany and Austria at the end of the nineteenth century. Nietzsche's pronouncements about the death of God and the degenerate slave mentality of the Christian tradition as well as his call for a "transvaluation of values" articulated the growing contradiction between the realities of the new technological world and the outmoded value system of a previous period: inherited tradition and authority lost their ability to help the modern urban man orient himself in a quickly changing world. By the first decade of the twentieth century, this sociocultural malaise had reached epidemic proportions, having become, in Kleefeld's terms, a "social identity crisis" (81). It is no doubt this aspect of Trakl's expressionistic antagonism which led 1950s critic Eduard Lachmann to argue that Trakl was essentially a Christian poet, whose poetry rests upon "the truth of Christian salvation . . . in a world far removed from

36. See Basil, *Georg Trakl,* 47.

God."[37] To a large extent the expressionist era—Trakl's era—was a period of conscious reaction to this psychosociological identity crisis. Expressionism, much like the late eighteenth-century *Sturm und Drang* movement, was an aesthetic revolution of young artists and intellectuals who felt compelled to renounce their fathers' outmoded and stifling value systems. Not surprisingly, a common motif or theme during the expressionist period pits rebellious sons against oppressive fathers.[38]

Don Juans Tod: *Language and the Broken Mirror*

From his juvenilia on, Trakl's work shows signs of the turn-of-the-century skepticism about the insufficiency of language—the "terrible helplessness of words," as he put in his letter to his friend Buschbeck (1:477). Such skepticism is clearly visible in his early and groping drama fragment, *Don Juans Tod* (The death of Don Juan; 1:449–51). This work, as so much of the writing from this early period, exhibits a problematic relation to language and is linked to a rather transparent psychological exploration in which Trakl's particular "specular" obsessions are revealingly manifest.

Before I begin my discussion, which is essentially an analysis of certain psychological determinants "motivating" the speech and actions of the psychodrama's three main characters (Don Juan, Catalinon, and Fiorello), I want to make clear that I am not treating these characters (or, of course, the various lyrical personae in

37. Lachmann, *Kreuz und Abend*, 9.

38. See Sokel, *Writer in Extremis*, 96–100, and Kleefeld, *Das Gedicht als Sühne*, 73–81. This theme is graphically demonstrated in Fritz Lang's 1925 expressionist film *Metropolis* in which a young protagonist defies his inordinately powerful industrialist father by joining the masses of dehumanized workers. In turning against his father, he is also rebelling against the authority of the new technological ethos and its overpowering machines—ominous and impersonal machines, which appear to be on the verge of extinguishing the human spirit.

Trakl's poems) as if they were real individuals by imputing to them a conscious or unconscious faculty governing their behavior. They will be treated, rather, as fictional personalities who exemplify certain psychological dispositions which are a point of convergence of literary and psychic process, on one hand, and social structuralization and cultural inscription on the other—a convergence that mediates, ultimately, between reader, text, and author. The three characters of this drama fragment dwell, as it were, in an intermediate textual zone between the extremes of author on one side and reader on the other. Though Kathrin Pfisterer-Burger does not include the reader in her analysis of the impersonal "space between boundaries" (*Grenzraum*)[39]—a space Trakl opens up or "evokes" in his writing "between himself and his work" (8)—her thesis that Trakl's writing constantly evokes this intermediate zone would seem to substantiate something that Ludwig von Ficker, Trakl's friend and publishing mentor, noticed in Trakl's lifetime about the poet's language. Responding to the sometimes harsh tone of his speech, Ficker wrote to Trakl: "Your . . . word[s] come from a depth that no longer belongs to you, a depth which has risen out of you, presented itself to me and now belongs to me. It is a depth which cancels out and rises above the personal" (2:762). Writing from a depth beyond the control of his conscious ego, Trakl was able to create a psycholinguistic textual space that mediates between poet and reader.

The act of reading a Trakl text becomes a productive psychological dialogue, which, by analogy to Freud's concept of transference, takes place in a *Zwischenreich* (intermediate realm) between the analyst (reader) and analysand (writer). Although I do not think that we can, as Peter Brooks suggests, "willingly bracket the

39. Pfisterer-Burger, *Zeichen und Sterne,* 23. Trakl's evoking of a "lyrical existence," Pfisterer-Burger concludes, produced in his poetry an "aesthetic life-space" (*ästhetischer Lebensraum*), which arose "out of existential necessity" (134–35).

impossible notion of author" from this *Zwischenreich,* I think that Brooks's (Freudian) transference model of reading goes a long way toward understanding the process of reading where "meaning . . . is not simply 'in the text' nor fully a fabrication of the reader (or a community of readers) but comes into being in the dialogic struggle between the two, in the activation of textual possibilities."[40] The traces on the surface of the text's complexly overdetermined structure elicit a response whose selective structurings and organizations always reflect something of the reader's psychological "investments." These investments then take form but also evolve in the interpretation of the text, that is, in the ongoing dialogue with the investments contained in the text. Brooks concludes, and I concur: "The advantage of such a transferential model . . . is that it illuminates the difficult and productive encounter of . . . the text and the reader, and how their exchange takes place in an 'artificial' space—a symbolic and semiotic medium—that is nonetheless the place of real investments of desire from both sides of the dialogue" (155).

In the first speech of the *Don Juan* fragment a poignant mistrust of language, tinged with anger and hostility, finds a forceful expression.[41] Irritated by an insistent scratching at the door to his room, Don Juan's servant Catalinon opens the scene by crying out:

> Was scharrt dort an der Tür! Nur immer zu!
> Ich rühr mich nicht.—Es scheint geduldig wie
> Ein Tier, das selbst dem Schweigen eine Antwort
> Entlocken möchte—scharrt und scharrt! He du
> Gib acht! Hier ist Hölle—sagt' ich Hölle?

40. Brooks, "The Idea of a Psychoanalytic Literary Criticism," 156. Further references to this article appear parenthetically in the text.

41. F. J. Fischer reports: "Trakl read the complete, three-act Don Juan tragedy to his friend Bruckbauer after which—as far as Bruckbauer can remember, in 1912—he burned the manuscript" ("Die Trakl-Handschriften im Salzburger Museum Carolino Augusteum," 163).

Vielleicht des Himmels Eingang auch. Wer weiß!
Dem Unfaßbaren hascht das träge Wort
Vergeblich nach, das nur in dunklem Schweigen
An unsres Geistes letzte Grenzen rührt.
Nur nicht so laut, ich komme schon und öffne!

(Er geht zur Tür und schiebt den Riegel zurück)

Tritt ein, du Unermüdlicher! Bist du
Ein Mensch, laß deine Sprache draußen,
Daß du vorwitzig sie nicht brauchst. (Emphasis added;
2:449.)

[What is scratching so at the door! Just keep at it! / I'm not going to budge.—It seems to be patient like / An animal, that would try to even coax an answer from silence! Hey you / Watch out! Here is hell—did I say hell?/ Perhaps also the entrance to heaven. Who knows! / *The indolent word is always grasping / In vain at the ineffable / Which rests in dark silence at the last bounds of the spirit.* / Not so loud, I'm on my way to open! / (He goes to the door and pushes back the bolt) / Come on in you insatiable one! If you're / A human being, leave your language outside, / So that you don't use it impertinently.]

Though Trakl was surely aware of the turn-of-the-century skepticism about the efficacy of language, the urgency and aggressive tone of this passage, combined with the intertextual undertones of blasphemy, perverse sensuality, seduction, and murder, suggest that the prominent position of these disparaging words about "the indolent word" may be more than a fortuitous rendition of an intellectual vogue.[42]

42. Sharp suggests that this early lament about the insufficiency of language "attests to Trakl's involvement in this [*fin-de-siècle*] intellectual atmosphere" (56–57). Kurrik, however, contends that the roots of this lament were aesthetic in nature: "The very restlessness of the adolescent imitations and experimentations

Although it is not clear from the text why this scratching at the door should elicit such a strong and unexpected reaction, one can see that language was a problem of sufficient gravity to emerge with little (or no) explanatory context at the very beginning of the act. Looking to the larger context of the speech, one notices that Catalinon wishes to remain alone in the room; disturbed by an insistent irritation, "scratching," from without, he reacts in an emotional, somewhat incongruous way by directing his frustration at the pre-eminent medium of social intercourse, language. When something threatens to intrude, language becomes the convenient target for the displacement of irritation. This observation is then reinforced by the implication contained in Catalinon's wish to banish language, that language is somehow inhumane: "If you are a human being, leave your language outside" suggests that it would be cruel and inhuman—perhaps even beastly—to bring language into this interior space. This suggestion is further strengthened if one considers that there is no knocking at the door, but rather a subhuman scratching which is likened to that of an animal that would try to coax an answer from silence. That which supposedly distinguishes man from animal (language) takes on, somewhat paradoxically, an inhumane and brutish character.

More will be said later about the relationship of language to silence ("schweigen" conspicuously occurs here twice), but let me suggest in passing that it is associated with a dark, quasi-mystical state "at the last bounds of the spirit," which, in analogy to Cata-

---

serves to point to his discontent with the poetic language that he inherits. The discontent emerges . . . as a continual lament and complaint about language" (*Georg Trakl,* 10). "Trakl's last cathexis," Kurrik concludes, "is to words" (41). Hans Esselborn is the first critic to undertake a systematic analysis of a pervasive language problematic in Trakl's work. This problematic, he contends, far outstrips any trendy rendition of an intellectual vogue: "One finds even in Trakl's . . . juvenilia the theme of language skepticism. No longer discussed in his later work, it is integrated right into the structure of his work" (*Georg Trakl,* 3).

linon's room, ought not to be disturbed by the loud external world of words. In a sense, this passage juxtaposes two realms, a threatening, loud, and irritating external world and a quiet, introverted, and antisocial inner world. It is thus a complex metaphor for a subject-object relation in which a defensive (regressive) subject is threatened by the social exigencies of the outer world. If one then factors into the metaphor the aggressive displacement of displeasure onto language, one can align this regressive subject with the narcissism of the Imaginary, which is threatened by the impinging *linguistic* forces of the Symbolic. The threat of the external world is tied to the problem of language; it produces anxiety, regressive tendencies, aggressive reactions, and paranoia. It is in this sense that Lacan believes that the "ontological structure" of the human world contains a "paranoiac" component that engenders aggressive impulses: "Aggressivity," he writes with respect to the child's early development, "is the correlative tendency of a mode of identification that we call narcissistic [exemplified in mirror-stage visual identifications], and which determines the formal structure of man's ego and of the register of entities characteristic of his world (16–17).[43]

Catalinon is thus a literary figure who is caught between the regressive pull of the Imaginary and the threatening forces of the Symbolic. Fiorello—who, we find out, is the scratcher at the door—is thus a counter figure whose loud and intrusive ways represent the deeper motivations that trigger Catalinon's psychic conflict. Imagined in the act of poetic creativity, they together

43. Further: "The ego appears to be marked from the very origin by this aggressive relativity" (Lacan, *Ecrits,* 19). Fredric Jameson articulates this point as follows: "The mirror stage, which is the precondition for primary narcissism, is also, owing to the equally irreducible gap it opens between the infant and its fellows, the very source of human aggressivity; and indeed, one of the orginal features of Lacan's early teaching is its insistence on the inextricable association of these two drives" ("The Imaginary and the Symbolic in Lacan, 353).

evoke a *Zwischenreich*, which, to paraphrase Ficker's comments, comes from a depth that no longer belongs to Trakl, a depth that has risen out of him and presented itself to the reader. Their conflict is carried out in an imaginative textual space whose psycholinguistic "investments" can mediate between poet and reader, who share a (subliminal) aversion to the socializing effects of words. Like the Classical aestheticians of the eighteenth century, who wished to counter the abstract and alienating effects of language with the Imaginary effects of absolute visual mimesis, Catalinon and his modern readers are linked and motivated by a narcissistic desire to experience (reexperience) a visual unity of self and other. Language is, in Catalinon's figural world, that troublesome disturbance from without, that incessant scratching at a door, which, to his—our—dismay, cannot be kept forever locked.

Indeed, Catalinon unlocks the door, whereupon his faithful servant Fiorello—"whose whole body is trembling"—enters bearing the horrible tidings of an "atrocity,"[44] an "unnameable crime" (30). In his short exchange with Fiorello, who despite the previous warning, has not left his disquieting language "outside," Catalinon twice aggressively orders Fiorello "to be silent." In two successive lines, Catalinon brusquely uses the informal imperative form of the verb "schweigen" ("Schweig, alter Mensch; Schweig du, wie ich gesagt"). Once this garrulous intruder has finally been silenced, however, Catalinon appears to retreat back into his private world by "humming to himself" the following song:

> In deine erloschenen Augen
> Pflanz ich ein loderndes Licht
> Ich entreiß dich dem Todesdunkel
> Und Gott und Teufel, sie hindern es nicht!

44. Parenthetical references in this discussion refer to line numbers in the *Don Juan* fragment.

[Into your extinguished eyes / I plant a blazing light / I tear you from the darkness of death / And God and Devil can do nothing to stop me!]

Catalinon's song is an expression of desperation, a wish to reverse the alienating effects of those impinging words (language), which bear the responsibility for the traumatic "deflection" from the radiance of the "specular I" to the darkness of his "social I." He seeks visual contact with a *you* whose shining eyes will reciprocate his gaze, not the "darkness of death." His song to himself is a dream wish in which an alienated psyche fantasizes relighting an extinguished I Thou relationship.[45] Such a relationship, however, is doubly imaginary, for it is a figment of an *imag*ination that retroactively projects a "dimension of images, conscious or unconscious, perceived or imagined,"[46] which preceded the noisy acquisition of language. Catalinon longs, in other words, to retreat from his dark state of paranoiac alienation in the Symbolic order (of a socialized I) back to the fanciful security of his preverbal specular existence in which his psyche had been at one with its environment in a resplendent Imaginary world of visual plenitude.

Catalinon's song to himself wells from a deep-seated aversion to the alienating medium of socialization. Language is thus not only the brutish paternal agency of Oedipal force and social taboo, it is also the obscuring agency that broke the Imaginary visual reciprocity of subject and object. "Your extinguished eyes" are nonreciprocating, nonloving eyes; they are dark eyes and signal a psychological death, which ensues when the linguistically objectified psyche must face a world darkened by the absence of radiant visual integration. It is the autumnal world evoked in Georg Trakl's poetry, a world of an "unsheltered being" who—to borrow Erich

45. One can, of course, identify this "thou," in a surface-level reading of a play about Don Juan, with the murdered Donna Anna.
46. Alan Sheridan, Translator's Note to Lacan, *Ecrits*, ix.

Neumann's Jungian characterization of Trakl's psyche—"has lost its connection with the maternal—with the ground root of the psyche"[47] and has been cast out of the unitary world of integration into the "nocturnal" world of "grown-ups" (166). Writes Neumann: "The birth of the world-ego with its ego-consciousness . . . necessitates the death of the childish ego. . . . That is why the childish ego reverts to a mythical ego to which the world appears as a unitary world. It is in this realm that the childish ego and its world are integrated. Trakl's life and poetry are determined by the conflict between the world of the day and the nocturnal world and by the movement of withdrawal" (166). Neumann's conclusion would complement the assertion that a subliminal hostility toward language surfaces in these lines. Adjusting slightly his Jungian terminology, one could say, very generally, that his "world-ego with its ego-consciousness" would correspond to post-mirror-stage consciousness in which the child gains, through the alienating acquisition of language, a differentiated and self-conscious awareness of itself at the expense of preverbal integration. Neumann's reverting "childish ego" is as such a regressive, narcissistic I, and his "mythical ego" would correspond to a (subliminally) idealized prelinguistic and undifferentiated mirror-stage specular I, a "mythical-specular-ego," as it were, for which the world quite literally "*appears* as a unitary world"—the unitary world of undifferentiated visual experience prior to the acquisition of language. Catalinon's desire to withdraw is motivated by a desire to reverse the process of socialization; he longs to "withdraw" from "the nocturnal [Oedipal] world" by warding off the social "grown-up" world of words and rekindling the lost radiance of extinguished eyes and mirror-stage visual plenitude: "Into your extinguished

47. Neumann, "Georg Trakl," 173. Further references to this work appear in the text.

eyes / I plant a blazing light / I tear you from the darkness of death."

The underlying aversion to language expressed in Catalinon's actions, his irritation at Fiorello's loud intrusion, and, most important, his song to himself bring into clearer focus a deep-seated distrust, a negative emotional investment, of language emerging in this early work. This subliminal aversion then brings the poet's writing subject—not necessarily Trakl's conscious "world-ego"[48]—fancifully to idealize in the process of poetic creation a brighter, unspeakable realm just out of reach of words. It is a quasi-mystical, prelinguistic state, which, to the poet's unending vexation, is forever receding into the recesses of "dark silence at the last bounds of the spirit." His indolent poetic words are forever trying to catch ("haschen vergeblich nach") something which, for a post-mirror-stage and self-conscious ego, is palpable yet uncatchable ("Unfaßbar"). It is a frustrating experience because Trakl catches, in and through the writing process, in and through his literary personae, fleeting flickers of something bright and unsayable. As a poet Trakl faces at this point in his career an irresolvable dilemma. Words will always fail him because they will never be able to illuminate that which they have helped to obscure—"extinguish."

48. Although it is not crucial to my analysis, one could argue in a Freudian vein that this paranoia and aggressivity are tied to Trakl's own problematic stage of primary narcissism (the mirror stage, in Lacanian terms), which, as the evidence seems to indicate, was neither normal nor healthy. This (Kleefeld believes) manifests itself in a narcissistic fixation that rendered Trakl incapable of dealing with the Oedipal trauma, incapable of submitting to the usual process of socialization, which, from a Lacanian view, would exacerbate his "paranoic alienation," primal aggressivity, and an imaginary fixation. Failure to relinquish such an imaginary fixation, Toril Moi suggests, leads to psychosis: "The subject may or may not like the order of things, but it has no choice: to remain in the Imaginary is equivalent to becoming psychotic and incapable of living in human society" (*Sexual/Textual Politics*, 100).

The theme of eyes and vision is further elaborated in the remaining lines of the drama fragment. Of the sixty-nine lines, sixty-seven are a monologue by Don Juan, who, immediately following Catalinon's song to himself, had entered from a door "through which one sees in a dimly lit room the corpse of Donna Anna lying on a sofa" (56). It is interesting that Otto Rank's psychoanalytic interpretation of the Don Juan legend casts the figure of the servant (Catalinon, in Trakl's drama[49]) as a "secondary division" of the primary Don Juan figure.[50] He is as such Don Juan's "ego ideal" and "stands for the criticizing and anxiety-oriented conscience of the hero in general" (52). This means, Rank points out, that the servant has its roots in primary narcissism—which might shed light on Trakl's interest in the figure in the first place. The Don Juan legend as a whole, he argues, derives from the Oedipus complex: "Clearly the endless series [of seduced women] . . . the many women whom he must always replace anew represent to him the *one* irreplaceable mother" (41). Although Rank altered and revised his analysis of the legend several times between 1922 and 1934, his later revisions treat as primary the version in which ghosts of female victims return to haunt Don Juan. The ghost of the seduced and murdered Donna Anna figure is, as "a fragment of the original motivation," a "champion of the violated moral law [who] walks in the footsteps of the mother [and] avenges the murder of the father" (101). Though we cannot be absolutely certain that Trakl's Don Juan kills Donna Anna's father, it is safe to assume that Trakl, like nearly all of his literary predecessors who wrote Don Juan dramas, did not deviate from this central aspect of

49. Critics generally agree that Niklaus Lenau's "dramatic poem" *Don Juan* was the model upon which Trakl based his Don Juan drama. See Stupp, "Beobachtungen zu Georg Trakls Fragment *Don Juans Tod,*" 34, and Fischer, "Die Trakl-Handschriften im Salzburger Museum Carolino Augusteum," 163.

50. Rank, *Don Juan Legend*, 51. Further references to this work appear in the text.

the legend. There seems to be little room for doubt, as the above-cited stage directions alluding to Donna Anna's corpse indicate, that Trakl's Don Juan murders the daughter, Donna Anna. There are, moreover, striking parallels in theme, imagery, and motif between this drama fragment and another early passion-murder drama (*Blaubart: Ein Puppenspiel*) in which an ecstatic lover murders his beloved. "Blaubart's love," concludes Kleefeld, "is deadly, it demands of its object total self-sacrifice, its life" (138). Trakl's passion-murderer Don Juan, it would seem, is but a variation on the Blaubart theme, or perhaps it is the other way around because *Don Juan* was most likely written before *Blaubart*.[51]

Kleefeld argues in his discussion of *Blaubart* that this sex-murder motif is central to Trakl's oeuvre and that the many and varied feminine victims populating his work "form a long series of symbolic object representations of the mother."[52] In killing the father, moreover, Don Juan would become a rebellious Oedipus who avenges the fracturing agency that broke the reassuring mirror of mother's eyes by casting the hapless child out of a unitary world of visual plenitude into the nocturnal world of deferring signifiers, arbitrary social orders, taboos, and endless guilt and self-recrimination.

Though I do not want to offer a reinterpretation of the Greek

51. Gunther Kleefeld's argument that Trakl's narcissistic fixation derives from his disturbed mother's inability to provide the love and support he needed would appear to be indirectly substantiated by Rank's remark that Donna Anna is closely aligned with the legend's "prehistoric sense," where "the daughter becomes not only the bad mother, but also the faithless mother" (Rank, *Don Juan Legend*, 101). In having Donna Anna killed, Trakl would be fulfilling a subliminal wish to avenge his own mother's supposed failures. (Trakl once told his close friend and supporter Ludwig von Ficker that he hated his mother so much that he could have murdered her with his own hands.) Yet, in taking Donna Anna as his lover, Don Juan, alias narcissistically fixated Georg Trakl, would also be carrying out his incestuous desires for his mother.

52. See Kleefeld, *Das Gedicht als Sühne*, 138, 146.

myth of Oedipus, I think that it is relevant to Trakl's interest in the Don Juan legend that blindness, knowing, and guilt are interconnected in the ancient myth. Upon learning, that is, coming to know, the horrible truth of his guilt—that he had slain his father and married his mother—Oedipus blinds himself. This self-blinding is, in the orthodox Freudian reading, a symbolic manifestation of (psychosexual) guilt and a resulting self-castigation (surrogate castration)—introjected (masochistic) aggression. But it can also be read in a Lacanian sense as a figure for the absence of pure visuality in post-Oedipal self-consciousness: the human subject must renounce the pull of the primary narcissism and blind itself to an Imaginary visual unity of self and other. In other words, the self-consciousness and knowledge of the social I necessitate a self-blinding surrender, a repression, of the specular I. Oedipal blindness is, then, the result of *know*ledge and self-recognition and stands for the loss, lack, and repression of an Imaginary—specular—symbiosis of self and other. It is interesting that in Greek, "I know" (*oida*) is the present perfect form of "I see"; "I know" thus means literally "I have seen."[53] Since the Greek present perfect form also expresses the resultant state of the active, present-tense verb form, "I know" would also express a state of no longer seeing,

53. I am indebted to Frank Graziano for this observation. See his introduction to *Georg Trakl*, 18. Graziano is also the first critic to suggest that a Lacanian reading could open up a new perspective for viewing Trakl's work (see 9 and 11). As to Trakl's language problematic, he writes: "The Trakl/Hauser affinity offers the greatest insight into the source of Trakl's poetry when we follow the lead of Peter Handke's 1968 drama *Kaspar* and suggest that language bears the ultimate responsibility for the loss of innocence. One is drawn out of the perceptual, unnamed One-world by language and then made to not only function in a cognitive mode that artificially orders a world with grammar, but also to there be manipulated by the very instrument (language itself). . . . The process of self-discovery initiated by the acquisition of the pronoun *I* results in the termination of the not-yet-born state which Trakl idealized in [his poem] 'Caspar Hauser'" (17).

that is, "I know" would imply "I no longer see." The bane of Oedipal knowledge is the blindness of no longer seeing.

Don Juan's concluding monologue consists essentially of two opposing parts. In the first, roughly two-thirds of the monologue, Don Juan raves melodramatically about a ghostly face, "a horrible face," whose persistent hovering disturbs a blissful state filled with visions of "superhuman faces." The presence of this ghost would seem to indicate that Trakl followed what Rank calls the "original motivation" of the legend in which Donna Anna's ghost returns to haunt her seducer and murderer, Don Juan. The monologue begins as Don Juan enters from the room in which Donna Anna's corpse lies:

> Weg, schreckliches Gesicht!
> Was scheuchst du mich von meinem Lager auf
> Da dieser Stunde tiefster Wonneschauer
> Mir noch im Blute bebt und mich erfüllt
> Mit übermenschlichen Gesichtern. Weg, Weg! (59–63)

[Away, you horrible face! / Why are you shooing me from my couch / At this hour when the most profoundly shuddering bliss / Still quivers in my blood and fills me / With superhuman faces. Away, away!]

It is noteworthy that Trakl here uses "Gesicht" (face, vision) in both a positive and negative sense: the "superhuman faces" populating his blissful state contrast with the "horrible face" which threatens to undermine that state. Faces are thus invested with both good and bad value; they are two-faced, as it were, and can associate with the extremes of "Wonne" (bliss) as well as "Schreck" (horror). Trakl compresses this good-bad, positive-negative association into the neologistic compound *Wonne-Schauer*, a constellation that not only melds bliss and horror but also suggests that this bliss could be associated with seeing because "Schauer" is ambiguous, meaning both "horror" and "looker." The neologism is also redolent of Catalinon's *Zwischenreich* psychic conflict, which he, for reasons mysterious to himself, characterizes with the extremes of heaven and hell: "did I say hell? / Perhaps also the entrance to heaven." Indeed, both Catalinon and Don Juan are plagued by intruding disturbances that evoke expressions laden with visual imagery. Catalinon responds to this impinging threat by fantasizing in his song to himself the resplendence of radiant eyes—a positive face—while *Wonne-Schauer* Don Juan, who is in danger of losing the positive face(s), fancifully evokes, as we shall see in the final lines of his monologue, a unitary world of color and sound.

Donna Anna's ghost is variously cursed in the intervening lines as a "Fratze" (grotesque face), a "verfluchtes Gebilde" (cursed figment), a "Tiergesicht" (animal face), or as something that looks at Don Juan "aus toderstarrten Augenhöhlen" (from eye sockets rigid with death). This last designation immediately recalls the "extinguished eyes" of Catalinon's song to himself. Indeed, a closer look at the text surrounding the ghost's "eye sockets rigid with death" reveals further parallels. The immediate context reads thus:

> Ah! Schwebst du mir noch vor und blickst mich an
> Aus toderstarrten Augenhöhlen, worin
> Die Finsternis, die noch kein Lichtstrahl je
> Erhellte, weint. (70–74)

[Ah! Are still hovering there looking at me / From eye sockets rigid with death where / Darkness, which has never been illuminated by a beam of light / cries.]

Common to both passages is the opposition of light and dark with respect to dead or extinguished eyes: the eyes, light, and darkness of death in Catalinon's song correspond, superficially, to the dead eyes, beam of light, and darkness of the monologue passage. The two passages, however, appear to contrast in that the extinguished eyes in Catalinon's song were once illuminated, whereas those of the ghost were never illuminated. This apparent contrast seems less contradictory if one recalls Otto Rank's observation that the ghost of the Donna Anna figure is, in psychoanalytic terms, a representation of the "bad . . . faithless mother." These eyes thus evoke a maternal agent who is now aggressively denigrated, blinded, with the hyperbole of eyes that were never illuminated. They are the dark eyes of sorrow in which darkness cries, not the bright eyes of a *Wonne-Schauer* who sees superhuman faces and visions. It is interesting that the only other occurrence of *Augenhöhlen* in Trakl's work literally involves a "boy" who finds no reciprocity in the eyes of a maternal figure:

> Ein Knabe legt die Stirn in ihre Hand.
> Oft sinken ihre Lider bös und schwer.
> Des Kindes Hände rinnen durch ihr Haar
> Und seine Tränen stürzen heiß und klar
> In ihre Augenhöhlen schwarz und leer. (1:103)

[A boy lays his forehead in her hand. / Her eyelids often sink down evil and heavy / The child's hands run through her hair / And his tears stream down hot and clear / Into her eye sockets black and empty.]

Trakl's Don Juan is a kind of reversed Oedipus who retaliates by killing a representation of the maternal and then blinding its ghost rather than himself. His aggression is channeled outward, not inward, and is directed at a maternal image, who, in psychoanalytic terms, is paradoxically the object of both aggressive impulses and incestuous desires.[54]

54. "This juxtaposition of aggression and regressive wish for integration," Kleefeld holds, "characterizes Trakl's psychic life and provides the basic pattern which his poetic imagination follows" (*Das Gedicht als Sühne*, 291). Kleefeld's Freudian analysis relates the numerous variations of utopic "lost paradise" imagery to Trakl's regressive "primary narcissistic fantasy" and "incestuous wish for integra-

In the four lines preceding this metonymic blinding of the mother, Don Juan curses his ghostly tormentor and threatens to strangle it/her with his own hands:

> . . . So faß' ich dich verfluchtes
> Gebilde du Auswurf meiner heißen Sinne
> Erwürge dich mit diesen Händen . . . (66—68)

[. . . so I'll grab you cursed / Figment, you discharge from my impassioned senses / And strangle you with these hands . . .]

Trakl uses here, interestingly, a very similar expression to the one he once used in a conversation with Ludwig von Ficker when he claimed that he hated his mother so much that he could have strangled her with his own hands. The occurrence of such biographical reminiscences in Trakl's work provides, as Jost Hermand remarked in 1959, "proof about the psychic succinctness of Trakl's figural language" and the various "psychic levels" that surface in his poems.[55] It is, in any case, also significant that Don Juan recognizes that this ghostly tormentor—"you cursed figment"—is a product of his own internal (psychic) conflagration. This horrid ghostly image, referred to in line 42 as a "grotesque face born of lecherous horror," comes from within; it is the ugly discharge (*Auswurf*) of a "nameless evil deed" (20); it is the guilt-inducing product of an infernal chaos of murderous-passionate impulses which lead, via Donna Anna, back to a desired but hated maternal imago.

In the lines immediately following the metonymic blinding of the mother, Don Juan continues his excoriation of the ghost:

tion." See esp. the sections entitled "das narzißtische Klischee" (275—315) and "Inzestwunsch und Vernichtungsangst" (103—9). See further Esselborn's discussion of Trakl's "regressive[r] Zustand des Dichtens" (*Georg Trakl*, 237—50).

55. Hermand, "Der Knabe Elis," 228.

. . . Und füllst den Raum mit Schweigen,
Das blaß, grufttief sich schleicht in meines Herzens
Aufschäumend Pulsen und schlangengleich sich windet
Um meiner Sinne trunkene Entzückung, (73–77)

[And you fill the room with silence, / Which pale, deep as tomb, slithers into my heart / Frothing pulses and like a snake it wraps itself / Around the intoxicated delight of my senses,]

Don Juan's world is at the point of breaking; his perilous distress has reached a feverish pitch. Images of seething sexuality fuse with claustrophobic visions of darkness and silence as the ghost's evil influence tightens, like a constricting serpent, its stranglehold on his *Wonne-Schauer* state of intoxication. But there is much more at stake than a threatened Eden of blissful intoxication: this satanic serpentine influence, we learn in the next lines, also threatens to eclipse both the sights and sounds of Don Juan's life:

Daß ferner immer ferner mir des Lebens
Vielstimmiges Geräusch verklingt, sich brechend
An ekler Öde. Es engt der Raum sich und
Verschlingt, der nahen Dinge sichere
Gestalt. Es steigt an mir empor. . . . (77–82)

[So that the many-voiced sound of life / Fades away and breaks apart / In a disgusting wasteland. The room is closing in / Devouring the certain form of near things. / It's climbing up me. . . .]

Don Juan's claustrophobic vision culminates with an image of engulfing darkness—foreboding darkness that threatens to eclipse the certainty and/or security of visual forms, "the certain form of near things." The bad face of Donna Anna's ghost, a negative maternal imago, has gained the upper hand and appears to be on the verge of obscuring, banishing into the recesses of "dark silence at the last bounds of the spirit," the (positive) superhuman faces that populate Don Juan's ecstatic visionary state.

That a snake should be used to characterize these pernicious effects is especially significant because it joins in one figure the negativity of Satan's destruction of paradise (and Eve's sinful temptation) with the negativity of an imposing paternal (phallic) agency of the Symbolic order. The snake carries the curse of instinctual repression, social taboo, denial, and prohibition and renders the Imaginary world of (pre-Oedipal) specular reciprocity a "high tragedy, a paradise lost."[56] The effects of Donna Anna's ghost thus combine with an intruding paternal force to negate the paradise of visual plentitude fantasized in Catalinon's song to himself and implied in the positive faces, the "superhuman faces," of the first lines in the Don Juan fragment. Fading into the obscurity of silence, Don Juan's thwarted ecstasy is banished to the realm of dream wish, to that fanciful Imaginary realm where a "specular mythical-ego" enjoys the preverbal security of visual integration.

Indeed, Don Juan's monologue concludes with such a fantastic dream wish. Suddenly everything is changed. Don Juan miraculously succeeds in banishing the ghost at the very moment when its slithering darkness is about to swallow "the certain form of near things." As quick and unexpected as a flash of lightning, Don Juan's claustrophobic visions of paranoia and alienation burst into an intensely egocentric—narcissistic—bright synaesthesia of sound and color. The monologue (and fragment) ends in a manic reversal: as the serpentine force is about to close its death grip, "It's climbing up me and is threatening to envelop me," Don Juan shrieks out:

> . . . Weg Wesenloses!
> Noch widertönt mein Blut von dieser Welt
> Die Erde hält mich und ich lache dein. (82–85)

56. Gallop, "Lacan's 'Mirror Stage,'" 118.

[. . . Away you thing of no substance! / My blood still echoes with the sound of this world / The earth holds me and I laugh at you.]

In desperation Don Juan calls out to an external world, to an earth which, like a nurturing mother, would securely hold and protect him from the darkening Oedipal negativities. Laughing in the face of his pursuers, Don Juan enacts an ardent wish that yet echoes in his impassioned blood of (re)establishing a felicitous connection with the external world by throwing open the window to the bright sights and sounds of day:

> (Er taumelt ans Fenster, und stößt es auf)
> Hier öffne ich dem Leben weit die Pforten,
> Und tönend braut's herein, mich zu umfassen,
> Mit seinen Schwingen hüllt's mich ein—und ich—
> Bin sein!
> Und atme ein die Welt, bin wieder Welt
> Bin Wohllaut, farbenheißer Abglanz—bin
> Unendliche Bewegung—bin. (85–93)

[(He stumbles to the window, and pushes it open) / Here I open wide the gates to life, / And sounding it surges in to embrace me, / It envelops me with its wings and I / Belong to it! / And [I] breathe in the world, [I] am again world / [I] am pleasing sound, color-hot reflection—[I] am / Endless motion—[I] am.]

In flinging open the window to the world, Don Juan attempts to break out of his dark and introverted Catalinonian chamber. He performs a rite of exorcism on his nocturnal impulses by exposing them, as it were, to the radiance of the daylight world. Forcing—suppressing—them, for the moment at least, back into a dark corner of his tormented psyche, he regains a narcissistic visual reciprocity and unity with his surroundings: "[I] am again world / [I] am pleasing sound, color-hot reflection—[I] am / Endless motion—[I] am." Don Juan's exorcism at the window is an image of psychic implications which occurs in various forms in Trakl's work, especially in his earlier work. The window, Alfred Doppler remarked in his discussion of Trakl's childhood nostalgia poem "Kindheit," suggests "the way out of enclosure to the outside . . . which can lead from 'present moment' [*Augenblick*] to the 'sight' [*Anblick*] of the world."[57] It is a way which registers the psychic polarity in Trakl's work between the "nocturnal world of grown-ups" and the regressive, narcissistic "childish ego."[58] Threatened by the Symbolic, Don Juan opens the window to the Imaginary world of narcissistic self-containedness.

Don Juan's evocation of this narcissistic realm in which he is held and embraced ("umfassen," "einhüllen" [86–87]) by a world of bright color and sound, "Noch wiedertönt mein Blut von dieser Welt / Die Erde hält mich" bears a strange resemblance to Goethe's earlier version of "Auf dem See" (On the Lake) written when the Olympian poet was twenty-five years old. In the first stanza of Goethe's poem, an egocentric poetic persona speaks of an infantile union with (maternal) nature: "Ich saug' an meiner Nabelschnur / Nun Nahrung aus der Welt" ("I suck upon my umbilical cord / Sustenance now from the world"). Cradled in a rocking boat, which is at once on the lake and headed for the heavens, the poetic persona is suspended in a blissful state of undifferentiation:

> Ich saug' an meiner Nabelschnur
> Nun Nahrung aus der Welt.

57. Doppler, "Die Stufe der Präexistenz," 277.

58. See Neumann, "Georg Trakl," 166. Pfisterer-Burger characterizes the bright "dream-wish" side of this polarity as a "utopic counter-image to the guilt of incest and theme of decline" (*Zeichen und Sterne*, 61). It is a "moment of delight" in which "things show themselves directly and primordially [to the lyrical I]" (60). Esselborn relates this utopic moment to Trakl's creativity as a "modern poet." "Here he is able to write poetry as a consequence of his retreat into the harmonious and sheltering 'blue cavern' of childhood, seen in terms of both an individual and a collective past" ("'*Blaue Blume*' or '*Kristallene Tränen*,'" 220).

Und herrlich rings ist die Natur,
Die mich am Busen hält.
Die Welle wieget unsern Kahn
Im Rudertakt hinauf,
Und Berge wolkenangetan
Entgegnen unserm Lauf.[59]

[I suck upon my umbilical cord / Sustenance now from the world. / And glorious is nature all around, / Which holds me at her breast. / The waves rock our boat / Upward to the rhythm of the oars / And cloud-shrouded mountains meet our course.]

The reverie of the poetic persona's tranquil state of narcissistic self-containedness and connection to the world is broken in the second stanza by a yet more beautiful image—a golden dream. Goethe's response, "Away, you dream! no matter how golden you may be; / Here is also love and life" is also strikingly (intertextually? psycholinguistically?) close to Don Juan's call "Away you thing of no substance! / My blood still echoes with the sound of this world." In any case, the persona in Goethe's poem chooses to relinquish the more beautiful dream (of mimetic desire) in favor of the life and love in the here and now:

Aug mein Aug, was sinkst du nieder?
Goldne Träume, kommt ihr wieder?
Weg, du Traum, so gold du bist,
Hier auch Lieb und Leben ist.

[Eye, my eye, why do you sink down? / Golden dreams, do you return? Away, you dream! no matter how golden you may be; / Here is also love and life.]

Occasioned by what would appear to be a self-reflection on the surface of the water ("Aug mein Aug, was sinkst du nieder?"), this vi-

59. Goethe, *Hamburger Ausgabe*, 1:102.

sionary dream conjures an archaic (Imaginary) image of "a golden age" of visual reciprocity which now resides in the memory—preconscious, unconscious—of the psyche. Whereas Don Juan's pursued persona is faced with antithetical good versus bad alternatives, the poetic persona in Goethe's poem need only choose between good and better. Its choice is thus more a matter of willful renunciation than forced suppression and leads, ultimately, away from the narcissistic state of Imaginary self-containedness, "I suck upon my umbilical cord," to a state of natural maturation, which is expressed in the visual reflection of the ripening fruit of the poem's final line:

> Auf der Welle blinken
> Tausend schwebende Sterne,
> Liebe Nebel trinken
> Rings die türmende Ferne,
> Morgenwind umflügelt
> Die beschattete Bucht,
> Und im See bespiegelt
> Sich die reifende Frucht.

[Sparkling upon the wave / Are a thousand swaying stars, / Gentle fog all around / Drinks in the towering distance, / Morning winds swirl about / The shaded bay, / And reflected on the lake / Is the ripening fruit.]

In renouncing the eye's golden dream, the persona resists the regressive allure of self-reflection. The image mirrored on the water at the end of the poem is thus not of the self; it is, rather, a (progressive) image of maturation which points beyond the narcissism of self-containedness. Appropriately, *ich* is completely absent from the final third of Goethe's poem. Aware but wary of the narcissistic allure of self-reflection, Goethe wrote in November 1772 to Sophie von La Roche: "Alas, it is the fate of the most noble of spirits to sigh in vain for the mirror of themselves." But Goethe also realized the need in adult life to look away from the alluring mirror to achieve true self-awareness. A few months before writing "Auf dem See," Goethe expressed this sentiment to Auguste Gräfin zu Stolberg in a letter of February 1775: "One only comes to know who one is when one finds oneself in another."[60]

Linking the problem of narcissism found in Goethe's "Auf dem See" to artistic creativity, Brigitte Peucker writes: "Alienated from infantile oneness, the speaker must fend off the temptation to return to that state; he banishes the dream to the realm of the unconscious, and affirms the here and now. . . . To become the mirror of art and not the mirror of self-love, the watery surface must become less permeable: a distance must somehow be fixed between self and other."[61]

A fruitful avenue for further investigation of Trakl's relation to Goethe might make use of Harold Bloom's psychoanalytic reception theory. I think a very good case may be made that much of Trakl's (especially) early work is a "psychic battlefield"[62] upon which Trakl's writing subject struggles to free itself from the textual influence of Goethe's work. The manic reversal at the end of this scene shows signs of what Bloom characterizes as a (subliminal) antithetical misreading of the precursor which attempts to

60. Quoted by Pietzcker, in *Trauma, Wunsch und Abwehr*, 29. See also Wellbery, "Specular Moment," 1–41, for an excellent study of the role of visuality in Goethe's early poem "Willkommen und Abschied."

61. Peucker, "Goethe's Mirror of Art," 43–49. Analyzing Goethe's poem "Prometheus," Pietzcker makes a similar claim to Peucker's about the mirror problematic in Goethe's early work: "And thus aesthetic creativity of mirroring becomes the balm for the narcisstic wound" (*Trauma, Wunsch und Abwehr*, 29). Pietzcker's claim that the "motor of Goethe's creativity" is bound up with his incestuous leanings toward his sister Cornelia (31–37) would suggest that Trakl's documented incestuous relationship with his sister Grete had a direct bearing not only on his poetic creativity but also on his clearly ambivalent relationship to Goethe.

62. Bloom, *Poetry and Repression*, 2.

"clear an imaginative space for" the younger poet.[63] One might also compare the striking similarities (and antithetical reversals?) between Trakl's imagery with the following section from Goethe's "Illmenau":

> Disappear dream!
> . . . The cloud is fleeing, the fog is falling
> The shadows are gone . . .
> The true sun illuminates me
> A more beautiful world lives within me
> The fearful face has dissipated into the air
> 'Tis new life. . . . [64]

The depressive-manic vacillation of Don Juan's monologue also bears a striking similarity in tone, structure, and vocabulary to a letter written by Trakl at about the same time as *Don Juans Tod*. Writing to his sister Minna on October 5, 1908, Trakl describes with great interest his psychological response to his recent move to the alienating metropolis of Vienna: "I am very much interested in what has happened to me in recent days, because things seemed so unusual—yet not so unusual, if one considers all of my predispositions. When I arrived here it was as if I could see for the first time life in all its clarity as it is without any personal interpretation, naked without preconceptions, as if I were perceiving all the voices, which reality speaks, gruesome and painfully perceptible. And for a moment I sensed something of the pressure that ordinarily burdens people, the driving force of fate" (1:471–72). The stress and trauma associated with his move to the "city of filth" (*Dreckstadt*), as he later referred to Vienna (1:528), appears to cast his delicate psyche back upon itself; the sordid effects of Vienna's

63. Bloom, *Anxiety of Influence*, 15.
64. Goethe, *Hamburger Ausgabe*, 1:107. See Adams, "Scene of Instruction," 467–513, for an insightful Bloomian analysis of Mörike's "defensive" reading of Goethe's "Illmenau."

rapid, late nineteenth-century industrialization serves to intensify and focus his attention on his own psychological state, which then merges with his perceptions of life and reality. This *Dreckstadt* thus gives him the impression that he is observing the real horrors and animalistic impulses that lie beneath the surface of all life. Trakl continues his letter: "I think that it must be terrible to always live like this, to be completely in touch with all of the animalistic drives which roll life through time. I have sensed, smelled, and felt the most horrible possibilities within me and heard in my blood the demons howl—a thousand devils whose urgings drive the flesh insane. What a horrible nightmare!"

Trakl's move to Vienna put him in touch with the howling demons and devils of his blood, which he seems to think are the driving force of fate. The letter's next paragraph, however, abruptly switches, like the end of the *Don Juan* fragment, to an antithetical view of reality. The parallels in vocabulary and tone between the letter and the drama fragment are striking: "Gone! Today this vision of reality has sunk again into nothingness. Far from me are things, and farther yet are their voices, and I listen again with an inspired ear to the melodies which are within me, and my winged eye dreams again its images which are more beautiful than all of reality! I am at home with myself and I am my world! My whole, beautiful world full of endless pleasing sound."[65] The nightmare vision of reality with its demonic host of subterranean pursuers is banished by the recovery of an antithetical vision of narcissistic reverie: "and my winged eye dreams again its images which

65. Kleefeld's Freudian reading construes the last line of this letter as "a fantasy of incestuous integration" in which "the separation between self and object is totally negated—this is the world of primary narcissism, the world of oceanic feeling in the womb of the archaic mother." Kleefeld continues, stating that "the flip-side of incestuous integration wish fantasy . . . this fantasy of omnipotence, is the feeling of utter weakness, which he senses in the large city" (*Das Gedicht als Sühne*, 104–5).

are more beautiful than all of reality! I am at home with myself and I am my world!" Trakl, unlike Goethe, does not have the option of renouncing the glorious visions of a mythical-specular-ego, for he lives not in a world of *Lieb und Leben* and the comforting maternal embrace of "gentle fog" (*liebe Nebel*) but in a *Dreckstadt* inhabited by demons, devils, and dark constricting serpentine forces. His only option, it would seem, is a narcissistic reverie, the synaesthetic intoxication of the senses and, ultimately, an art form that might appease those demons and perhaps also keep those "images" of his "winged eye" and the "endless pleasing sound" of his "inspired ear" from fleeting back into dark silence at the bounds of his spirit.

Dating also from the same time as these poetic-psychological explorations is the review in which Trakl praised the psychological acuity of Gustav Streicher's *Seelentragödie* (Trakl's term) *Monna Violanta*, that drama which sought "to solve a psychological problem of the most subtle kind by means of modern psychoanalysis [*Seelenanalyse*]." When read in connection with the letter describing his reflections on his own psychological state, it becomes clear that Trakl took an active interest, from the period of his early writing on, not only in his own psychological state but also in questions of psychology in general, an important fact which is often overlooked in the Trakl criticism. The plot and subject matter of *Monna Violanta* bear a striking resemblance, with one major difference, to those of Trakl's *Don Juan*. In Streicher's play, it is the female character, Monna Violanta—not the male character— who, in Trakl's words, is pursued by "the ghost of a dead person . . . with its horrible, lecherous gestures" (1:208). It is not surprising that Trakl was especially pleased with the manic reversal of the play's denouement: "It is only in the last scene . . . and in an elevating intensification that the drama is resolved in a Dionysian song about the joyousness of life." The character Monna Violanta ultimately eludes the repulsive and "terrible power of a deadly force," Trakl explains, by conjuring "the most crude of life's forces." She must, in other words, unleash the demonic, animalistic drives to exorcise them and, in the final analysis, transcend them, like Don Juan, in a manic "Dionysian song about the joyousness of life."

Of particular interest in this regard is Trakl's praise of the prerational, prelogical emotional effect of this neoromantic piece, which, as Trakl explains, "transports some into a cool ecstasy, while it allows others to dream; its plot, however, should not be recapitulated, because so much would be lost in the process." This effect, as Trakl reformulates neoromantic theory, derives not from the rational sense of language but rather from the *melos* of words themselves. Streicher's play was successful, Trakl felt, precisely because its "sweet feminine rhetoric" was able to express the ineffable and hold fast the fleeting moment of mood: "It is strange how these verses penetrate the problem, how often the sound of the word expresses an inexpressible thought and holds fast the fleeting mood. In these lines there is something of the sweet feminine rhetoric which seduces us to listen to the *melos* of the word and ignore its content and meaning; the minor key of this language puts the mind into a meditative mood and fills the blood with dreamy fatigue" (1:208). The implication is clear: the sound of the word, the "minor key" of language, has a sensuous incantatory power which is superior to the ordinary sense of words. That this sensuous power is attributed to a "feminine rhetoric" suggests that Trakl's remarks may have, at least in part, a deep psychosexual motivation that brings him to fantasize escaping in and through a feminine element the rational grasp of language's "content and meaning." The sense of escape is strengthened by Trakl's allusion to a state of intoxication which lulls the mind and "fills the blood with dreamy fatigue." Put in the context of Trakl's alcoholism and drug addiction, this allusion to the intoxicating effects of the "minor key of language" begins to make poetic sense. The desirable incantatory effects of *melo*dious poetic words, like the narcotic effect of drugs, provided him with a sensually pleasing means of escaping the torment of self-consciousness, a torment that he sensed, vaguely perhaps, was somehow linked to the rational "content and meaning" of language, which can destroy the intoxication of Dionysian song. Trakl accordingly ends his review with a final praise of the work's "mood-inducing power" and the following words about Streicher's public recitation of the work: "The public gladly followed him [Streicher] into his world and rewarded him with gratitude, for allowing them to look for an hour into the depths of a strange existence." Praising here an art form of psychological vision that *looks* into the strange depths of "an" existence, Trakl is careful not to equate this impersonal, evocative existence with the conscious intentions of its creator, Gustav Streicher.

The mania and synaesthetic realm of "pleasing sound" of the final lines of Don Juan's monologue, the narcissistic world of beautiful images and infinite harmonies of Trakl's letter to his sister, Catalinon's song to himself and his subliminal aversion to language, as well as Trakl's praise of the sweet, feminine *melos* of words beyond their semantic significance, all point to an idealized mythical-specular state of egocentrism which would partake of a more primal, feminine element and seal itself off from the intrusive patrocentric forces of deferring signifiers. Speaking to such an idealized realm of retreat, which he ties to the Jungian "mother-anima archetype," Erich Neumann writes:

> Intoxication, dream and mental derangement reach a unique accord in Trakl's poetry, but the yearning for a deeper and more sheltered reality finally overwhelms him in the form of a craving to escape from the hostile, alien world of normal reality. . . . With the emergence of the mythical dimension in Trakl's poetry, all the plastic elements relating to this world fuse into a unity

that nevertheless gives the impression not simply of a dream but of the shaping of a deeper and "other" reality. In many ways the music of the poems, with its strange rhythm, follows the techniques of self-expression which are employed by the unconscious and which we have learned to understand in the interpretation of dreams. His poems are alive with fusions, displacements, and identifications, expressed in a picture language of symbolic significance that conveys to us the world of the prelogical, with its dissolutions and nonconceptual plastic forms.[66]

This mythical, dreamlike state engendered in the act of writing brought Trakl's writing subject to fantasize at this point in his career about a bright intoxication of "Dionysian song." But to conjure this manic "elevating intensification," he needed, it would seem, somehow to override or bypass the censuring effects of the ego's "defensive armour"[67] so that he might submit to the (depressive) requisite "terrible power of a deadly force." He had to court his demons, unleash their seething dark force, and hope to find some momentary relief from their pressure by, if he were so fortunate, achieving a fleeting moment of synaesthetic brilliance. Thus his "indolent words" led him to the dark bounds of his ego's consciousness, where his feverish "fusions, displacements and identi-

66. Neumann, "Georg Trakl," 181–82.

67. See Lacan, *Ecrits*, 17. Lacan believes that the ego is an alienating objectification which holds the subject captive by systematically misreading the message of the unconscious. "Thus Freud introduced the ego into his doctrine by defining it according to the resistances that are proper to it. What I have tried to convey is that these resistances are of an imaginary nature . . . and can be reduced in man to the narcissistic relation introduced by Freud" (168). One could argue in a Lacanian vein that Trakl's weakened ego was incapable of conjuring the usual "imaginary resistances" and thus was, especially in the *writing* process, in touch with the frightful *linguistic* "message of the unconscious" (169). Sharp also takes a similar line of reasoning. Following the lead of Michael Hamburger and with the help of Laingian antipsychiatry, he suggests that Trakl's work manifests the "fictitious" character of the ego. See Sharp, *Poet's Madness*, 58, 82, 110–36.

fications" followed the repetitive, paradigmatic pulse of words, the combinatory laws of the primary process of signifiers themselves. Powered by a deep-seated aversion to the socializing influence of language and a concomitant longing (retroactive fantasizing) about a prelinguistic state, Trakl's writing pushed him ever further into the impersonal symbolic matrix of the linguistic other, the unconscious, where desire is forever channeled through the paradigmatic under*tones* of language and the grammatical, narrative force of conscious speech had loosened its grip on the words he used. By his own admission, his poems were a fusion of disparate elements which "forged in four lines of verse, four individual image-parts into one impression"—a product of a "living fever," which, for reasons unknown to him, "produced this particular form" (1:478). It is significant that Trakl should use a masculine image of forging (*der Schmied, schmieden*) to characterize his struggle with a recalcitrant language. The symbolic register of words, in Western culture at least (according to—among others—Lacan, Derrida, and Kristeva), is the medium through which the "patrocentric" laws of culture and society are transmitted to ("inscribed within") the human subject. Trakl works within the authority of this masculine inscription trying to overcome its limitations to conjure a prelinguistic, feminine *melos,* which, to speak with Kristeva, "produces in poetic language 'musical' but also nonsense effects . . . and is later reactivated as rhythms, intonations . . . in psychotic discourse."[68]

Trakl's earlier poetry sustains its power from an induced state of fever, a Rimbaudian derangement of the senses. By submitting to the paradigmatic pulse of freely associating composition, he was able to disengage his writing from explicit intentionality and the logic of narrative—syntagmatic—discourse to evoke in and through his writing the pleasing *Zwischenreich* between an

68. Kristeva, *Desire in Language,* 133.

Imaginary "feminine rhetoric" of *melos* and Symbolic register of patrocentric order. Trakl became, as we will see in the following chapters, increasingly skilled at using the more impersonal paradigmatic axis of language so that he could draw from a preconscious level of significance which might secure some relief from a gloomy existence of fragmentation and alienation. In his feverish paradigmatic forging and reforging, substituting and displacing his small elemental vocabulary into single linguistic impressions, he struggled to synthesize a melodious and densely imagistic cohesion whose assuaging unity might momentarily close the wound of man's problematic entry into the grown-up world of words. What results is a profoundly modernist mode of writing poetry that allowed him to explore a psycholinguistic dimension that underlies all discourse.[69] This modernist mode of writing, one could say, was itself a kind of psychoanalysis, of "literary self-analysis," as Esselborn has aptly put it.

69. In musing that the truth of Trakl's poetry lies in his fusing of the unconscious with literary expression, Esselborn comes close to recognizing that Trakl is creating poetry out of the unconscious structures and orders of language itself. "Trakl's search . . . for an authentic form of expression demands . . . the development of a scenic language as a way of presenting unconscious psychic processes. . . . The breakdown of the traditional lyrical I and the . . . individual allow . . . for a true expression, the *identity of person and language*" (emphasis added; *Georg Trakl*, 225).

CHAPTER 6

The Twilight of Romanticism:
Trakl's *Fleurs du Mal*

The nineteenth century dislike of Romanticism is the
rage of Caliban not seeing his own face in a glass.—
Oscar Wilde, *The Picture of Dorian Gray*

The Twilight of Romanticism

THE PSYCHIC POLARITY motivating Don Juan's manic-depressive mood swings informs Trakl's poetry from his earliest adolescent verse to the poems written in the final weeks of his life.
Though increasingly refined, tempered, and perhaps aesthetically
disguised, Trakl's verse reflects a sustained effort to explore in
the medium of verse the psychic *Zwischenreich* between Imaginary
brightness and impinging darkness. The more abrupt juxtaposition of opposites aligned with light and dark in his earlier work
is transformed into complex images which differentiate, through
multileveled, metaphorical displacements, the play of opposites.

Early on Trakl was often content with creating first-person
poetic personae who couch their pronouncements of existential
trauma in antithetical images of light and dark, as exemplified in
the following stanza taken from "Gesang zur Nacht" (Song to the
Night), written in

> Das Dunkel löschte mich schweigend aus,
> Ich ward ein toter Schatten im Tag—

Da trat ich aus der Freude Haus
In die Nacht hinaus. (1:225)

[Darkness extinguished me in silence, / I became a dead shadow in the
day— / As I stepped out of the house of joy / Out into the night.]

From 1909 on, Trakl became increasingly interested in exploring
the psychopoetic implications of stepping "out into the night" as a
"dead shadow in the day," of exploring, in other words, the creative possibilities the process of darkening makes possible. The
somewhat simplistic presentation of opposites in the above lines
thus gives way to such complex metaphorical imagery of a world in
decline as is found in the last stanza of Trakl's well-known poem
"Untergang" (Decline) written in 1912:

Immer klingen die weißen Mauern der Stadt.
Unter Dornenbogen
O mein Bruder klimmen wir blinde Zeiger gen Mitternacht. (1:116)

[The white walls of the city sound forever. / Beneath thorn arches, / O
my brother, we blind hands climb toward midnight.]

Here Trakl concludes the poem's thematic of autumnal darkening
with an evocative constellation of images of light and dark to create an unsettling, nighttime "soulscape" in which the blind hands,
signaling—among other things—the haunting disintegration of
pure vision, is related to the alienating noise of civilization. This
chapter will examine how Trakl's earlier attempts to explore the
poetic implications of the "stepping out into the night" set the
stage for the modernist aesthetics of his mature work that necessi-
tated a definitive break with the epistemological assumptions underlying the classical-romantic tradition of confessional poetry. In
Trakl's early work, one finds a form of poetic expression very similar to the *Erlebnislyrik* model of the *Goethezeit* in which a stable

poetic persona, often a protagonist speaking in the first person, appears to relate the details of some experience to impart to a sympathetic and congenial reader a more general spiritual or emotional truth. Trakl's early poems often tell stories;[1] they are generally linear in development, thematically cohesive, and attempt by means of aesthetically controlled and articulated language to reach a sympathetic reader. In tone and content, however, this verse is markedly different from that of the classical-romantic tradition. It is not the expression of an inspired poet but almost exclusively a lament about inner turmoil and alienation. The form is classical-romantic, but the content is modernist-expressionistic.

The early sonnet "Dämmerung" (Twilight), written in 1909, is typical of this period. Alluded to immediately in the title is the pervasive influence of the philosophical mentor of the young and rebellious expressionist generation: Nietzsche.[2] His razor-edged critique of Western values found in his *Twilight of the Idols*[3] sets the resonant stage upon which an (apparently) stable poetic persona tells its woeful tale of fragmentation:

1. Of course, *Erlebnislyrik* involves more than telling stories. As we saw in Chapter 1, the *Erlebnislyrik* poem has a strong narrative moment; the poet speaks as if he or she were relating/communicating a message about a particular state of affairs. Because this genre is supposed to originate in and center around the poet's personal (subjective) experience, it frequently is written in the first person, which adds to its narrative tone. "Narrative" is thus used here to designate not so much storytelling per se as the illusion of relating/communicating a message. See Esselborn, *Georg Trakl*, chap. 2.

2. Esselborn sees Nietzsche's Dionysian/Apollonian antithesis as a dominant experience-structuring principle in Trakl's work. See ibid., chaps. 3 and 4. See further Doppler, "Orphischer und apokalyptischer Gesang," 219–21, 231, for a discussion of Nietzsche's influence on Trakl.

3. Nietzsche's *Twilight of the Idols* was to become part of his planned but never completed "transvaluation of values." The pernicious overestimation of reason and intellect, Nietzsche had proclaimed, was a false idol, an expression of spiritual decay, which is most effectively countered by the Dionysian intoxication of creative artists who stand above the false values of rationality.

Dämmerung

Zerwühlt, verzerrt bist du von jedem Schmerz
Und bebst vom Mißton aller Melodien,
Zersprungne Harfe du—ein armes Herz,
Aus dem der Schwermut kranke Blumen blühen.
Wer hat den Feind, den Mörder dir bestellt,
Der deiner Seele letzten Funken stahl,
Wie er entgöttert diese karge Welt
Zur Hure, häßlich, krank, verwesungsfahl!

Von Schatten schwingt sich noch ein wilder Tanz,
Zu kraus zerrissnem, seelenlosem Klang,
Ein Reigen um der Schönheit Dornenkranz,

Der Welk den Sieger, den verlornen, krönt
—Ein schlechter Preis, um den Verzweiflung rang,
Und der die lichte Gottheit nicht versöhnt. (1:218)

[You are uprooted and distorted by every pain / And you quiver from the dissonance of all melodies, / You fractured harp—a poor heart, / From which the sick flowers of melancholy bloom. // Who sent to you the enemy, the murderer, / Who stole the last sparks of your soul, / Oh how he has removed the divine from this bare world / And made it into a whore, ugly, sick, and pale with decay! // From the shadows swirls yet a wild dance, / To the crookedly torn, soulless sound, / A round dance about the thorn-crown of beauty, // Which, wilted, crowns the victor, the lost one / —A bad prize, for which despair has fought, / And unreconciled is he with the luminous divinity.]

Ignoring for the moment its patently poetic features (rhyme, rhythm, alliteration, assonance, metaphor, and the like), it would be safe to say that this language functions much like the language of everyday discourse. In the first quatrain, for example, one gets the distinct impression that a speaker, or writer, intends to relate

176

something—re-present a particular experiential situation—to a listener or reader. Though the situation is a bit bizarre, a naive reader—one who is unaccustomed to poetic language—could without undue difficulty grasp and recapitulate the basic story line, which might go as follows. The speaker addresses a you (*du*), someone who is upset and torn by every pain, someone who quivers from the dissonance of all melodies and whose heart is likened to a shattered harp from which blossom forth the diseased flowers of melancholy.

The narrative import, however, is not so patently clear. At first blush the assertion "And you quiver from the dissonance of all melodies" seems to be readily intelligible: dissonance causes the addressed "you" to quiver. Were the line to end with "dissonance" the assertion would be unmistakably clear and in consonance with the preceding line. This, however, is not the case because with the last word ("melodies") the reader is informed that, contrary to normal expectations, the source of dissonance is melody; melody and dissonance are not causally connected, as implied here, but are rather antithetically related.[4] Melody, we are accustomed to believing, is a pleasantly flowing arrangement of tones. Like the romantic song, it pleases the senses. *Mißton* (dissonance), by contrast, displeases the senses, it is not a pleasant tone, but a mis-tone, a nerve-rattling annoyance. Melding the mismatched *Mißton/ Melodie* pair creates a tension that begins to undermine the coherence of the original narrative reading. If, however, one were to strike the *Mißton* from the second line, the result would be an assertion

4. For a contemporary musicologist, melody and dissonance would probaly not seem as antithetical as they would for someone unfamiliar with the more avant-garde music of this century—the work of Schönberg or Stravinsky, for example. By the same token, Trakl's generation probably sensed a stronger antithesis in this pair than the present, "postmodern generation." What was discordant for the early twentieth century has long since been adopted, commodified, and mass produced by the popular culture industry.

which is not only more purely narrative (and less "difficult" to comprehend), but also closer in spirit to the early romantic view of poetry. The "you," it could then be said, quivers from melodies, being an excited, creative, and productive organ of what Novalis called the "musical soul-relationships" of the cosmos. Through the poet, the pure music of the spheres was to ex-press itself and magically unite the kindred hearts of poets and readers with the divine. In a sense, pure melody—melody without *Mißton*—is a figure for the idealism underlying the early romantic song. It also stands for romantic poets' optimism, their reverence for nature, and the quasi-mystical power of the poetic word.

Given the force of this *Melodie/Mißton* tension, one could take this stanza as a figure for the antiromantic streak pervading Trakl's earlier poetry. The positive, romanticism, is shadowed by its negative, dissonance. The contrary force of the *Melodie/Mißton* pair is then thematically related to the shattered harp, which produces broken melodies—dissonances—and to the flowers (a metonym for burgeoning life and exalted poetry of divine origin), which are countered by disease—"the sick flowers of melancholy." These flowers, moreover, are not only sick, they are the product of sickness—the mental malady of melancholy. Positive and negative— music, melody, and blooming flowers, on one hand, and dissonance, depression, disease, and shattered harps, on the other—are counterposed. The *Mißton* of the modern era, it might seem, has blighted irreparably the purity of romantic melody. That melody, a song that was to blossom forth like springtime flowers from the inspired and exalted romantic heart, is now shattered by the dissonance, perhaps, of existential trauma and a post-Baudelairian era of alienating cities and nerve-jangling machines. The poetic result is sick flowers springing from the depression of a "poor heart"— *kranke Blumen*—which are likened to the fractured chords of a broken harp. Art and disease, to move to a more abstract level, are intimately related and aligned. Shadowing romantic confessional form is the negativity of "dissonant" content—the sickness of deformed melodies, deformed harps, and deformed flowers: the modernist content of "Dämmerung" threatens to break the romantic mold—to deform romantic form.

Sick Flowers, Ich and Du

As in the *Erlebnislyrik* poem, the poetic persona speaking in "Dämmerung" appears to tell its story (narrate) by communicating with an empathetic reader. The sense of narration is strengthened by the various second-person pronouns (*du, dein, dir*)—informal pronouns of address which imply a speaking *ich* and thereby create the illusion of an intimate relation between two persons. The reader, in other words, cannot help but feel on some level that this *du* is the *du* of interpersonal address, that he or she is being addressed by a speaking *ich*. Looking again to the first quatrain, one notices immediately that these second-person pronouns do not address another person but rather the poetic persona, which has cast itself as a "shattered harp" and "poor heart." Through these metaphoric displacements (and a poetic convention that allows one to address oneself by addressing the heart), Trakl's writing subject is able to indulge in a narcissism of self-referentiality while at the same time maintaining both the sense of narrative cohesion and the illusion of communication. This *Erlebnislyrik* poem thus builds, on one hand, from an involuted self-address motivated by a narcissistic impulse to establish a self-sufficiency that would not be "uprooted and distorted by every pain." It is poetic speaking that wells from an unchecked but impossible desire to find and identify with a *du*, with an other, which is not strange and alienating. But "Dämmerung" also builds, on the other hand, from the writing subject's desire to establish a compensatory unity of narrative cohesion which might also control and counter the fragmenting effects of socialized, postspecular existence. "The psychic function of narrative and fantasy," Fredric Jameson reminds us, is an attempt "of the subject to reintegrate his or her alienated image."[5] In other words, the desire for narrative cohesion and contiguity would be a surrogate unity which itself wells from the primal, narcissistic desire to reverse the constitutional fragmentation that, in psychoanalytic terms, was created when the perceptual unity of the Imaginary was ruptured by the paternal agency of the Symbolic order.

Moving on to the second quatrain, one notices how this narcisstic persona now, in a similar fashion to Don Juan's metonymic blinding of a maternal image, denigrates a feminine image (*"die Welt"*) by transforming it, "the world," into a sick and repulsive whore:

Wer hat den Feind, den Mörder dir bestellt,
Der deiner Seele letzten Funken stahl,
Wie er entgöttert diese karge Welt
Zur Hure, häßlich, krank, verwesungsfahl! (1:218)

[Who sent to you the enemy, the murderer, / Who stole the last sparks of your soul, / Oh how he has removed the divine from this bare world / And made it into a whore, ugly, sick, and pale with decay!]

Though the poetic persona does not attempt and is perhaps incapable of answering the rhetorical question posed here—whose question mark is conspicuously absent—it is suggested that a negative agency, an anonymous enemy and murderer, is to blame. The psychoanalytic implications are striking: not only is this negative agency masculine, but it is also held responsible for the darkening of the *du*'s soul, having stolen its "last sparks" and transformed its world—*die Welt,* mother nature—into an ugly, degenerate whore.

5. Jameson, "The Imaginary and the Symbolic in Lacan," 353.

In one figurative move, the Imaginary fantasy of a romantic idyll is dashed and the maternal is denigrated and defiled.

Taken together, the two quatrains of "Dämmerung" present, similar to Bonaventura's *Nachtwachen,* a "reverse-side of early romanticism."[6] Their imagery runs squarely counter to the early romantic belief that art and life were related manifestations or expressions of the same positive force of the cosmos. The world has been transformed—the divine has been removed—it has become the antithesis of the early romantic vision of a divinely creative nature: mother nature is now a whore, an ugly and sick woman whose sinful activity leads not to procreation, but to fallow decomposition—decadence. Romanticism's positive pathos has turned negative, and the high poet-priest has become a degenerate lamenter who sings not about the exalted cosmic origin of poetry but about diseased flowers springing from disease.

The frequent occurrence of such words as "Hure" (whore) or "Dirne" (prostitute) in Trakl's earlier work evidence, perhaps, what Harold Bloom calls, in *The Anxiety of Influence,* the "language

---

6. See Richard Brinkmann's "Nachtwachen von Bonaventura." Brinkmann comments that the *Nachtwachen* constitute a parody or satire of the early romantics' idealism as well their reverie for the "transcendental" ramifications of *die Nacht.* In, for example, the fourteenth *Nachtwache,* the watchman visits an insane asylum, where he encounters an actress who became deranged playing the role of Ophelia in Shakespeare's *Hamlet.* Shakespeare, we are told, "had affected her too strongly" (Bonaventura, *Die Nachtwachen,* 112). It is interesting to note that the watchman states that her crazed singing produces disharmony: "I heard Ophelia singing jagged pieces of her ballads . . . which seemed to become one big *disharmony*" (emphasis added; 122). Pure melody, as it is sung by a person made ill by art, disintegrates into disharmony, dissonance. Trakl's writing subject, it might seem, has defensively aligned itself with the night watchman, whose words not only satirize early romantic poetics but also begin to articulate what will become known as a thematic of *fin-du-siècle* literary decadence. "Oh friend poet," calls out Bonaventura's night watchman into the night, "he who wants to live now, should not write poetry" (*Nachtwachen,* 122).

181

of taboo."[7] Bloom argues that the veneration of genius and the emphasis on originality in post-Enlightenment poetry produces in poets an underlying tension or anxiety about the originality of their work. This tension, or "anxiety of influence," occasions subliminal defense mechanisms, whereby poets struggle to establish and maintain their autonomy from strong precursor poets. One such mechanism is the use of taboo words—words inappropriate or even unutterable by a previous generation of poets—which are used by the poet to clear a creative space free of the pervasive influence of "father" precursors. Trakl's use of words designating "whore" ("Hure" and "Dirne"), words inappropriate in "father" Goethe's era, would be plausible candidates for such a language of taboo.[8] They might also evince signs of a more general defense mechanism, one which underwrites the poignant antiromantic streak in much of Trakl's work.[9]

To cast the modern/expressionistic tone and content of these quatrains solely in negative terms as an antithetical reflection of— or psychic reaction to—early romanticism, however, misses the playful ambivalence pervading these lines. No matter how sick, flowers do bloom in the first quatrain. And no matter how "dissonant" and malformed they may be, flowers are—by virtue of a pervasive, intertextually mediated tradition in which they connote beauty—potentially beautiful. This ambivalence emerges elsewhere. Though less explicit, the *Mißton/Melodie* pair also evinces an ambivalence, for these melodies, no matter how much disso-

7. Bloom, *Anxiety of Influence,* 66. Trakl was no doubt motivated by his reading of Rimbaud to use such unlyrical words.

8. See ibid., 66–68.

9. Sharp points out that Otto Weininger's theory of hermaphroditism, about which Trakl had definite (documented) opinions, also had a strong influence on his early writing: "Otto Weininger's differentiation between two extreme feminine types, the prostitute and the mother . . . has left its mark on these [early] poems" (*Poet's Madness,* 62). See also Kleefeld's discussion of *die Hure, Das Gedicht als Sühne,* 204–6.

nance they contain, are nonetheless melodies. They are dissonant melodies, a succession of tones that, as melodies, have the potential to please. "Bebst" (quiver) likewise contains this ambivalence. Though usually the physical sign of psychological stress, "beben" can also signal positive emotion, extreme happiness, for example, or the thrill of anticipation and accomplishment. In the context of these four lines, "the thrill of accomplishment" cannot be ruled out. Indeed, something potentially thrilling takes place and is accomplished: the fractured harp continues to sound and sick flowers continue to bloom. One cannot, without an act of interpretative exclusion or suppression, dismiss the positive semantic potential of (quivering) harps, (dissonant) melodies, or (sick) flowers. This constellation of ambivalences in "Dämmerung" thus brings to the reader's attention the possibility—to use the figural language of the first quatrain—that from the ground of sickness can grow strange flowers and tones, which, all negativity notwithstanding, are capable of thrilling. One could also say that this quatrain counterposes the negativities of dissonance and sickness with the possibility of a new poetics in which, to speak with Hans Magnus Enzensberger, " 'negative' behavior is poetically impossible; the reverse side of any poetic destruction," Enzensberger reminds, "is the construction of a new poetics."[10]

Such a poetological reading of "Dämmerung" is strengthened by the poignant ambiguity of the poem's title: "Dämmerung" can refer to the passing of a day (twilight) or to the arrival of a new day (dawn). In that the poem problematizes both the pervasive influence of the poetic tradition and the status of lyrical poetry in a postromantic world, one could say that the irreconcilable ambiguity of the title prefigures the poem's basic inability to reconcile past and present. It is thus caught between the *Dämmerung* of de-

10. Enzensberger, *Museum der modernen Poesie,* 11. See the section "The Proliferation of Theory" in Chapter 4.

cline—the twilight of romanticism—and the *Dämmerung* of a dawning new era in which the "flowers" of poetry manage to bloom in a "godless and cursed century," as Trakl once referred to his era (1:518–19).

There is another aspect, though certainly not a unique feature of Trakl's poetry, that should be addressed in conjunction with this discussion of ambivalences. As the words "Dämmerung," "Blume," or "Hure" would suggest, this poem is embedded in and to a certain degree plays off a rich intertextual history. Nearly every line "echoes," to borrow Wolfgang Preisendanz's characterization of Trakl's earlier verse, with conspicuous bits and pieces of preexisting "already written" discourses. The poetological mention of diseased flowers, for example, clearly echoes Baudelaire's *fleurs du mal*,[11] whereas the title itself signals, as discussed above, the cultural pessimism expressed by Nietzsche's *Götzendämmerung* (*Twilight of the Idols*) or perhaps even Richard Wagner's *Götterdämmerung* (*Twilight of the Gods*). The complicity of art and disease resounds with *fin-de-siècle* decadence. Perhaps even Bonaventura lurks on the periphery of the quatrain. Goethe's presence, and perhaps induced absence, likewise manifests itself subtextually. The *Schmerz-Herz* (pain-heart) rhyme pair (lines 1 and 3) would betoken, for instance, his earlier *Erlebnislyrik*. It is an intriguing fact that this very same rhyme pair occurs in two of Goethe's most well-known and often anthologized earlier poems "Willkommen und Abschied" and "An den Mond." One cannot help but wonder whether there might even be a touch of self-conscious "Bonaventurian" satire motivating this echo, or whether there is perhaps an anxiety defense mechanism at work here as well—a subliminal mechanism that has brought Trakl's writing subject to defy the

11. Preisendanz writes: "One could almost mistake the Trakl-Sonette *Dämmerung* for something from Heine's *Junge Leiden,* so similar are these works in motif, vocabulary, and diction" ("Auflösung und Verdinglichung," 234).

strong "father" poet by perversely twisting the precursor's "primal words."[12] Clearly *Herz* and *Schmerz* could be listed as "primal" vocabulary for the exuberant younger Goethe.

Turning again to the first quatrain, one will see that *ich*, by contrast to much of the *Erlebnislyrik* of the early nineteenth century, is not spoken (or in this poem in general). In place of explicit first-person references, the poetic persona makes, through a series of objective correlatives (harp, heart, sick flowers) indirect reference to itself. By referring to itself indirectly and as an other (e.g., as a harp, a poor heart, or *du*) and then talking about the creations of this other-*du* (dissonant melodies and sick flowers) the poetic persona calls attention not only to the absence of a unified/unifying *Ich* (ego) but also to the problematic presence of a series of preexisting impulses which inform its own sick flowers of poetry. The other-*du* of this quatrain, very importantly, quivers, as it is stated in the third line, from the dissonance of *all* melodies—which necessarily includes those from the past. Thus the *du* is not only split from the *Ich*, but it is also a passive medium through which the dissonances of the "already played" melodies sound. There is, moreover, a certain anonymity expressed in the *Mißton/Melodie* figure which serves to reinforce the irrepressible nature of this *other*, for the *du* of the quatrain is ultimately a harp, a (inanimate) musical instrument that is not strummed by a harpist, but rather vibrated by the "dissonance of all melodies" that precede its own productions. Trakl's writing subject, one could say, has created a constellation of self-referential images which foreground the possibility that the poetic pulse that informs its echo-filled *fleurs du mal* does not well solely from the poet's inspired heart. Surfacing in the creative process thematized here is a ghostly set of fractured "melodies" which pass through the poet's words on their impersonal course from another place, from the "already played" melo-

12. Bloom, *Anxiety of Influence*, 66.

dies and fragmenting dissonances of early romanticism, French symbolism, and the preromantic *Hainbund* group,[13] and/or the alterity of the unconscious labyrinth of impersonal signifiers in the symbolic register.[14] Placed in the context of Trakl's work, these foregrounded forces (and probable psychic defense mechanisms) signal a young poet's struggle, subliminal perhaps, with the past— a struggle in which his writing subject seeks to free itself from the weight of traditions so as to find and establish a poetic idiom that would be appropriate to its particular situation and time. In a way, these intrusive resonances and echoes represent a potentially disruptive semantic impulse which always thwarts and undermines the poet's attempt to control language for his or her own narrative purposes. Ironically, Novalis's idea of the poet as medium (through which the transcendental spirit speaks) seems to have found expression in this poem. Only here the poet-medium is not so much vibrated by the originality of the "spirit of the world," but rather by, among other things, the secondhand versions of singers

13. Wolfgang Preisendanz points out a striking similarity in tone and vocabulary between Trakl's earlier verse and that of the *Hainbund* poets, especially the verse of F. Mathisson and J. G. Salis-Seeweis (Preisendanz, "Auflösung und Verdinglichung in den Gedichten Georg Trakls," 255–57). Furness, "Trakl and the Literature of Decadence," 82–95, adds to the list of borrowings and echoes in Trakl's "poetry of quotation" another early eighteenth-century quarry, namely Georg Büchner's *Lenz*. See also Schier, "Büchner und Trakl," 1052–64, esp. 1062.

14. Brigitte Peucker's study *Lyric Descent in the German Romantic Tradition* hinges upon Trakl's struggle with the growing awareness that "poetry does not issue from voice" (173). In reference to the poem "Melusine," she writes: "The point of all this ambiguity is, in any case, that voice is now here, now there, but never in the possession of the 'speaker'" (175). Sharp, by contrast, sees the multiple voices and personae of Trakl's verse (as manifest, for example, in the poem "Helian") as "tremors of his own personality": "The richest sources which Trakl exploited for his poem were doubtless the fluctuation and tremors of his own personality structure," which, Sharp believes, are linked to the "shattered eyes," "broken visions," and the like of Trakl's imagery. See Sharp, *Poet's Madness*, 98–101.

of the past and the alterity of the linguistic register. "Dämmer-ung," we begin to realize, is a complexly self-referential and poet-ological poem which contains (or produces) a lateral message about the origins of the poetic pulse. It considers as such its own "conditions for possibility" and becomes what Novalis and Schlegel had termed one hundred years earlier *Transzendental-poesie*.

This poetological strain is taken up again in the poem's first tercet:

> Von Schatten schwingt sich noch ein wilder Tanz,
> Zu kraus zerrissnem, seelenlosem Klang,
> Ein Reigen um der Schönheit Dornenkranz,

[From the shadows swirls yet a wild dance, / To the crookedly torn, soulless sound, / A round dance about the thorn-crown of beauty,]

Out of the shadows (of the past? of the already written? of the dark Oedipal agency of the unconscious?) comes a wild round dance that encircles the thorn-crown of beauty. The mysterious, imper-sonal origin of this round dance is highlighted by the "soulless sound" of the second line. The torn ("zerrissnem") character of this soulless sound, moreover, thematically relates back to the bro-ken harp of the first quatrain, for a broken harp, which is vibrated by the anonymous and alienating "dissonance," would likely pro-duce "crookedly torn, soulless sound." Mention of beauty (a sine qua non of classical-romantic poetics) in connection with these clangs, adds to the poetological character of this lateral message. This tercet also contains the fracturing ambivalence seen in the first quatrain: beauty is likened to a thorn-crown, a problematic crown that adorns, elevates, *and* pains its bearer. Like the *fleurs du mal,* both good and bad, the "thorn-crown" of beauty is both good and bad. Tie to this the Christian implications of a thorn of crowns (which could signal the painful departure of a thorn-crowned divinity from the fellowship of man) and one can again talk of a deromanticized early romantic dream: the divine has receded, having taken with it the faith in the *pure* and *divine* melody sought by Novalis's generation.

The final tercet of "Dämmerung" does not resolve the poem's tensions and ambivalences; if anything, it adds to them with a series of paradoxical and perplexing images:

> Der Welk den Sieger, den verlornen, krönt
> —Ein schlechter Preis, um den Verzweiflung rang,
> Und der die lichte Gottheit nicht versöhnt.

[Which, wilted, crowns the victor, the lost one / —A bad prize, for which despair has fought, / And unreconciled is he with the luminous divinity.]

The wilted thorn-crown of beauty, we learn, is a *bad* prize, which is presented to the victor, who, paradoxically, is also the *lost one*. In the poem's final line the Christian divinity implied in the thorn-crown emerges again. What this luminous divinity has to do with the poem as a whole is mysteriously unstated—though Esselborn conjectures, in a Nietzschean vein, that "Apollo, the luminous and illuminating god, figures here."[15] In any case, all we learn is that the lost victor receives the ambivalent accolade—the bad prize of the wilted thorn-crown of beauty—which does not propitiate the luminous divinity. This divinity is, as its isolated position in the final line would suggest, marginal at best, at a remove from the dark, de-deified ("entgöttert") world of sick flowers, soulless sound, and dissonance. Darkness, if anything, is the victor here, for the divinity of light is unaffected, unpropitiated, by the wild Dionysian dance that "swirls yet" from the shadows. There is no salvation, no reconciliation with a luminous but absent deity, for this victor, this

15. Esselborn, *Georg Trakl,* 156. Further references to this book appear in the text.

lost one, must remain in a world plagued by the vertiginous dark forces of a wild Dionysian "round dance." The figural relationship between a *deus absconditus* and a dark world of evil forces is reminiscent of a conversation Trakl once had with several of his friends. When one of them suggested that the poet move to the country from the city, Trakl retorted that he, unlike Christ, had "no right to flee from hell." Surprised by such an expression of orthodox Christian faith, one of his friends then asked him how he could account for such phenomena as Buddha or the Chinese sages. "They also received their *light* from Christ" was Trakl's response.[16]

In this dichotomy of a luminous divinity and the darkness of a wild, earthy dance, Esselborn sees a poetological figuration of "the failure of writing poetry," which stems from an incommensurability of the Apollonian and Dionysian impulses in Trakl's earlier work. "This stanza presents," he writes, "the failure to achieve a transition from Dionysian to Apollonian assumptions of poetry" (156).[17] Perhaps it would be more accurate to say that this stanza points to the problem of writing poetry in a world devoid of Apollonian (or Christian) light. The aesthetic failure enacted here is not so much a failure to achieve a transition from "Dionysian to Apollonian assumptions" as a failure to evoke in the creative process the Imaginary security of resplendent visual integration. This poetological stanza thus moves the psychic polarity that motivated Don Juan's manic-depressive behavior onto the aesthetic plane; it thematizes as such its failure to reconcile the unconscious (Dionysian) impulse with a mimetic desire for a unitary world of (Apollonian) light. In an undated letter of 1910 or 1911 to Irene Amtmann, Trakl made a cryptic remark about beauty which suggests

16. *Erinnerung an Georg Trakl*, 117 (emphasis added).
17. This poem is characteristic of what Esselborn sees as the basic content-form conflict and discrepancy underwriting Trakl's poetic development, e.g., "the discrepancy between the possibilities presented in the traditional canon and Trakl's own individual experiences" (138).

that he was to some degree aware of the psychological implications of his aesthetic dilemma: "One should take care to guard against perfect beauty [*vollendete Schönheit*] before which there is nothing but dumb looking [*blödes Schauen*]" (1:551). Perfect beauty occasions a kind of dumb *looking,* a kind of selfless specularity, one might say, which, like a preverbal Imaginary *unio* with the world, would entail a highly desirable but impossible transcendence of self-consciousness. Immediately following his comment on the *blödes Schauen* of perfect beauty, Trakl continues: "No, our fate is: forward to your self!" Human beings cannot go back, no matter how beautiful and alluring that may be; one must, rather, go forward to oneself.

Trakl's aesthetic dilemma is further complicated by his adherence to a Nietzschean aesthetics of Dionysian intoxication. Though he may have ascribed to such an aesthetics, he was at this point in his career unable or, perhaps, unwilling to put the Nietzschean insight into poetic practice so that he could more fully explore the creative potential of unconscious desire. The Dionysian unconscious, figured in the negativity of the round dance issuing from the shadows, is thus a disruptive and uncontrollable force that would make a mockery of any poet who might wish to propitiate or evoke a luminous divinity, be it Christian or Apollonian. Thus the dark pulse of unconscious desire thwarts here any Don Juan manic evocation of beautiful images and "endless pleasing sound." What is left, the poem implies about itself, is the "soulless sound" and the "dissonance of all melodies," which, ultimately, fall short of the idealistic standards demanded by a classical-romantic aesthetics of mimetic desire.

Though Trakl may have flirted in "Dämmerung" with the disruptive impulse of the Dionysian unconscious, the poem nonetheless remains within the bounds of traditional confessional poetry. The poem moves from expressions about a particular situation (personal anguish and discord) to a more general, abstract level, that is, to an obtuse statement about an aesthetic dilemma (and/or the complicity of art and disease in the postromantic era). To this end Trakl wove a series of images, ambivalences, poetic figures, and "dissonances" into cohesive, albeit ambiguous, statements that produce the illusion of an intended narrational unity of experience and poetry. "Dämmerung" is thus governed, superficially at least, by the representational logic of classical-romantic lyrical expression. Whether the poem is ultimately a negative or positive statement about itself, its creator's existential/psychological situation, or modern poetry in general is left undecidedly open by the word *Dämmerung* and the ambivalence pervading the figures of sick flowers and dissonant melodies. Is this poem an ode to the twilight of romanticism, the lost purity of melody and all that entails, or is it a hymn to the dawning of a new poetry which manages to bloom forth from the sickness and decay of a frightening era? Where is the poem situated? *Dämmerung* of dawn, or *Dämmerung* of dusk? Or both?[18]

In creating a poetic persona that alludes to the anonymous and impersonal character of its own "creations" in a series of ambivalent objective correlatives ("harp," "heart," "dissonance"), Trakl has brought together a constellation of images which accentuates a disjunction between the *Ich* and what the *Ich* says. It is a disjunction through which his writing subject articulates not only a certain self-estrangement but also the possibility of a more objective form of poetic discourse which is not grounded in or constrained by the explicit, conscious intentions of the poet's empirical self. In an un-

18. Referring to Trakl as the poet of the *Abend-land*, Heidegger suggests that the abounding *Abendland* figures in Trakl's work refer to "the Occident" or literally the "Evening-land," which is really a concealed "dawn," a new, more authentic beginning. See Heidegger, "Georg Trakl," 190. This essay has been translated by Peter Hertz as "Language in the Poem: A Discussion of Georg Trakl's Poetic Work," in *On the Way to Language* (New York: Harper & Row, 1971), 159–98.

dated letter from late 1911, Trakl, in one of his rare reflections upon his poetic creativity, wrote to his friend Buschbeck about a process of "depersonalizing." Describing a reworked version of a poem, he states: "It is much better than the original version, since it is now impersonal, full to bursting with movement, faces, and visions. I am convinced, that it will say and mean more to you in this universal form than it did in the limited personal form of the first version" (1:485). Trakl has reforged his poem and filled it with semantic possibilities whose free-floating "movement, faces, and visions" have burst the limiting "personal" form of the original version. He has achieved, in other words, a more "universal form," whose semantic density (its ability to "say and mean more") derives from the increased semantic potential of modern, polyfunctional expression. Moreover, in stressing that the new poem will mean and say more to his friend, Trakl emphasizes the role of the recipient and shifts the signifying power of his words further away from himself. The result of such depersonalization would be a more objective language whose increased semantic potential resonates in a psychic *Zwischenreich* between poet and reader.

The Confessions of "Confiteor"

The aesthetic dilemma of irreconcilable impulses informing "Dämmerung" occurs in another early and subtly poetological poem, which, as its title, "Confiteor" (Latin: "I confess"), might suggest, presents a reflection upon its position vis-à-vis the classical-romantic tradition of confessional poetry.[19] Typical of his earlier work, Trakl uses the conventional form of rhymed, first-person verse to convey a baroque message of death and decay. After indulging in a series of extravagant lamentations about a horrible,

19. This poem cannot be accurately dated. It is conceivable that it was written as early as 1906, when Trakl was still a *Gymnasiast,* since it was included in a collection of poems—found in his *Nachlaß*—which he assembled in August 1909.

dark world filled with anxiety, pestilence, and distorting shadows, the poetic persona appears to reflect upon the nature of its confessional speaking:

Confiteor

Die bunten Bilder, die das Leben malt
Seh' ich umdüstert nur von Dämmerungen,
Wie kraus verzerrte Schatten, trüb und kalt,
Die kaum geboren schon der Tod bezwungen.

Und da von jedem Ding die Maske fiel,
Seh' ich nur Angst, Verzweiflung, Schmach und Seuchen,
Der Menschheit heldenloses Trauerspiel,
Ein schlechtes Stück, gespielt auf Gräbern, Leichen.

Mich ekelt dieses wüste Traumgesicht.
Doch will ein Machtgebot, daß ich verweile,
Ein Komödiant, der seine Rolle spricht,
Gezwungen, voll Verzweiflung—Langeweile! (1:246)

[The colorful images painted by life / I see darkened by dusk, / Crude distorted shadows, gloomy and cold, / Subdued by death already at birth. // And since the mask has fallen from every thing, / I see only fear, despair, disgrace and pestilence, / The heroless tragedy of humanity, / A bad play, performed on corpses and graves. // Reviled am I by this desolate dream vision, / Yet, a powerful commandment compels me to tarry, / An actor who speaks his role, / Forced, full of despair—boredom!]

As in the poem "Dämmerung," a strong narrative impulse is organized around the perceptions of a poetic persona. Here, however, first-person reference is explicit: *ich* occurs three times, once in each stanza. Though the decadent theme and expressionistic excesses are at odds with the "inspired heart" poetry of the classical-romantic tradition of the nineteenth century, the poem's structure and thematic development are still very much under the sway of the narrative constraints of that tradition. Accordingly, the poem moves in a conventional romantic fashion from a particular situation to a more general level of abstraction. First, the poetic persona recounts the particulars of what it sees—"colorful images painted by life"—and then states, in a more general vein, how these colorful images" degenerate into the decadent imagery of a repulsive world in which it, ultimately, is forced by an anonymous commandment to mouth its boring role. Underscoring this movement from particular to abstract is a thematic of vision. In the first two stanzas, visuality plays a major role; the poetic persona relates what it *sees,* from the more purely sensory "colorful images" of visual perception in the first stanza, to the more abstract objects of perception in the second stanza: "I see only fear, despair, disgrace and pestilence." Then, in the third stanza, the visual element gives way to the general effects of what has been seen: "Reviled am I by this desolate dream vision."

Taken alone, the poem's first line is positive. Life paints colorful pictures, inspiring romantic images, as it were, which the remainder of the poem then disfigures. It is against this bright background that the lyrical I makes its gloomy "confiteor." What others might see as colorful images painted by the vital force of life, it sees distorted by cold shadows which forever darken its visual experience and reveal life to be a "heroless tragedy" performed badly upon "corpses and graves." In a sense, the first line represents a Goethean vision prior to the Traklean consciousness of "paranoiac knowledge,"[20] where the objects of the visible world are invested with an alienating and menacing threat. "Confiteor" is, then, the confession of a self-conscious but alienated "social I," which forever sees itself at odds with a world in which "the mask has fallen from every thing." It is interesting that the "colorful images"—

20. Lacan, *Ecrits,* 16–17.

what might be construed as a romantic idyll of unmediated pure visuality—begin to disintegrate in the second line at the point at which the lyrical I first appears and *ich* is spoken. In saying *ich* to speak about what it sees, the persona marks a subject-object differentiation, which it articulates in the series of decadent visions in the following lines. The pure vision of line 1 deteriorates into a baroque tragedy that de-masks everything in the visual world and transforms the poetic persona into a self-conscious speaking subject who despairs about its inauthentic speech. The poem thus begins to articulate a split between seeing and speaking, which the young poet was incapable of further elaborating at this stage in his career.

The deromanticizing, *de*-masking of visual experience in "Confiteor" denigrates and inverts the enthusiastic affirmation of life which pulses through the first five stanzas of young Goethe's well-known poem "Maifest" (Mayfest):

Wie herrlich leuchtet
Mir die Natur!
Wie glänzt die Sonne
Wie lacht die Flur!

Es dringen Blüten
Aus jedem Zweig
Und tausend Stimmen
Aus dem Gesträuch

Und Freud und Wonne
Aus jeder Brust.
O Erd', o Sonne,
O Glück, o Lust,

O Lieb', o Liebe,
So golden schön

195

Wie Morgenwolken
Auf jenen Höhn,

Du segnest herrlich
Das frische Feld,
Im Blütendampfe
Die volle Welt![21]

[How gloriously nature / Glows for me! / How the sun shines! / How the fields laugh! // Blossoms burst / From every twig / And a thousand voices / From the bushes // And joy and bliss / From every breast. / Oh earth, Oh sun! / Oh happiness, Oh delight! / Oh love, Oh love, / So golden-beautiful, / Like morning clouds / Upon yon hill! // You bless with beauty, / In the blossom-mist / The full world.]

Goethe's poetic persona poeticizes a world of blissful egocentricity in which the "colorful images" of life reflect the positive productivity of nature. Behind these beautiful images, it would seem, is the divine force of love, not a masquerade of death and pestilence. In the resplendence of this glowing spring day, the poetic persona also finds, in the sixth stanza, a reaffirmation of its narcissistic joy reflected in the gleaming eyes of a girl:

O Mädchen, Mädchen,
Wie lieb' ich dich!
Wie blinkt dein Auge,
Wie liebst du mich!

[Oh girl, Oh girl, / How I love you! / How your eye gleams, / How you love me!]

This poetic persona's blissful reverie is not disturbed by an awareness of narcissistic allure (which broke the spell of mimetic desire

21. *Goethes Werke*, 1:30–31.

in Goethe's later "Auf dem See"[22]), and so the poem can move to the unproblematic conclusion in which the lyrical I praises the girl's love as the inspiration for its "new songs." One begins to sense, however, that the exuberant affirmation of life and love in "Maifest" presents more of an Imaginary vision than a "total unity *in language* of man and nature," as Erich Trunz succinctly formulates the more traditional view of the poem.[23] "Maifest," one could argue, presents, rather, a poetic subject's attempt, whether conscious or not, to counter its estrangement from nature—its postspecular disunity *in language*—by means of a fanciful union with a feminine counterpart, be it the maternal ground of *die Natur* (Mother Nature) or the gleaming eyes of a loving girl.[24]

Though "Maifest" and "Confiteor" contrast with respect to visual perception, there is one intriguing point of intersection between the poems: both contain a pronounced poetological turn. In the last two stanzas of Goethe's poem, the poetic persona addresses the connection between eros and lyrical creativity and reflects upon the girl's role in its creative process. Rather than leading to the despair of an actor who is compelled to mouth lines, however, this reflexivity reinforces the persona's egocentric joy and sense of originality: the poetic persona rejoices over the cosmic energy of love which unites girl, nature, and art—a divine energy which, it feels, always leads to "new songs":

> Wie ich dich liebe
> Mit warmem Blut,

22. See the discussion of "Auf dem See" in Chapter 5.

23. Trunz, "Anmerkungen des Herausgebers," in *Goethes Werke*, 1:454 (emphasis added).

24. It might be interesting to note in this context that the Greeks believed that falling in love with someone entailed being "entrapped by one's own vision" reflected in the lover's eyes. See Knoespel, *Narcissus and the Invention of Personal History*, 11.

Die du mir Jugend
Und Freud' und Mut

Zu neuen Liedern
Und Tänzen gibst.
Sei ewig glücklich
Wie du mich liebst.

[The way I love you / With warm blood, / Gives to me youth / And joy and courage / For new songs / and dances. / Be eternally happy / The way you love me.]

The lyrical persona in "Confiteor," however, does not rejoice about new songs, but rather despairs at its lack of originality and freedom. It also, by contrast to the personae of both "Maifest" and "Dämmerung," makes explicit reference to itself as an artist— albeit a problematic "Komödiant," which, besides "actor," carries the sense of "buffoon," "deceiver," or even "hypocrite." This actor-buffoon, moreover, suffers under the force of an anonymous commandment that it remain to speak a tragic role. The commandment to stay and speak, the compulsion, perhaps, to produce art, holds the *Komödiant* captive in a hostile and decaying world. Art and commandment thus strike up a tenuous collaboration, for the *Komödiant* is both/either a hero who defiantly speaks its role and/or a mere pawn forced to play its part in a tragedy poorly executed.

The anonymity of the commandment and its juxtaposition to the *ich* in the second line of the third stanza recall the undercurrent of anonymity pervading "Dämmerung." Like the strange *Mißton*, the origin of this commandment is not clear. It does not well from an inspired heart nor does it, in its anonymity, represent a willful and fully self-conscious act. As in "Dämmerung," a schism between *Ich* and expression is highlighted. In "Confiteor" the *Ich* is not vibrated by alien *Mißtöne* but rather impelled by an uncompromising force that makes it into an actor in humanity's "heroless tragedy." It is compelled to speak an already written role (roles by their very nature are already written when they are spoken), a role from the anonymous human past, inherited, as it were, from expired speakers upon whose "corpses and graves" it now stands. The "boredom" at the end of the poem punctuates the persona's lack of contact and identification with what it speaks, that is, what *speaks it*, and underscores the boring and repetitive nature of its "soulless sound."

In ending its confession with a reference to itself as an actor who despairs about the boring role he is forced to speak, this early poetic persona takes a reflexive turn that subtly problematizes the tradition which up to Trakl's time had taken the confessional (*Erlebnislyrik*) poetry of Goethe's era as the paradigm of authentic lyrical expression. The speaking of confessional poetry, it would seem, can no longer satisfy the expressive needs of this poetic persona. What it speaks has become an empty compulsion, an inauthentic mouthing of a "role," a repeating of the *already written* lines of an inappropriate tradition. It is trapped in the heroless human tragedy that transforms the bright images of life into the horrific imagery of literary decadence. In using the paradigm of confessional poetry to question the appropriateness of that paradigm, this early poetic persona struggles to articulate its troublesome clash with the tradition and in so doing produces a somewhat confused statement about an aesthetic dilemma whose paradoxical nature registers the need to escape the narrative constraints of the *confiteor* mode.

CHAPTER 7

Trakl's Aesthetic of Mirrors

Und in silbernen Augen
Spiegeln sich die schwarzen Schatten unserer Wildnis,
—Georg Trakl, "Passion"[1]

"(WHO MIGHT HE HAVE BEEN?)" queried Rainer Maria Rilke in 1915 after reading Georg Trakl's first volume of poetry, published posthumously in that same year. Who was this obscure Austrian poet, who in a few short years before his early death at twenty-seven transformed such a patently narrow range of depressive motifs into poem after poem of bizarre autumnal landscapes, which, like the visual fullness of mirror images, deny access to the space behind their glassy surface? "I imagine," Rilke wrote, "that even the initiated experiences these views and insights as an outsider pressed against panes of glass: for Trakl's experience occurs like mirror images and fills its entire space, which, like the space in the mirror, cannot be entered. (Who might he have been?)[2]

Deflected by the mirrorlike opacity of this seemingly inaccessible "mirror-image world,"[3] Rilke's frustrated interpretative desire appears to project the difficulty back upon the person of the poet. Is it not Georg Trakl, ultimately, who is responsible for this her-

1. "And in silver eyes / Is mirrored the black shadows of our wildness," (1:393).
2. *Erinnerung an Georg Trakl*, 11.
3. In another passage, Rilke referred to Trakl's work as a "mirror-image-world" (quoted by Storck, "Arbeitsgespräche," 158).

metic house of mirrors? Does he not hold—or withhold—the key to this locked "space in the mirror"? Sensitive to the prosaic demands placed by his deflected desire, Rilke demurely bracketed his question within the safely disqualifying space of a parenthetical mention. No matter how rhetorical or prosaic, Rilke's question cannot be disqualified; it emerged in his writing about reading Trakl. Though literary theorists are quick to warn of the reductive dangers of entering the "space" of poems through the back door of biography, of searching for the *what* of poetry in the *who* of the poet, Trakl's mirror-image world continues to deflect the critical gaze of his readers, who, like "outsider[s] pressed against panes of glass," cannot help but wonder whether there are, to quote Rilke again, just a "few facts and reminiscences about the poet"[4] which might make this recalcitrant verse a little more accessible. Though Rilke's metaphor of the mirror is frequently cited as a poignant image for evoking that "alienated realm of [Trakl's] poetic experience which is fundamentally inaccessible"[5] there is a second—and invariably overlooked—aspect of Trakl's work which is reflected in Rilke's response: the image of the mirror itself. In characterizing the deflecting opacity of Trakl's writing with the figure of the mirror surface, Rilke has made use, perhaps unwittingly, of one of the poet's most important, if not central, experiential metaphors. How the mirror or reflecting surface figures in the poet's groping exploration of the dark origins of his poetic creativity is the topic of this chapter.

The Darkening Process of Decline

In his mature work, Trakl effectively distanced himself from the confessional mode of classical-romantic *Erlebnislyrik* and achieved an objective austerity and concentrated precision which broke

4. Ibid., 161.
5. Sharp, "Trakl," 254.

new ground for German poetry. Here, under the sway of Friedrich Hölderlin and Rimbaud,[6] Trakl put the frenzied, egocentric excesses of his earlier writing behind and began to produce controlled, almost dispassionate imagistic verse largely devoid of first-person references and overt confessional content. The often anthologized poem "Untergang" conveys the crisp efficiency and soft, muted tone of this breakthrough period. With terse elemental terms Trakl aligns an evocative constellation of images to create an unsettling landscape in which a haunting autumnal atmosphere casts its dark shadow on everything in both the natural and human spheres. Like a quiet autumn evening, this "decline" softly descends from the heavens, with their foreboding departure of birds and cold wind, and ends, after passing over "our" graves, in the city at the depth of night ("midnight"). The poem "Untergang" (Decline) was dedicated to Trakl's poet friend Karl Borromaeus Heinrich. Though less directly reflexive and self-referential than "Confiteor," the poem does nonetheless present a subtle poetological reflection upon the relationship between (obscured) vision and poetic creativity.

Untergang
An Karl Borromaeus Heinrich

Über den weißen Weiher
Sind die wilden Vögel fortgezogen.
Am Abend weht von unseren Sternen ein eisiger Wind.

Über unsere Gräber
Beugt sich die zerbrochene Stirne der Nacht.
Unter Eichen schaukeln wir auf einem silbernen Kahn.

---

6. See Böschenstein, "Hölderlin und Rimbaud." Recent scholarship has explored Trakl's deep affiliation with the German romantic poet Novalis. See Pfisterer-Burger, *Zeichen und Sterne*, and Esselborn, "'*Blaue Blume*' or '*Kristallene Tränen*'?" 203–32.

Immer klingen die weißen Mauern der Stadt.
Unter Dornenbogen
O mein Bruder klimmen wir blinde Zeiger gen Mitternacht.

[Above the white pond / The wild birds have flown away. / An icy wind blows from our stars at evening. // Above our graves / The shattered brow of night is bowed. / We rock beneath the oak trees in a silver skiff. // The white walls of the city sound forever. / Beneath thorn arches, / O my brother, we blind hands climb toward midnight.]

Since the poem's subtle poetological implications are more generally a product of its dense weave of imagery as a whole, it would be helpful to begin with general observations about the poem's particular structure and content: one is immediately struck by its tight structure and repetitive vocabulary. This structural tightness is most apparent in the symmetrical repetition of "über-über" and "unter-unter" in the initial position of lines, the twice occurring "weiß" and "Nacht," as well as the punctuation pattern of the first two stanzas and its variation in the third. The sensuous quality of this poem, by contrast to Trakl's earlier work, produces a hypnotic flow of resonating sounds and somber rhythms; most notable are the hollow "o's," the eerie "i's," the haunting "ei" assonances and "w" alliterations, and the various sibilants whose hissing waxes and wanes to suggest the swirling of a chilling autumn wind.

Also typical of Trakl's mature work is the dense intratextual cross-referentiality, which Trakl establishes here through a play of assonance and alliteration. In the first stanza, for example, the repetition of "w" and "ei" in the "weißen Weiher" of the first line resonate in the "eisiger Wind" of the third line. More than an arbitrary play with sound, this resonance serves to associate these four elements and reinforce the sense that the white pond of the first line is frozen and lifeless. The "weißen Weiher," moreover, echo in the "weißen Mauern" of the third stanza, where the analogous position of "weiß" sets up a symmetry between these two stanzas' first lines and, in effect, contrasts the white *pond* with the white *walls*. "Weiß" is the structural tie which contrasts the openness of the natural sphere (pond) with the closure of civilization (the white walls of the city). Trakl's choice, in this context, of the word "Weiher" is also significant. He did not use the perhaps more common term "Teich" (pond)—which would have maintained the "ei" assonance but lost the cross-referential potential of "W"— likely because "Weiher" also conjures certain religious associations that enrich the poem's nature-civilization contrast. The German word "Weihe" ("blessing," "consecration," "solemnity"), it should be pointed out, is closely related to "Weihestätte" ("holy place") and derives from a Germanic root which means "holy," "magical," or "religious." Trakl's white pond thus suggests a holiness that is absent in the cold sterility of the "white walls of the city." If one then considers the German expression, "Er ist dem *Untergang geweiht*" ("he is doomed to die/fall"), the choice of "Weiher" becomes all the more meaningful in this poem of death and decline entitled "Untergang."

In any case, the openness of the foreboding autumnal scene in the first stanza is intensified by the distant origin of the "icy wind" in line 3. But why is this icy wind coming from "our stars"? Are they *our* stars because they bring the celestial message of our fate, our *Untergang*—"our graves" (line 4)? Such an associative reading of this typically indeterminate imagery would be strengthened by the first stanza's (southerly) flight of birds, a natural sign for the inevitable darkening decline of fall. Parallel bird imagery also occurs in a poem entitled "Dezember" (December), which likewise progresses from a "flight of wild birds" (crossing dark) waters, in the first stanza and ends, similar to "Untergang," with a nighttime image of verticality: "the night follows with shattered masts." Indeed, the flight of birds, and especially birds themselves, often figure in Trakl's verse as a foreboding natural sign for autumn and decline (literally "Untergang"). Unfortunately, tracing down such abounding parallel imagery in this verse, where "each new sad-beautiful image encountered . . . is somehow already known and already read,"[7] inevitably leads to endless circuits through Trakl's "self-plagiaristic"[8] oeuvre and yields at best vague general trends but never interpretative keys. The nighttime "broken masts" in the poem "Dezember" (1:377) seem, for instance, to resonate in "zerbrochene Stirne der Nacht" in "Untergang," which in turn resonates in the strikingly similar "zerbrochene Stirne im Munde der Nacht" (1:308; "shattered brow in the mouth of the night") in a poem entitled "Am Rand eines alten Brunnens" (At the Edge of an Old Spring). A "bowing brow" likewise occurs in various poems in contexts whose similarity would invite comparative analysis. Various permutations and combinations of virtually every image in "Untergang"—with the exception of "we blind hands climb"— show up in literally dozens of poems. The eerie "an icy wind blows from our stars," for example, turns up almost verbatim in two other poems as "from our stars blows a snowy wind" (1:321, 330). Another related and equally mystifying aspect of Trakl's verse was brought to light, as mentioned in Chapter 5, in 1969 with the publication of the new critical edition to his work. Presented for the first time in a lengthy critical apparatus are the numerous manuscript draft versions of a majority of his poems. In an earlier version of "Untergang," for example, the word "dark" in the final line "O my brother in *dark* sighs" was replaced in succession by "long," "pale," "deep," "black," "dark," "frail," "silent" ("langen," "bleichen," "tiefen," "schwarzen," "dunklen," "schmächtigen,"

7. Killy, *Über Georg Trakl*, 41.
8. Hamburger, "Georg Trakl," 204.

"schweigend" [see 2:195]), and then reworked in the final version of the poem to become "O my brother, we *blind* hands."

The strangeness of blind hands climbing toward midnight is partially the result of an untranslatable aspect in the German word "Zeiger," which, in addition to "hand of a clock," can also mean "indicator" or "pointer."[9] This semantic aspect allowed Trakl to cast, in a typically expressionistic manner, the human being as an inanimate thing, as an alienated being objectified, as it were, by the dehumanizing forces of the modern world. By objectifying the brothers as the "blind hands" of ticking time in a stanza beginning with "the white walls of the city sound forever," Trakl brought together a constellation of motifs in which the disintegration of pure vision (implied in "blind") interplays with images connoting the disintegrating forces of time and the alienating effects of civilization. The inescapability of these threatening forces and effects is reinforced by the temporal infinity of the city's endlessly sounding walls—sterile, blinding "white walls," which "sound forever," enclosing and entrapping the human being in the alienating and unnatural noise of civilization. Reiterating the sense of threatening entrapment is the unfriendly image of "thorn arches" beneath which the brothers are transformed into the blind hands—the indicators—of the eerie darkness of "midnight."[10]

If one then construes "my brother" of the final line as a fraternal allusion to Karl Borromaeus Heinrich—Trakl's poet friend to whom the poem is dedicated—one begins to see that this tersely imagistic poem is, like so much of Trakl's work, also self-referential

9. "Zeiger" is derived from the verb "zeigen" (to show, point, indicate) and thus signifies, on a primary semantic level, "something which shows, points, or indicates."

10. One might also argue that these brothers stand outside of the bright city and, by analogy with the story *Dornröschen* (Sleeping Beauty), they have been excluded by a thicket of thorns ("Dornenbogen"). In both cases, the figural result is essentially the same: the brothers are isolated and alone in the dark.

and poetological. With the words "O my brother, *we* blind hands climb toward midnight," the distanced and restrained poetic persona quietly calls out to a kindred soul, a poetic brother who like himself blindly points to the darkness of midnight, to, perhaps, an empty transcendence in the cold, dark void of the cosmos. It is as though the very existence of these objectified indicator brothers, standing alone in their alienation, has itself become a signifying event. Exposed to the process of darkening autumnal decline, they become a groping gesture that registers, like a cosmic weather vane, the darkness—blindness—of a postromantic era that can no longer *see* a reassuring bright unity in the "colorful images painted by life." This reading is indirectly confirmed, perhaps, by the final line of the poem's second version, which reads "Oh my brother, the landscape of the soul is darkly transformed." In becoming itself a darkening landscape, this (objectified) soul is, by contrast to its romantic brothers, incapable of reflecting the radiant display—the "colorful images"—of the natural world. It is a soul that reflects only the dark transformation of the romantic landscape.[11] Iris Denneler has also commented on the poetological potential of these final lines, musing that one may see in the words "Bruder" and "Zeiger" an allusion to the shared poetic calling of Heinrich and Trakl, who had carried on a kind of "communication . . . in the medium of literary texts."[12] Heinrich and Trakl had requested Ludwig von Ficker to publish Trakl's "Untergang" along with an article by Heinrich in the same *Brenner* issue. It is also significant that Trakl had removed from the final version of the poem (pub-

11. The poetological implications of this stanza are perhaps confirmed in a yet earlier version of the final stanza in which "Saitenspiel" ("the play of a stringed instrument") occurs. Borrowed apparently from Hölderlin, this motif often figures in Trakl's work as a metonym for lyrical poetry. In, for example, a poem named after Novalis, Trakl alludes to the early death of this "holy stranger" as the peaceful cessation of his "Saitenspiel" (1:324).

12. See Denneler, *Konstruktion und Expression,* 212, 215.

lished in the *Brenner*) possible allusions to Hölderlin and an arcadian landscape and in so doing strengthened both the poem's antiromantic content and its nature and civilization contrast.[13]

The Psychology of the Mirror

As we saw in Chapter 2, the faith in the "pure music" and divine nature of early romanticism became increasingly problematic for the generations of poets following Baudelaire. The assumptions and motivations that informed the work of Goethe and Novalis no longer rang true in the era of rapid industrialization, wildly fluctuating free-market economics, and mass urbanization. For Trakl, such faith seems to have been all but eclipsed. Writing to Ludwig von Ficker on June 26, 1913, Trakl confides to his friend, in a letter filled with self-recrimination and guilt: "I long for the day when my soul will neither want nor be able to live in this wretched body defiled by melancholy, the day when my soul will leave this mockery of a body of excrement and decay that is an all-too-accurate mirror image of a godless, cursed century" (1:518–19). The world to which Trakl's life is in tune is not the divine and pure nature posited by the early romantics but a godless and repulsive world of decay. He is imprisoned by a body that mirrors the fallen state of the present and makes a mockery of the idealism of the past. To be sure, the extreme nature of Trakl's graphic abhorrence for his body also contains signs of psychological trauma which goes beyond a Nietzschean cultural skepticism or early twentieth-century "social identity crisis." In casting himself as an "accurate mirror image" of a cursed and godless world of excrement and decay, Trakl, to speak with Lacan, throws "back onto the world the disorder of which his being is composed."[14] Here is no reassuring visual reciprocity, but

13. See Trakl, 2:196, and Denneler, *Konstruktion und Expression*, 215.
14. See Lacan, *Ecrits*, 20.

a negative reflexivity in which Trakl forever *sees* himself at odds with an inhospitable world of guilt and denial.

Knowledge of the world, as we saw in the discussions in the preceding chapters, can have a threatening, paranoia-inducing effect. It signals the human subject's frightening finitude and lack of self-sufficiency, for the ability to articulate the objects of the world entails an awareness—subliminal, at least—of self as opposed to, and in a sense opposed by, the world. In throwing "back onto the world the disorder of which his being is composed," Trakl is not only aggressively responding to the threat contained in the opposing world of objects, but he is also responding to a troubling disorder, which, to his "mirror-image" self, is an all-too-accurate reflection of his own fragmenting lack of unity. It is as if he is able to see through the duplicitous ruses and defenses of the grown-up ego, whose existence depends upon its ability to maintain the fiction or illusion of the unified self that was formed in those original visual—Imaginary—identifications.

This psychovisual problematic manifests itself in various ways in Trakl's poetry, from explicit figures of distorted mirror images, water reflections, and hauntingly absent self-reflections, to more complex images of vision, optics, and eyes which—both good and bad—express a profound ambivalence toward specular experience. Trakl's obsession with specularity—what likely prompted Rilke to characterize his work as a "mirror-image-world . . . totally in decline"[15]—suggests that the reflective surface functioned as an important, if not central, experiential metaphor in Trakl's psychopoetic exploration of an autumnal world in decline.

Trakl's specular motifs are found most frequently in contexts that undermine or negate the positive value of the reflecting surface. The figural result, which ranges from a denigration of visual experience in general to an alienating distortion of self-perception,

15. See note 2, above.

registers, on a more purely psychological level, a deep-seated anxiety about the tenuous nature of self-consciousness and/or the "illusion of unity," which, Lacan would point out, "entails a constant danger of sliding back again into the chaos from which his [the human] being started."[16]

In his treatment of Trakl's specular imagery, Hans Esselborn argues that self-reflections—be they figured in mirrors, reflective surfaces, eyes, or the various forms of the *Doppelgänger*—served Trakl as a means of objectifying the process of "self-encounter" and "self-recognition" (*Selbstbegegnung* and *Selbsterkenntnis*).[17] These two processes, Esselborn ascertains, can result in a "confirmation of self," or, more frequently, they lead to a "negative counterimage" in which "the threatening side of the ego is revealed." Though very helpful in charting out the general function and development of Trakl's use of the mirror, Esselborn's analysis considers neither the underlying psychological motivations that prompted Trakl to key upon the mirror, nor what the larger psychoepistemological implications of this "mirror-image world" might entail beyond and apart from the particulars of Trakl's writing.[18]

The following list contains a small sampling of images in which the mirror is explicitly mentioned:[19]

16. Lacan, "Some Reflections on the Ego," 15.

17. Esselborn, *Georg Trakl*, 127–38. An exhaustive study of Trakl's mirror imagery would have to include the many motifs and images, such as the reflecting water surface or the *Doppelgänger,* which suggest or allude to a mirroring process or function. See note 18, below.

18. This likewise applies to Wolgang Held's dissertation, "Mönch und Narziß." Held relates the motif of the mirror in Trakl's poetry to death and the unconscious.

19. This list does not list the scores of images—such as the following—that imply or suggest specular experience, mirror images, or the watery self-reflection of Narcissus: "Über seufzende Wasser geneigt / Sieh dein Gemahl: Antlitz starrend von Aussatz" (1:393; "Bent over sighing waters / Look at your spouse: face rigid with leprosy"). Though there are only a few explicit mentions of Narcissus in

Silver her mirror image looks at
Strangely glowing twilight (1:12)[20]

The boy strokes the cat's hair,
Spellbound by the mirror of its eyes (1:271)

There are shadows which embrace before a blinded mirror (1:55)

And in silver eyes
Is mirrored the black shadows of our wildness (1:393)

From the mirror's deceptive emptiness
Arose slowly . . . a face: Cain! (1:220)

Loudly the pond-mirror shatters (1:27)

Rosy mirror: an ugly image,
Which blackly appears from behind (1:302)

And I see, like a sabbath of mad witches,
Blood-colored blossoms in the brightness of the mirror (1:222)

Softly blinds the mirror-pond (1:107)

From a ghostly mirror-pond / Wave fruits (1:265)

In the black waters are mirrored leprous ones (1:72)

Possessed ones are mirrored in cold metals (1:301)

Oh! You quiet mirrors of truth.
. . . There appears the reflection of fallen angels (1:68)

Trakl's work, his poetry is replete with allusions to the mythological figure. See
Doppler, "Die Stufe der Präexistenz in den Dichtungen Georg Trakls," 273–84.
Doppler lists forty-five "Narcissus- and mirror-motifs" (281, n.21); see also the
following discussions of the Narcissus motif in Trakl's work: Esselborn, *Georg
Trakl*, 175–77; Held, "Mönch und Narziß," 126–39; Schier, *Die Sprach Georg
Trakls*, 70–71.
20. The original German may be found in the Appendix.

Blue firn sink into a barren room,
Which are the deceased mirrors of lovers. (1:501)

Trakl's obsession with mirror imagery was given impetus by two noteworthy sources largely unexamined in the Trakl literature. The first was Rudolf Kassner, a contemporary of Trakl's whom he had briefly met in 1913. Kassner had argued, as Sharp has pointed out, "against the pejorative, narcissistic significance of the mirror."[21] Though Kassner did not publish his book *Narciss oder Mythos und Einbildungskraft* (Narcissus or the myth and imagination)[22] until 1928, it is possible that their discussion touched upon the psychological implications of the myth of Narcissus or some related topic. It is also possible that Trakl had learned indirectly of the "metaphysical physiognomics" of Kassner's work through his meetings with a circle of friends and intellectuals in Vienna. In any case, there are several general ideas in Kassner's mystical psychology which could shed light on Trakl's interest in the mirror. First, Kassner related the psychological significance of the mirror to the discovery of self and identity, stating: "The self needs the mirror, namely, for its being and as a measure of its existence . . . when the human being stands in front of the mirror, there is only one being present, and thus he says: I" (28). (One might also wonder whether Kassner's work found a—intertextual, at least—resonance in Lacan's speculations about the mirror stage.) This process of visual identification, however, presupposes the quasi-magical power of the prerational imagination to circumvent, Kassner believed, any "interference between seeing and being" (62). Such an imaginative seeing of the "connection between body and soul" (30) has been, with the exception of certain visionary individuals and artists, all but lost to the modern, rational human being. Kassner thus elevated the mythical figure of Narcissus to the status of

21. Sharp, *Poet's Madness*, 151.
22. Kassner, *Narciss*. Further references appear in the text.

the original and prototypical poet (31–33). Though the influence of such thinking does seem to resonate in Trakl's aesthetic of mirrors, we cannot be sure to what extent he was familiar with Kassner's ideas. Suffice it to say that such ideas were in the air that both Trakl and Kassner were breathing during the first decades of the twentieth century.

The second and most direct influence on Trakl's aesthetic of mirrors, and certainly a quarry for vocabulary and ideas, was Oscar Wilde's work,[23] especially his novel *The Picture of Dorian Gray,* which, as Otto Basil remarks, was one of his "favorite books . . . to which he was attached with all his heart."[24] Trakl's initial fascination with the story may have been fostered by an uncanny resemblance between his own childhood and that of Dorian Gray, which Wilde sketches as follows: "Months of voiceless agony, and then a child born in pain. The mother snatched away by death, the boy left to solitude and the tyranny of an old and loveless man. Yes; it was an interesting background. It posed the lad, made him more perfect as it were. Behind every exquisite thing that existed, there was something tragic. Worlds had to be in travail, that the meanest flower might blow."[25] Wilde's novel, a sustained treatise on the late nineteenth-century aestheticist worldview, revolves around Dorian Gray's narcissistic obsession with the painted image of his face. Trakl's interest in the story was likely piqued by Wilde's description of the portrait painter who so accurately captured Gray's image: "From a psychological point of view, how interesting he was! The new manner in art, the fresh mode of looking at life, suggested

23. That Trakl possessed no fewer than five works by Oscar Wilde suggests his debt to Wilde may be extensive. With the exception of a short study by Peter Cersowski, Trakl scholars have shown practically no interest in the Trakl-Wilde connection. See Cersowski, "Georg Trakl, Oskar Wilde, und andere Ästhetiker des Schreckens," 231–45.

24. Basil, *Georg Trakl,* 113–14.

25. Wilde, *Picture of Dorian Gray,* 35. Further references appear in the text.

by . . . one [the painter] who was unconscious of it all" (36). It is easy to see how Trakl could identify with an artist who so unselfconsciously is able to capture—mirror—the image of another. Seduced then by the glib intellectual wit of the older Lord Henry Wotton, who serves in the novel as the spokesman for the decadent aestheticist view, Dorian Gray, in a moment of youthful hedonism, wishes that the face in his portrait, that is, "picture" (*Bildnis* in the German version) would age rather than his own. His wish comes true, and in trying to live out his life as an aesthetic event, Gray becomes increasingly debauched and eventually is led to murder, to take refuge in opium, and, ultimately, to take his own life. After driving his innocent lover (Sybil Vane) to suicide, Gray's relationship with his aging portrait-countenance becomes highly troublesome. There he recognizes "cruelty round the mouth as clearly as if he had been looking into a mirror after he had done some dreadful thing" (90).

Wilde consciously plays off the classical myth of Narcissus, once explicitly mentioned ("Once, in boyish mockery of Narcissus, he had kissed, or feigned to kiss, those painted lips" [109]) and then alluded to in the following passage: "You had leant over the still pool of some Greek woodland and seen in the water's silent silver the marvel of your own face" (114). This passage bears a strange similarity in vocabulary and tone to the passage from Trakl's late, psychological prose-poem "Offenbarung und Untergang" (Revelation and Decline): "And as I bent over the silent waters with silver fingers, I saw that my face had left me."[26] Both passages exhibit similarities to Ovid's description of Narcissus: "there was a pool silver with shining water . . . he [Narcissus] sees his eyes, twin stars . . . white fairness."[27] Trakl, it would seem, reworked the

26. "und da ich mit silbernen Fingern mich über die schweigenden Wasser bog, sah ich daß mich mein Antlitz verlassen" (1:169).

27. Ovid, *Metamorphoses,* 70.

classical myth—whether consciously or not—along Dorian Gray lines to include the horror Gray experiences in the later stages of psychological disintegration whenever he looks at either his mirror image or his aging portrait.

Trakl's wary fascination with the narcissism of self-reflection and his passion for *Dorian Gray* suggest that his ambivalence toward the mirror was a complex mixture of mythic intertextuality, personal disposition, and a certain awareness of a psychological discourse taking form at that time—a discourse that culminated in the years following Trakl's death in the work of such thinkers as Freud, Rank, Kassner, and Lacan. Freud's essay on narcissism was published in 1914, Rank's book *The Double: A Psychoanalytic Study* in 1925,[28] and Kassner's book *Narciss oder Mythos und Einbildungskraft* in 1928, while Lacan's mirror-stage essay was presented in 1936. Trakl, it appears, was responding to what Hofmannsthal alluded to as the deeper "double-life 'of this very strange epoch.'"[29]

Rank's work on the double is of particular interest because he includes in his discussion an analysis of Dorian Gray's ambivalence toward his (loved but feared) double, which, Rank believes, expresses defensive feelings about his narcissistic self-love. The existence of the double in myth, religion, and literature, Rank asserts (in expanding upon Freud's 1919 analysis of the double[30]), was rooted in the universal problem of narcissism. The double stems, in his view, from a fear of mortality and a wish to perpetuate

28. Rank, *The Double*, 71–73. Rank's German title was *Der Doppelgänger; eine psychoanalytische Studie* (Leipzig, 1925). Parenthetical references in the text are to the English translation.

29. Quoted by Doppler in "Die Stufe der Präexistenz in den Dichtungen Georg Trakls," 274. In his discussion of the turn-of-the-century interest in the double, Doppler writes: "The perceiving ego is irreconcilably opposed to the thinking ego, although they belong to the same person. This leads to a split in consciousness: the ego, which feels itself to be in and part of nature . . . meets the *Doppelgänger*, who is the thinking ego" (274).

30. Cf. Freud, "The Uncanny," in *Standard Edition*, 17:219–56.

oneself after death—the Judeo-Christian concept of the "double" of the immortal soul or the conceptualization of mortal man being created in the image of an immortal God would be two manifestations of this. In extreme cases such as that of Dorian Gray, the double takes on sinister forms and becomes a compensatory antidote for an overindulgent self-love, whereby the guilt is defensively transferred onto a devilish double who is thus made responsible for such reprehensible behavior. Kassner likewise addressed the relationship between narcissism, death, and guilt (sin), all of which, he believed, are connected to imagination: "For the sake of imagination, Narcissus must die or go through death, in order to find unity with himself and the primal essence of things. . . . If there were no death, there would be no sin. . . . Sin is imagination" (31). Once again, Kassner's thought shows possible points of affiliation with Trakl's work, especially if one considers the aphorism in which Trakl characterized his poems as a form of "incomplete penance" for the "unresolved guilt" which follows "moments of deathlike being" (1:463).

Though Lacan only alludes to Rank's work on the double,[31] it would appear that he was not unsympathetic to Rank's notion that, in addition to a fear of death (thanophobia), the double can express, as in the case of the *Brothers Karamosov,* a "rivalry toward the hated competitor" (77–78). The formation of the fictional construct of the ego, Lacan contends, always engenders aggressive impulses. This is because the subject is forced in the mirror stage to "assume the armour of an alienating identity,"[32] that is, to identify with a double (in the form of an alienating external image of another) whose ideal (visual) unity can never be matched by the subject's inexorable psychic disunity. This is why, Lacan argues, the ego—the product of this visual identification—becomes dur-

31. Cf. Lacan, *Ecrits,* 3.
32. Ibid., 4. Cf. Sharp, *Poet's Madness,* 151.

ing the mirror stage a rival for the subject or self, whose origin is rooted in the existential insufficiency that gave rise to mirror-stage identifications in the first place. Trakl's problematizing of visual reciprocity could thus be read from a Lacanian perspective as a subliminal uneasiness about the tenuous state of the ego's Imaginary—narcissistic—stability, a stability which is always under the threat of psychic disintegration. The mirror image would be a threatening rival, a frightening omen of the ego's illusory unity, which is in "constant danger of sliding back again into the chaos from which his [the human] being started."[33]

The threatening character of specular self-reflection is especially prominent in Trakl's early poem "Das Grauen" (The Horror), written in or before 1909. Here we find, as is so often the case in his early work, an explicit and somewhat simplistic use of the mirror motif:

> Ich sah mich durch verlassene Zimmer gehen.
> —Die Sterne tanzten irr auf blauem Grund,
> Und auf den Feldern heulten laut die Hunde,
> Und in den Wipfeln wühlte wild der Föhn.
>
> Doch plötzlich: Stille! Dumpfe Fieberglut
> Läßt giftige Blumen aus meinem Munde,
> Aus dem Geäst fällt wie aus einer Wunde
> Blaß schimmernd Tau, und fällt, und fällt wie Blut.
>
> Aus eines Spiegels trügerischer Leere
> Hebt langsam sich, und wie ins Ungefähre
> Aus Graun und Finsternis ein Antlitz: Kain!
>
> Sehr leise rauscht die samtene Portiere,
> Durchs Fenster schaut der Mond gleichwie ins Leere,
> Da bin mit meinem Mörder ich allein. (1:220)

33. Lacan, "Some Reflections on the Ego," 15.

[I saw myself walking through lonely rooms. / —The stars were dancing wildly in the blue firmament, / And in the fields the dogs were
howling loud, / And in the treetops swirled the foehn. // But suddenly: Stillness! The dull glow of fever / Released poisonous flowers
from my mouth, / From the branches fell the dew like from a wound /
Palely shimmering, and fell, and fell like blood. // From the mirror's
deceptive emptiness / Arose slowly, and as if headed nowhere / Out of
horror and darkness a face: Cain! // So quietly the velvet curtain
rustles, / The moon looks into the room as if into emptiness, / Here I
am alone with my murderer.]

The poem begins with an image of visuality in which a lyrical I
reports on its vision of itself walking through deserted rooms.
Immediately following this scene of self-perception are disconcerting natural images of vertiginously dancing stars, howling dogs,
and a wildly whirling foehn wind—an unpleasant wind widely
believed to cause headaches and psychological malaise. The lyrical
I sees itself as frightfully alone in an inhospitable world of fragmentation, not one of reassuring visual integration.

   In the second quatrain this problematic self-perception co-
alesces in a sudden moment of stasis and clarity: "But suddenly:
Stillness!" Now in the immediacy of present-tense forms, the lyrical I describes its focused perceptions, beginning with the sick
flowers (of poetry?) issuing from its own mouth and culminating
in the horrific perception where it meets the deadly rival of its own
mirror image (which reverberates in the "murderer" of the poem's
final line):

> From the mirror's deceptive emptiness
> Arose slowly . . .
> Out of horror and darkness a face: Cain!

Whether this is construed as a double omen of death (Rank), a
mirror-stage rival (Lacan), or a threatening *Ich-Ideal* superego

(Freud), one thing is perfectly clear: this specular self-encounter is far from comforting.

It is intriguing that Trakl chose to depict the specular rival as Cain, the firstborn son of Eve, "the mother of all living" (Gen. 3:20). Cain and Abel were, significantly, the first children of a post-Fall union of Adam and Eve. Jealous of his brother, who had found favor in the eyes of God, Cain slays his sibling rival, and, after being discovered by God the father, castigates himself: "From thy face I shall be hidden and I shall be a fugitive and a wanderer on the earth, and whoever finds me will slay me" (Gen. 4:15). And so "Cain went away from the presence ["Angesicht" (face) in the German Bible] of the Lord, and dwelt in the land of Nod, east of Eden" (Gen. 4:16); he has become a hunted fugitive who is expelled from Eden and separated from the "mother of all living." Cain is thus a figure in "Das Grauen" for a paranoid and guilty (post-Imaginary) existence which forever engenders utopic longings for a *unio mystica* in the eternal light of God. But Cain is also a figure for the impossibility of fulfilling the demands of mimetic desire, be it in life or, as suggested in the poem, the feverish fusions of the poet's cursed *giftige Blumen*.

Ultimately, Trakl parts ways with the Dorian Gray who in the narcissism of self-reflection senses utopic perfection of a *l'art pour l'art* existence. When Wilde writes, "You had leant over the still pool of some Greek woodland and seen in the water's silent silver the marvel of your own face. And it had all been what art should be, unconscious, ideal, and remote" (114), Trakl responds, "und da ich mit silbernen Fingern mich über die schweigenden Wasser bog, sah ich daß mich mein Antlitz verlassen. Und die weiße Stimme sprach zu mir: Töte dich!" (1:169) (And as I bent over the silent waters with silver fingers, I saw that my face had left me. And the white voice spoke to me: Kill yourself!). The absence here of narcissistic visual reciprocity and the impossibility of fulfilling mimetic desire trigger suicidal wishes, which, when read in the context of Trakl's poetry of "incomplete penance," would also signal the problematic nature of any art form that seeks to evoke the perfect (unconscious) beauty of a unitary world of visual integration. If art and poetry are to exist in the modern world, the pull of Narcissus, Trakl seems to realize, must be overcome: "for the sake of the power of imagination, Narcissus must die."[34]

In another early poem, entitled "Drei Träume" (Three Dreams), the lyrical I reflects upon an inability to understand its bewildering dreams and visions. Though it may not understand these visions, it does recognize that they are "tragically fantastic," that is, unfulfillable Imaginary creations which are in some way related to the problem of obscured visual (narcissistic) reciprocity:

> In meiner Seele dunklem Spiegel
> Sind Bilder niegeseh'ner Meere,
> Verlass'ner, tragisch phantastischer Länder,
> Zerfließend ins Blaue, Ungefähre. (1:215)

[In the dark mirror of my soul / Are images of never-seen seas, / Desolate, tragically fantastic lands, / Dissipating into the blue, nowhere.]

The Sister and the Mirror

Otto Rank's comment that Dorian Gray's "imposing egoism, his inability to love, and his abnormal sexual life" that allowed him "to obtain only the crudest of sensual pleasures" (71) from women suggests that Trakl's interest in Narcissus and the Oscar Wilde

34. Rudolf Kassner, *Narciss,* 31. Rudolf Schier sees in Trakl's allusions to Narcissus a process whereby the poet distances himself from romantic theories of imagination that posit an analogous relation between spirit and world, language and nature. "The Narcissus figure," he writes, "is a fitting expression for the limits of figural language based on the [romantic] concept of analogy" (*Die Sprache Georg Trakls,* 70).

story may run even deeper, if one considers that Trakl's love life, which consisted of visits to prostitutes and his (documented) incestuous relationship with his sister Grete, was also far from normal. "Just as we have no real love poem from Trakl," reports Theodor Spoerri, "there is also no evidence about his life that suggests that . . . he was ever genuinely in love, or that he ever had—except for his sister and mother—a deep relationship with a woman that went beyond the everyday superficial."[35] Trakl seems to have suffered from what Rank calls a "defective capacity for love" and perhaps also a narcissistic fear of the ego's "dissolution in sexual love"[36]—a fear of "sliding back again into the chaos" (Lacan) from which it started. Of particular interest is Rank's contention that "in the Narcissus legend there is a late but psychologically valid version which reports that the handsome youth thought he saw his beloved twin sister in the water,"[37] since "the sister" (*die Schwester*) often figures in Trakl's mirror motifs. That *die Schwester* is included in this constellation of motifs strongly indicates that her figuration in Trakl's work entails not only personal motivations but also deep psychological ones.

Trakl's sister Grete has been described as his "spitting image" (*Ebenbild*),[38] so similar were the siblings in physical appearance. An orthodox Freudian reading of Trakl's incestuous attraction to his sister might locate the origin of this desire in a narcissistic

35. Spoerri, *Georg Trakl*, 36. See also Trakl's letter of June 26, 1913, in which he laments: "Too little love, too little righteousness and compassion, but always too little love; all too much hardness, arrogance and all kinds of criminality—that's me" (1:519).

36. See Rank, *The Double*, 73, 85.

37. Ibid., 70. Cf. Sharp, *Poet's Madness*, 151. Esselborn sees Narcissus as a central figure in Trakl's work, especially the earlier poems in which Trakl makes use of the legend to create figures ("Identifikationsfiguren") through which he can then objectify the problematics of the "seherischer Dichter" (Esselborn, *Georg Trakl*, 174–77). See also Held, "Mönch und Narziß," 126–39.

38. See Spoerri, *Georg Trakl*, 39.

mother fixation which he transferred onto the sister as a surrogate mother. A Lacanian reading might make use of the *Ebenbild* similarity between the two; the sister would be an object of Imaginary narcissistic attraction, a reassuring visual similarity—self-reflection—which would also function as a subliminal reminder of the ego's tenuous, if not illusory, identity.

It might also be helpful in this context to mention that Achim Aurnhammer's study of androgyny in European literature reads Trakl's "sister-visions" as part of a "sister-mystery" or transcendental "light-mystery" (*Lichtmysterium*) which evokes a fanciful "mystical place" where all earthly oppositions are resolved. "The gleaming sister," he concludes, "depicts the yearning for that angelic creature of light, who is lost at birth and can only be regained in death."[39] Aurnhammer's analysis is complemented by Richard Detsch's research on the various late nineteenth-century notions of androgyny and "sexual mysticism" with which Trakl, his friends, and his sister Grete were familiar.[40] It seems that he and his sister were attracted to the idea of an androgynous unity that would transcend in death the problematic aspects of human—not to say, incestuous—sexuality. In any case, Trakl was devoted to Grete and was very close to her throughout his adult years. This would help to explain why the figure of the sister so often functions as a spiritual refuge, albeit at times defiled, which serves as a feminine counterpart to masculine figures. *Die Schwester* is thus part of a rich symbolic arena whose mythic-psychic dimensions range from the

39. Aurnhammer, *Androgynie,* 274–75. In his discussion of the myth of Narcissus, Aurnhammer suggests that the Bible also contains a mysticism of specularity: "Paul (in 2 Corinthians 3:18) characterized the mystical experience of God as 'seeing and mirroring' [*schauend und spiegelnd*]" (277). Note how the visual union of God and man involves a transformation from difference to visual identity (in the English translation of verse 18 of 2 Corinthians 3): "And we all, with unveiled face, reflecting the glory of the Lord, are being changed into his likeness."

40. See Detsch, "Unity and Androgyny," 115–33.

asexual androgynous unity of hermaphroditism[41] and an archaic, pre-Christian wedlock of brothers and sisters such as Zeus and Hera to Trakl's creations of *Mönchin, Jünglingin,* and Fremdlingin neologisms[42] which evince his attempt, in his struggle with a recalcitrant language, to forge ("zusammenschmieden") male and female into single poignant and expressive "impressions" (1:478). Belonging to this arena is also the mythical character of Narcissus, who by one account "saw his beloved twin sister in the water."[43]

Note the association of the sister with images of visuality and specularity in the following passages:[44]

The slender figure of the sister steps out of the blue mirror and he falls as if dead into darkness.

The strange sister appears again in someone's evil dreams. . . .

. . . .

The student, perhaps a Doppelgänger, watches her for a long time.

Behind him stands his dead brother. (1:55)

His hands touch the age of bluish waters
    Or in the cold night the white cheeks of the sisters (1:70)

41. See Sharp, *Poet's Madness,* 53–62.

42. Trakl feminizes the masculine terms of "Mönch" (monk), "Jüngling" (youth), and "Fremdling" (stranger) in the following: "Aus dunklem Hausflur trat / Die goldne Gestalt / Der Jünglingin" (from "Das Herz," 1:154); "Mönchin! Schließ mich in dein Dunkel" (from "Nachtergebung," 1:164); "und da ich frierend aufs Lager hinsank, stand zu Häupten wieder der schwarze Schatten der Fremdlingin" (1:168). These neologistic images of androgyny and hermaphroditicism, Michael Hamburger remarks, "stand for a mode of being exempt from original sin," which, like Trakl's "ungebornen" motifs, denote "a state of innocence more complete than the innocence of childhood" ("Georg Trakl," 200, 204). See also Kleefeld's discussion of the "sisterly counterpart of the 'Fremdlingin,'" in his article "Kaspar Hauser and the Paternal Law," 75–79.

43. Rank, *The Double,* 82.

44. The original German may be found in the Appendix.

As the eyes of the sister open round and dark in the brother
(1:314)

Are you speaking of your sister! I saw her face last night in a
starry pond (1:455)

One final example comes from the end of his prose-poem "Traum
und Umnachtung" (Dream and Derangement):

> A crimson cloud shrouded his head, so that he fell silently upon
> his own blood and image, a lunar face; and he fell stonily into
> emptiness, when in a shattered mirror there appeared a dying
> youth, the sister; and the night devoured the accursed race.
> (1:150)

To be sure, the openness of this suggestive passage of death and
darkness—containing the fractured specular encounter and the
fusion of brother with sister—would accommodate various interpretive perspectives. Suffice it to say that this constellation of imagery (which includes *das verfluchte Geschlecht*—of a cursed, incestuous brother-sister relationship?) is framed, or perhaps, shadowed,
by the father's house. Under the rigidity of this paternal structure—whose rigidity is underscored by the three occurrences of
steinern (stony)—there appears in the broken mirror image the
fleeting narcissistic hope of the brother finding himself in the reflection of the sister. It is also significant that the three occurrences
of *steinern* modify the face or eyes of the three principal characters
(mother, sister, and brother) who are thereby opposed to the father. This stony absence of visual reciprocity also figures in the
opening lines of the poem where signs of a language problematic
interplay with a father-mother, boy-sister constellation: "In the
evening the father became an old man; in dark rooms the face of
his mother turned to stone and the curse of the fallen race fell
heavily upon the boy. At times he remembered his childhood,

filled with sickness, terror and darkness. . . . The slender figure of the sister stepped out of a blue mirror and he fell as if dead into darkness. At night his mouth broke open like a red fruit and the stars shimmered above his speechless sorrow. His dreams filled the old house of the fathers" (1:147).[45]

The first line of the prose-poem displays a figural transformation or denigration of both parental images. Whereas the father's virility is invalidated in "old man," the reassuring and nurturing connotations of motherhood are also negated by the cold rigidity of stone. One also notices the primary position of the father, followed by the mother, whose petrifying face would signal the impossibility of visual reciprocity and/or Imaginary integration for the boy. Connected to this process of petrification is then the "curse of the fallen race," an image that points ahead to the prose-poem's final mirror scene where the night devours the "cursed race." Though no broken mirror figures in the opening lines, the sister's fleeting presence in the mirror reflection is, similar to the poem's final line, accompanied by darkness and death. Both scenes, moreover, enact the impossibility of securing a lasting (surrogate) Imaginary reciprocity in the sister. What is left, the opening lines suggest, is the "speechless sorrow," which remains speechless because words can never fully compensate for or represent what they themselves have helped to invalidate: the fantasy of a unitary existence of visual integration. And though the poetic persona may have aggressively denigrated the father in the very first line, his figural presence cannot be eliminated: the enclosing paternal realm (intensified in the plurality of "house of the *fathers*") can be escaped, the poem suggests, only in dream. Consequently, the "speechless sorrow" is followed by "His dreams filled the old house of the fathers"—a line that may also shed light on the poem's title, "Traum und Umnachtung," if one considers that *Umnachtung* signifies not only a

45. The original German may be found in the Appendix.

lack of "mental" clarity, or insanity, but also, literally, the result of the ineluctable, obscuring darkness of night. Of course, the complexity of the prose-poem should not be reduced to this constellation of psychoanalytically significant terms alone, nor, by the same token, should be figuration of *die Schwester* be equated simplistically with incestuous desire or a person named Grete. "Traum und Umnachtung" is a piece of exploratory prose poetry in which the figure of the sister reveals itself to be part of a larger complex of psychic symbols associated with guilt, problematic specularity, language, and, ultimately, a deep uneasiness about the demands of mimetic desire.

Kathrin Pfisterer-Burger devotes more than half of her recent study on Georg Trakl to a detailed analysis of "Traum und Umnachtung," which she reads as a distillation of various concerns underwriting Trakl's mature work.[46] Focusing on the poem's basic opposition between seeing and blindness, she shows how this opposition, manifested in utopic visions of brightness countered by dark images of incest and decline, is connected to the problematic visual encounters between brother and sister. "The meeting of siblings," she points out, "forms the 'basic pattern'" (43), which is repeated and varied throughout the prose-poem in the series of brother-sister encounters, which culminate in the specular image in the last line where brother and sister are fused in a fractured mirror. Though Pfisterer-Burger's insightful reading of the poem relates the sister to the themes of vision, blindness, and poetry[47]— and, ultimately, to a deep existential guilt—without reducing her to some form of veiled autobiographic reference, she fails to show

46. Pfisterer-Burger, *Zeichen und Sterne*. Further references appear in the text.

47. Pfisterer-Burger asserts that the speaker in "Traum und Umnachtung" is a "blinded seer" (*umnachteter Seher*) and a "possible emblem for the poet" (ibid., 77). She writes in this regard: "The main figure is both seeing and blind [*umnachtet*], proud and lonely, ascetically abstinent and instinctually desirous, humble and haughty. Not mutually exclusive, these antinomies create a boundary zone . . . in which this figure, and the poet, must live" (67).

how the sister and these related themes and images are connected to the poem's problematizing of language itself. Trakl's struggle with language does not, in her view, go beyond the aesthetic problem of trying to express the ineffable intensity and depth of the poet's experience of pain and guilt. "Petrification [*das Steinerne*] becomes the last dimension of the experience of pain," which, she concludes, "shows serious consequences on the level of creative process" and can lead to the poet's inability to speak—"zum lyrischen Verstummen des Dichters" (71). Yet Trakl, we know, did not cease to speak, but persisted in his existential—poetological—struggle with language, which is the topic of the following section.

Blindness, Mirrors, and Poetry

In the first stanza of a relatively late poem entitled "Herbstseele" (Autumn Soul), Trakl places the dazzling, reflective surface of a pond in a patently hostile environment. Here, typical of his later verse, he has "depersonalized" the specular experience so as to create more objective imagery:

> Jägerruf und Blutgebell;
> Hinter Kreuz und braunem Hügel
> Blindet sacht der Weiherspiegel,
> Schreit der Habicht hart und hell. (1:107)

[Cry of hunter, bay of hound; / Beyond the cross and the brown hill / Softly blinds the mirror-pond, / The hawk is shrieking hard and shrill.]

In itself, the pond is unproblematic; it is a natural surface whose sunny-day brilliant dazzle might blind the eye. Trakl did not choose, however, a verb that might convey such dazzling effects (e.g., "glänzen"—"to gleam, dazzle"), but created, rather, a decidedly negative verb out of the adjective for "blind." The resulting neologism thus focuses the attention on the "not seeing" of blindness. Within the context of this stanza, the sense of blinding characterizes, in addition to the dazzling visual effects of the pond, an obscuring of the reflective surface because Trakl's neologistic verb has no specified direct object. "Softly blinds the mirror-pond" can mean that the mirror-pond both blinds and becomes blind.

The sense of "not seeing" is then subtly reiterated in the first two lines of the next stanza, where "black silence" hovers ominously over "path and stubblefield":

> Über Stoppelfeld und Pfad
> Banget schon ein schwarzes Schweigen;

[Above the path and stubblefield / Black silence already cowers;]

That this "black silence" suggests the absence of vision is strengthened by Hans-Georg Kemper's observation that silence (*Schweigen*) is often modified in Trakl's imagery by attributes that connote "not seeing," which led him to conclude, "Ominous silence [*Schweigen*] corresponds to the black of not seeing."[48] This is an important insight which would reinforce the claim that the theme of obscured vision or specularity—blindness—is associated in Trakl's work with language (and ultimately poetry), since *Schweigen* can mean to keep silent, not speak.

By undermining the potentially beautiful specularity of the naturally reflective mirror-pond, Trakl has also undermined the "holy," "magical," or "religious" connotations of "Weiher."[49] "Weiher" frequently occurs in images involving natural reflections—especially the reflection of stars—as was pointed out above in the discussion of the first stanza of Trakl's poem "Untergang":

48. Kemper, *Georg Trakls Entwürfe*, 35, 194.
49. See the discussion of the poem "Untergang" (Decline) at the beginning of this chapter.

Über den weißen Weiher
Sind die wilden Vögel fortgezogen.
Am Abend weht von unseren Sternen ein eisiger Wind. (1:116)

[Above the white pond / The wild birds have flown away. / An icy wind blows from our stars at evening.]

The obscuring of specular reflection implied in the darkening autumnal skies over the white pond emerges again in the second stanza of the poem in the bowing darkness of the "shattered brow of night":

Über unsere Gräber
Beugt sich die zerbrochene Stirne der Nacht.
Unter Eichen schaukeln wir auf einem silbernen Kahn.

[Above our graves / Bows the shattered brow of night. / We rock beneath the oak trees in a silver skiff.]

By personifying the night with "brow," Trakl transforms the encroaching night into a face whose fractured darkness is incapable of reciprocating "our" gaze. This motif of a bowing brow or face occurs in other poems in images denoting or suggesting visuality and specularity, from the "brow which bends over bluish waters" (1:338), to the haunting Narcissus figure who "bends over silent waters to see" that his "countenance has left" him (1:169). In any case, the problematizing of visual reciprocity suggested in the bowing brow was explicitly present in draft versions of this stanza of "Untergang," which contain not only an "Antlitz" ("face," implied in the "bowing brow") but also a mention of the mirror. Lines 5 and 6 of the poem's first version read:

Umschlungen laß uns neigen auf blaue Wasser,
Die dunklen Spiegel männlicher Schwermut (2:191)

[Let us bend in embrace over blue waters, / The dark mirrors of masculine melancholy]

In the second version Trakl introduces another telltale word by replacing "männlich" (masculine)[50] with "schweigend" (not speaking), a term that brings into play not only the blindness of "not seeing" (which, as Kemper has noted, is associated with "Schweigen") but the subliminal presence of language (and poetry) as well. In the third version "schweigend" is nominalized and moved to the preceding line, which becomes, in a transitional stage, "Weht uns das Schweigen steinerner Wasser" ("The silence of stony waters blows over to us"). "Schweigen" is then replaced by "Antlitz" (face) in the final stage of the second version, leaving "Weht uns das Antlitz steinerner Wasser an" ("The face of stony waters blows over to us"). By replacing the "silence" with "face" Trakl, in typical fashion, puts the stress on the problem of "not seeing," which is especially significant here if one considers that romantic associations of blue in "blue waters" have been negated with an image that undermines the potentially beautiful specularity of a naturally reflective surface: "the face of stony waters."[51]

50. That there is often at least a subliminal psychosexual component to the various mirror motifs is suggested by the "masculine melancholy" of this line. Further signs of psychosexual motivation are also evident in a variation of this line in which Trakl replaced "mirror" with "cave," which, as Iris Denneler argues, "points to a repression of sexual associations" (*Konstruktion und Expression,* 73).

51. Esselborn notes a change in thematization of poetic creativity in Trakl's mature work which signals the poet's move from a romantic to a modernist conceptualization of poetry: "Trakl employs new ciphers in characterizing his wild song, especially that of metal, which represents the utmost contrast to the soft and living Nature of the idylls. . . . If the latter corresponded to spontaneous and immediate composition—as is invoked in the image of the blue flower—then inorganic metal and the city of stone is suitable only for that sort of production which proceeds from the deadening of feeling. The stone and metal of this mode of production suggest, as in symbolist theory, a technical principle of composition and aesthetic construction without consideration of the experiences and wishes of the author

In the fifth and final version of the poem, the version published in *Der Brenner,* the blindness implied in the various versions of the second stanza is made explicit in the poetological "blind hands" of the final stanza, in which the peaceful quiet of nature is broken by the sounding of the city's white walls:

> Immer klingen die weißen Mauern der Stadt.
> Unter Dornenbogen
> O mein Bruder klimmen wir blinde Zeiger gen Mitternacht.

[The white walls of the city sound forever. / Beneath thorn arches / O my brother, we blind hands climb toward midnight.]

It is as though the sound of civilization and human society is somehow implicated in a darkening process which first obscured the resplendent dazzle of the magical pond and then moved on to the "brothers" in the final line, transforming them into blind hands whose groping gestures point to the ominous dark silence of an alienating modern world.

A similar constellation of natural scenery and civilized, darkening decline occurs in one of Trakl's best-known poems, the "Kaspar Hauser Lied" (Kaspar Hauser Song, 1913). Here the poet plays off the motif of the noble and innocent savage destroyed by civilization by alluding to a legendary (and historically documented) foundling named Kaspar Hauser, who at the age of seventeen or eighteen mysteriously appeared in Nuremberg on Whit-Monday 1828, ignorant of both language and society. Hardly able to walk and incapable of speaking, this boy had been isolated since

---

which serve only as the raw material. In Trakl this is expressed in images of forging, joining and forming, as well as in the cipher of the crystal, with its pure and harmonic but also artificial and dead structure—both of which, like the metal shape, stand for the artistic product of the mind" ("*Blaue Blume*' or '*Kristallene Tränen,*'" 225).

birth, as he later recounted after acquiring the rudiments of lan-guage, in a dark, dungeonlike room. As enigmatic as his origin was his demise some five years later; he was stabbed to death in the Hofgarten at Ansbach by an assailant whose identity—like that of the perpetrators of his macabre upbringing—remains to this day a mystery. Trakl's "Kaspar Hauser Lied" belongs to a rich and varied imaginative response to the Hauser mystery, which includes, more recently, Peter Handke's 1967 *Kaspar* play and Werner Herzog's 1975 film *Every Man for Himself and God against All.*[52] Using motif and vocabulary borrowed from Paul Verlaine's "Gaspar Hauser chante" poem and (especially) Jakob Wassermann's 1908 semidoc-umentary novel on Kaspar Hauser,[53] Trakl constructed a typically enigmatic and abstract (modernist) poem which is only vaguely reminiscent of the Hauser story. Rather than harkening back to the foundling's dungeon-dark beginnings, Trakl's poem opens with the following measured and richly lyrical allusions to a bright, presocial world of innocence:

Er wahrlich liebte die Sonne, die purpurn den Hügel hinabstieg,
Die Wege des Waldes, den singenden Schwarzvogel
Und die Freude des Grüns.

Ernsthaft war sein Wohnen im Schatten des Baums
Und rein sein Antlitz.
Gott sprach eine sanfte Flamme zu seinem Herzen:
O Mensch!

Stille fand sein Schritt die Stadt am Abend; (1:95)

52. For an insightful analysis of the historical, cultural, and aesthetic determi-nants of the literary reception of the Hauser story, see Bance, "The Kaspar Hauser Legend."

53. Wassermann, *Caspar Hauser oder die Trägheit des Herzens,* translated by Caroline Newton under the title *Caspar Hauser.* References are to the German edition.

[He truly loved the sun, which, crimson, descended the hill, / The paths of the forest, the singing blackbird / And the joy of green. // Solemn was his dwelling in the shadow of the tree / And pure his countenance. / God spoke a gentle flame into his heart: / O man! // Silent his footstep found the city in the evening.[54]]

One immediately notices the bright, warm, and colorful Arcadian imagery; here is a joyous serenity, an Eden of authentic dwelling in which Kaspar ("he") and primal nature ("sun," "hill," "forest," and "tree") coexisted harmoniously before "his footstep" entered in silence "the city in the evening." Taken by itself, the first stanza depicts—in the past tense—a bright world, which, when compared with Trakl's abounding present-tense scenes of autumnal decline, appears to present a preexisting ideal state of peaceful coexistence and love. Even the setting sun, usually a foreboding sign of imminent doom, is (was) an object of love—in a stanza which itself is unified by one verb: "loved." "He truly loved" joins together all the elements of this natural scene as the objects of Kaspar's true love. It is significant, also, that the first object of this love, the sun, is a feminine noun ("die Sonne")—a primal feminine element that connotes the ultimate origin of all light and life.

Bathed in the primal warmth of the setting sun, Kaspar was at one with his world—a fanciful, quiet world undisturbed by the civilized noise of society. Here, in the Edenic "joy of green," he could listen to the sweet *melos* of the blackbird's song—a pure

54. This is, with the exception of the last line, Robert Firmage's translation (see his *Song of the West*). I have changed his rendition of this line ("His footstep found the city silent in the evening") because it strongly suggests that the city is silent. The original contains a typically undecidable ambiguity, in that "Stille" can be a noun, adjective, or adverb. I have followed the German syntax and placed "Silent" in the original position, which supports both translations. This brings the ambiguity into play in the English while suggesting, as does the original, that the silence applies more to the footstep than to the city.

melody in an Arcadian "minor key" untainted by the loud "content and meaning"[55] of the words forced upon him when he turned up in the city. Here there is a joyous serenity without the earlier synaesthetic "Don Juan" mania, an Eden of harmonious dwelling in the "pleasing sound" of a blackbird whose singing is a pure melody, a romantic *Melodie* without *Mißton*. Kaspar enjoyed, as long as he was safely isolated from the alienating world of words, a harmonious existence in a unitary perceptual world. He dwelled, to couch it in psychoanalytic terms, in the resplendent but doomed Imaginary world of a "mirror stage"—the fanciful preverbal state of a "specular I," which is conjured, or retroactively projected, by a linguistically objectified "social I." His psyche had, as it were, not yet been socialized, in Lacan's words, "objectified in the dialectic of identification with the other . . . before language restores to it . . . its function as subject."[56] Kaspar Hauser's Edenic innocence would suggest the Imaginary purity of a childlike Adam who has not yet fallen from the grace of a resplendent perceptual world into a civilized world of words. But this is an innocence that, as Meltzer puts it, "does not lie in childhood, it lies in fantasy; it does not lie in intellect, it lies in mimetic desire."[57]

A language problematic with social implications is also present in Wassermann's Kaspar Hauser novel. In a chapter entitled "The Mirror Speaks," Wassermann writes about how Hauser was saddened and troubled by his confrontation with language: "It was a long way from the thing to the word. Nonetheless, the same way also led to people; indeed, it was as if people stood behind a screen of words which made their expressions strange and horrible." The words that brought Wassermann's Hauser to the society of people

55. See 1:208 and my discussion of Trakl's review of Gustav Streicher's play in Chapter 5 above.
56. Lacan, *Ecrits*, 2.
57. Meltzer, *Salome and the Dance of Writing*, 155.

also produced a frightening estrangement, for words made people's features, especially their faces, strange and menacing. Not surprisingly, Hauser's "favorite fantasy" was "that he someday be permitted to go home."[58] He longed to return *home*, to an Imaginary home, which would entail an existence prior to the menacing, socializing influence of language.

The idea of an adolescent boy who is miraculously ignorant of both language and society seems to have conjured in Trakl's imagination a sensuous—intoxicating—vision of primal innocence. His Kaspar-Adam was thus happily "uncivilized"; he dwelled in a unitary world that contained no broken mirrors, shattered dark brow, blinded eyes, or alienating words. Unmarked by trauma, his "countenance" is "pure"—not the "mirror image of a godless, cursed century," as Trakl had referred to himself (1:519).

Trakl, it would seem, had little trouble identifying with the legendary foundling doomed by the anonymous brutality of the city and, in fact, once referred to himself as a "poor Kaspar Hauser" in a letter written from the city of Innsbruck—a place he described in that same letter as "the meanest and most brutal city that exists" (1:487). It is no coincidence that Trakl's prose-poem "Traum und Umnachtung" carried as its original title "Der Untergang Kaspar Münchs" (The Decline of Kaspar Monk). The purity of Kaspar, be he an ascetic monk or an innocent foundling, is doomed to decline—a darkening decline that in Trakl's later work transforms a boy named Kaspar Hauser into a complex psychomythic figure who evokes the beautiful but unattainable mythic state of a perceptual world of visual integration. The story of Kaspar Hauser was more than a literary source or a convenient set of symbolic props; it was a profound existential metaphor which both reflected and elaborated his dark visions of civilization and its discontents. It was

58. Wassermann, *Caspar Hauser,* 43, 45.

236

a legend which, as Frank Graziano has succinctly stated, "informs Trakl's poetry as much as his own biography."[59]

The impossibility of this myth of preexistence[60] is evoked already by the portentous setting sun in the opening scene of Trakl's Hauser poem. This Edenic landscape contains, moreover, like Adam and Eve's garden before the Fall, a potentially dangerous tree: "Solemn was his dwelling in the shadow of the tree." The bright (maternal) security of his fanciful existence in the sweet feminine *melos* of the blackbird's song stands in the shadow of a tree which conjures visions of the menacing paternal Tree of Knowledge created by God the Father. The paternal agency is and was there from the beginning (in Western culture, at least), inevitable and sure as the setting sun. Fittingly, the second stanza concludes with God's abrupt linguistic declaration—"God spoke . . . into his heart: / O man!"—which marks the end of Kaspar's innocent preexistence and sends him forth into the noisy world of words.

Trakl's Hauser poems ends, after an allusion to the passage of

59. Graziano, "Introduction" to *Georg Trakl,* 16. Gunther Kleefeld makes a similar claim about the figure of Kaspar Hauser: "The significance of Kaspar's killer . . . could not be found in, elucidated, or derived from either the Wassermann novel or the historic facts surrounding the legendary figure. This killer is and was a product of Trakl's imagination long before he ever encountered the Kaspar Hauser legend" ("Kaspar Hauser and the Paternal Law," 54). Bance also alludes to Kaspar's paradigmatic significance in Trakl's work, writing: "Kaspar Hauser was a particularly productive motif for Trakl. He was easily assimilated to such figures of his last years as Endymion, Helian, Elis, Sebastian, all representing innocence preserved by early death" ("The Kaspar Hauser Legend," 208).

60. "Preexistence" alludes to the concept of *Präexistenz,* which Hugo von Hofmannsthal used (in 1916) to describe his earlier, unselfconscious self. Alfred Doppler's farsighted essay of 1968 ("Die Stufe der Präexistenz," 273–84) not only relates the utopic moment of Trakl's work to the Hofmannsthal concept but also suggests that Trakl's creativity (and his bright visions of preexistence) are tied to the narcissism of the mirror: "As the unity of nature disintegrates, the poet's creative mirror throws back no image" (279).

seasons, "Spring and summer and beautiful the autumn / Of the righteous, his light footstep," with the following dark and violent images:

Nachts blieb er mit seinem Stern allein;

Sah, daß Schnee fiel in kahles Gezweig
Und im dämmernden Hausflur den Schatten des Mörders.

Silbern sank des Ungebornen Haupt hin.

[At night he remained alone with his star, // Saw, that snow fell into naked branches, / And in the dusky hallway the shadow of the killer. // Silver, the head of the unborn sank down.]

Kaspar never escaped the "shadow of the tree," whose latent menace is transformed, with each quiet step he takes toward the city and society, into "the shadow of the killer." There, the shining "righteous" one is murdered. Yet he departs from his alien world in an innocent unborn ("ungebornen") state, perhaps because he was never completely socialized and corrupted by the civilization of the city, but perhaps also because, to put it in Christian terms, his unbornness precluded his being reborn and redeemed within the Christian fellowship of man and God. Lost is the promise of rebirth and transcendental solace. The biblical myth of the Fall has become in Trakl's Kaspar Hauser world the reality of humanity's inexorable fall into the cold and brutal world of modern civilization.

Though blindness is not explicitly mentioned in the "Kaspar Hauser Lied," it is subtly implied in the denigration of innocent Kaspar's perceptual idyll. It is no coincidence that blindness figures, as Gunther Kleefeld has pointed out, in "Nachts" (At Night), the poem that immediately followed the Kaspar Hauser poem in the volume of poetry Trakl assembled in 1914. The "Kaspar death-scene," Kleefeld writes, "is followed by an image of blinding in a poem which condenses the drama of sexual desire, guilt, and punishment played out under the surface of the 'Kaspar Hauser Song.'"[61] It is interesting that Kleefeld's detailed analysis of Trakl's Kaspar Hauser poem also shows that the figure of the sister is an integral part of a "latent discourse" pervading the poem (and indeed Trakl's work in general). Also "under the surface" of Trakl's rendition of the Hauser legend is, as we now see, an implicit commentary on the psychomythic complex of narcissistic self-reflection. It too is an integral part of a pervasive but latent discourse which underlies and informs Trakl's autumnal poetry of doom and decline and manifests itself in various degrees in the many images involving blindness, specularity, and visual experience.

Trakl's late work is not always as patently apocalyptic as the "Kaspar Hauser Lied." Indeed, there are several late poems whose specular imagery hint at a creative or redemptive impulse which seems to derive from the Western world's decline—the "fall," perhaps, that Rilke saw in Trakl's work as "the precondition or pretext for ascension."[62] Two such poems are "Abendländisches Lied" (Song of the Occident) and "Abendland" (Occident), which—as their German titles might indicate—take a sweeping poetic view of the darkening "occident" (literally evening-land, *Abend-land*) of the Western world.

Completed at about the same time, perhaps within a month of each other, the Kaspar Hauser poem and "Abendländisches Lied" seem almost to form a complementary pair, so close are they in imagery, development, and tone. They contrast, however, with respect to visuality, in that the theme of vision and seeing—only implied in the deterioration of the perceptual idyll in the Kaspar Hauser poem—plays a crucial role in the final stanza of "Abend-

61. Kleefeld, "Kaspar Hauser and the Paternal Law," 82.
62. Storck, "Arbeitsgespräche," 158.

ländisches Lied." Preceded by what one critic has aptly described as "a compressed history of the Western world, progressing from prehistoric innocence"[63] to the fallen present, this stanza contains motifs of both resplendent visual brightness and obscured self-reflection:

> O, die bittere Stunde des Untergangs,
> Da wir ein steinernes Antlitz in schwarzen Wassern beschauen.
> Aber strahlend heben die silbernen Lider die Liebenden:
> Ein Geschlecht. Weihrauch strömt von rosigen Kissen
> Und der süße Gesang der Auferstandenen. (1:119)

[O, the bitter hour of decline, / When we see a stony countenance in black waters. / But the lovers lift their beaming silver eyelids: / One flesh. Incense streams from rosy cushions / And the sweet song of the resurrected ones.]

This transfiguration at the moment of despair is not unlike the forced manic reversal at the end of *Don Juans Tod*. Here, however, there is a redemptive and transfiguring song,[64] which overcomes obscured—petrified—visual reciprocity; it is a more restrained and measured reversal which signals, as Michael Hamburger writes, "an integration of the psyche—so that the individual is redeemed from narcissistic solitude."[65] This stanza suggests that

63. Detsch, *Georg Trakl's Poetry*, 33. Aurnhammer factors into this historical progression the narcissism of self-reflection: "Here [in "Song of the Occident"] is the culmination of series of cultures: antiquity—middle ages—the modern era of decline which is figured in the petrification of narcissistic self-reflection" (*Androgynie*, 284).

64. The musicologist Albert Hellmich sees in this "sweet song of the resurrected ones" a culmination of a Nietzschean "'affirmation of life in song'" (*Klang und Erlösung*, 130). Hellmich asserts: "The musical elements in Trakl's work symbolize more than life and an unbroken existence; as the components of a counter-world [*Gegenwelt*], they open the possibility of salvation from the real world of 'decline and decay' and make possible an overcoming in art of a frightful existence" (130).

65. Hamburger, "Georg Trakl," 191.

the failure of narcissistic self-reflection in the "black waters" of the present "hour of decline" need not necessarily end in the lonely demise of a Kaspar Hauser. It is as though the "silver" sinking of Kaspar's innocent head is countered by the uplifting "silver eye-lids" of lovers—lovers whose transfiguring unity would break the spell of guilt-inducing narcissistic allure and occasion a "sweet song" of redemption. In any case, the origin of such sweet song is directly related to the absence of pure visual reciprocity in an existence that seems to deny the Imaginary unity of the Kaspar Hauser idyll and the fulfillment of mimetic desire.

It should come as no surprise that the mythic singer Orpheus, whose doomed backward glance and yearning (for the lost feminine counterpart) gave rise to beautiful melodies of lament and loss, should appear in another late poem of epic proportions, "Passion," in which the redemptive power of poetic song is also related to the disintegration of bright specularity.[66] Here, the poetological impulse sounds already in the poem's first line:

> Wenn silbern Orpheus die Laute rührt,
> Beklagend ein Totes im Abendgarten—(1:395).

[When Orpheus touches silver his lyre, / Lamenting something dead in the evening garden—]

Following the appearance of the "boy" and "mother" (in the second stanza), a sister then appears in the fourth stanza:

> Wen weinst du unter dämmernden Bäumen?
> Die Schwester, dunkle Liebe
> Eines wilden Geschlechts,[67]

66. Cf. the various versions of the poem "Passion" (1:125 and 392–97).

67. The ambiguity of "Geschlecht" is impossible to render in English; the word means, in addition to "race" or "generation," "sex."

[For whom are you crying beneath dusking trees? / The sister, dark love / Of a wild race,]

The incest suggested here reemerges more explicitly in the tenth and eleventh stanzas in conjunction with a Narcissus figure who sees a horrific vision of his lover in a water reflection:

> Über seufzende Wasser geneigt
> Sieh dein Gemahl: Antlitz starrend von Aussatz
> Und ihr Haar flattert wild in der Nacht.
>
> Zwei Wölfe im finsteren Wald
> Mischen wir unser Blut in steinerner Umarmung ⟨.⟩[68]

[Bent over sighing waters / Look at your consort: Face rigid with leprosy / And her hair flutters wildly in the night. // Two wolves in a dark night / We mix our blood in petrified embrace ⟨.⟩]

In the redemptive scenery of the final stanzas, the poem's imagery turns again to the Orphic impulse.[69]

> Nächtlich tönt der Seele einsames Saitenspiel
> Dunkler Verzückung
> Voll zu den silbernen Füßen der Büßerin
> Im verlorenen Garten;
> Und an dorniger Hecke knospet der blaue Frühling.

68. Angle brackets indicate notations whose near illegibility may render the reading uncertain. Kleefeld claims, in reference to this leprous reflection of the sister-lover, that "Blindheit und Aussatz sind die Strafe für die Übertretung des Tabu, des väterlichen Inzestverbots" (Kleefeld, *Das Gedicht als Sühne,* 365). This also could be articulated as a loss of Imaginary reciprocity, the figural result of the mirror shattering paternal law and orders of language.

69. See Simon, *Traum und Orpheus,* esp. 122–54, for a detailed analysis of the Orpheus legend and its relation to Trakl's poetic self-understanding. Though he frequently conflates the lyrical personae of Trakl's poems with the poet himself, Simon brings to light the pervasive interplay (and conflict) between Christian and Greek mythological elements in Trakl's work.

Und unter dunklen Olivenbäumen
Tritt der rosige Engel
Des Morgens aus dem Grab der Liebenden.

[Nightly sounds the soul's lonely play of strings / Of dark delight / Fully at the feet of the female penitent / In the lost garden; / And blue springtime buds on a thorny hedge. // And beneath dark olive trees / Steps the rosy angel / Of the morning from the grave of the lovers.]

The Orphic allusion, "Nightly sounds the soul's lonely play of strings," replaces, very interestingly, a specular image in a variant version in which the lyrical persona sees a female penitent in a mirror reflection:

Daß die Schönheit reiner das Herz erfreue.
O der kristallene Spiegel,
Da in Schauern du erkennst die himmliche Büßerin (2:223)

[So that beauty more pure(ly) rejoices the heart. / Oh the crystalline mirror, / As you recognize in shudders the heavenly female penitent]

A similar intertwining of obscured vision and song figure prominently in the second stanza of "Abendland"—a poetological stanza which explicitly relates song to the stony absence of vision:

Leise verließ am Kreuzweg
Der Schatten den Fremdling
Und steinern erblinden
Dem die schauenden Augen,
Daß von der Lippe
Süßer fließe das Lied. (1:399)

[The shadow quietly leaves / The stranger on the way of the cross / And his seeing eyes become / Stony blindness / So that the song / May flow sweeter from his lips.]

Note how this song benefits from the blinding of "seeing eyes," how such "stony blindness" enables the song to flow sweet*er* from the lips. One cannot help but wonder whether there might also be Homeric resonances in this obvious connection of poetry and blindness. In any case, there arises, it would seem, in the absence of resplendent visual integration, a sweet song, a redeeming aesthetics of sweet *melos*. In this dark world, the blinded singer-poet is forced to listen to his own "inner melodies" (1:472) and transform them into a song that might help him deal with the trauma and alienation of a modern world that invalidates the Edenic joys of a fanciful, pre-Fall Kaspar Hauser existence. It is a song that would compensate for the "lost" purity of vision and sound represented by the blackbird's pure singing in the Arcadian setting of the "Kaspar Hauser Lied."

Returning again to the poetological "message" contained in the stony blindness and sweet song of the last stanza of "Abendland," we can now see that this stanza represents a fuller aesthetic realization of the problematic split between seeing and speaking which emerged in the frenzied lamentations of Trakl's early poetological poem "Confiteor," for example, and was further elaborated in the "semiotic" blind hands of the poetic brothers in "Untergang." Rather than despairing at the frightening, dark disintegration of life's "colorful images," this composed, late persona seems to recognize such disintegration—the failure of mimetic desire—as the Orphic impulse which motivates its compensatory sensuous songs of darkness, death, and decline.

What begins to come into focus as one reads through some of the stanzas and versions of these late poems is not so much variations on a theme—of incest perhaps—as a permutating set of words (sister, lover, eyes, face, mirror, blindness, cross, [lost] garden, resurrected [ones], Orpheus, lyre, song, and so on) whose interplay produces a complex of psychomythic imagery which evokes and relates such general notions as guilt, sensuality, androgyny, and redemption to the creation of poetry. This particular constellation of images, mythic-religious resonances, and concepts produces, in other words, a poetological reflection on its own Orphic origin, an origin in which the blinding impossibility of fulfilling mimetic desire is connected to the impossibility of escaping the alienating structures of self-consciousness. The sister, for example, is but one (psychic) nodal point in this poetological constellation[70] of imagery in which guilt is associated with the narcissistic allure of sensory perception and, perhaps, even a deeper, subliminal Judeo-Christian prohibition against image making.[71] And though Trakl may write about a sweet song of redemption, his *melo*dious words will never be able to secure a lasting transcendence of self-consciousness and guilt because such transcendence can be achieved only in annihilation of the self—in death.

Frustrated by the "terrible helplessness of words" and perhaps by a deep-seated aversion to the socializing effects of language, Trakl managed—despite his dementia praecox and Kaspar Hauser paranoia—to create a profound lyrical work which recorded his Orphic descent into the frightening underworld of human desire. He wrote a strangely cohesive verse whose "network of tentacular roots," to borrow from T. S. Eliot's Ben Jonson essay, reach "down to the deepest terrors and desires,"[72] which most people experience only in the safe world of dreams. Gloomy but compelling, Trakl's imagistic work brought together the poet's antithetical visions, specular obsessions, and Orphic impulses into an aesthetic accord which finds a sympathetic resonance in a postindustrial age of

70. That Trakl is reported to have said that his sister, who studied to be a concert pianist, was "the most beautiful girl, the greatest artist, the most unusual woman" (Basil, *Georg Trakl,* 76) would strengthen the claim that the sister figures in a psychomythic dimension and is linked (via art and music) to poetry.

71. Cf. discussion in Chapter 2.

72. Eliot, *Selected Essays,* 135.

computers, stultifying media barrage, and faceless urbanization. But this work also records an intense struggle with language that resonates in a *Zwischenreich* between poet and reader and speaks to and from the alienations of the modern era—an era struggling to come to terms with the visual dis-synchronization of words and world that generated in the first decades of the twentieth century the psychoepistemological discourse of mirrors. But it is also an era which finds the desire of poetry linked not only to the impersonal menace of the *Abend-land* but also to an unrequited need for myth in its various forms and disguises.

CHAPTER 8

The Play of the Paradigm

Only the man who has so much to give that he can
forget himself in his work can afford to collaborate,
to exchange, to contribute.—T. S. Eliot

The more plural a text, the less it is written before I
read it.—Roland Barthes

IN CHAPTER 6 we examined several of Trakl's early, echo-filled
poems that thematize on a subtextual level an irreconcilable clash
with tradition. In their *fleurs du mal* lamentations about dissonant
melodies and powerful, anonymous commandments, these early
poetic productions express an uncertainty about the origins of the
poetic pulse and signal a struggle in which a writing subject seeks
to free itself from the weight of tradition so as to find and establish
a poetic idiom that would be more appropriate to its particular
situation and time. While Trakl's poetological understanding of
his own creativity gradually evolved, he continued to borrow un-
abashedly throughout his career from his many precursors. This
plagiaristic habit, however, does not diminish the evocative power
of his language, but rather shows, as Reinhold Grimm has remarked, that for Trakl "poetry is no longer the private possession
of the poet but is simply verbal material of which anyone can make
use."[1]

1. Grimm, "Georg Trakls Verhältnis zu Rimbaud," 310; (further references to

After listing for nearly thirty pages parallels between Trakl's work and the 1907 German translation of Rimbaud[2]—images, motifs, and phrases that often correspond to the letter—Reinhold Grimm is able to link Trakl's aesthetic breakthrough in 1911–12 to the influence of Rimbaud's work. Trakl's intense reading and appropriation of the French poet provided him with a unique *"means of expression,"* which enabled him "to record and indeed speak about his experiences" (306).[3] Not only did Trakl acquire a more appropriate vocabulary from Rimbaud, but he also—and perhaps most important—learned an alogical "rhétorique" (310), which allowed him to break from the strictures of syntagmatic determination.

Bernhard Böschenstein, more recently, has shored up Grimm's analysis of Trakl's breakthrough by showing that his productive middle period—from about the end of 1912 to the end of 1913— was initiated not only by his reading of Rimbaud but also by his "simultaneous reception" of Hölderlin.[4] In Hölderlin he found a kinship of spirits, a poet of Dionysian madness, night, and winter. From this point on, Böschenstein shows, Trakl's poetry moves away from the kaleidoscopic imagery of the Rimbaud break-through period and assumes more and more the hymnic tone, diction, and differentiated rhythms characteristic of Hölderlin.

---

this article appear in the text). Following the lead of Grimm, Brigitte Peucker remarks in her recent book: "Although the influence of prior poets in the Romantic tradition remains important . . . the object of his descent [search for origins], is the revisionary language of descent itself, the language of exhaustion that all these poets appear to have exhausted" (*Lyric Descent in the German Romantic Tradition,* 166).

2. Rimbaud, *Arthur Rimbaud,* trans. K. L. Ammer.

3. Grimm continues: "Rimbaud's work in Klammer's [K. L. Ammer] German had suddenly loosened the poet's tongue so that he now saw the possibilities and found the courage to produce a new kind of poetry" ("Georg Trakls Verhältnis," 306–7).

4. Böschenstein, "Hölderlin und Rimbaud," 27. See also Fiedler, "Trakl and Hölderlin."

Böschenstein notes that the presence of Rimbaud is gradually supplanted in the final phase of Trakl's career (1914) by "the profound influence of Hölderlin's 'hymnal language.'"[5]

Trakl wrote the relatively unknown and unexamined poem "Melancholie" in early 1914, when Rimbaud's influence was on the wane. Although the poem's measured cadences and controlled pathos are indeed reminiscent of Hölderlin, Trakl does not fully submit to the hymnic tone of his spiritual brother.

Melancholie

Die blaue Seele hat sich stumm verschlossen,
Ins offne Fenster sinkt der braune Wald,
Die Stille dunkler Tiere; im Grunde mahlt
Die Mühle, am Steg ruhn Wolken hingegossen,

Die goldnen Fremdlinge. Ein Zug von Rossen
Sprengt rot ins Dorf. Der Garten braun und kalt.
Die Aster friert, am Zaun so zart gemalt
Der Sonnenblume Gold schon fast zerflossen.

Der Dirnen Stimmen; Tau ist ausgegossen
Ins harte Gras und Sterne weiß und kalt.
Im teuren Schatten sieh den Tod gemalt,
Voll Tränen jedes Antlitz und verschlossen. (1:332)[6]

[The blue soul has mutely enclosed itself, / In through the open window sinks the brown forest, / The silence of dark animals; in the depths grinds / The mill, clouds rest spilled out upon the footbridge, // The golden strangers. A team of horses /Bursts red into the village. The garden brown and cold. / The aster freezes, painted so delicately upon a fence / Nearly dissolved already is the gold of the sunflower. //

5. Böschenstein, "Hölderlin und Rimbaud," 27.
6. This poem (listed in the standard edition as "Melancholie I") is not a version of Trakl's better-known poem "Melancholia" (listed as "Melancholie II").

Voices of prostitutes; dew is spilled / Into hard grass and stars white and cold. / Look at death painted in precious shadows, / Every face full of tears and closed.]

Vestiges of Rimbaud's desecrating revision of romantic idealism are still present in "Melancholie," most notably in "der Dirnen Stimmen" and the poem's title. Specific vocabulary items such as "Dirnen," "Tau," and "Antlitz" may also suggest Rimbaud's presence, whereas the poem's second line, "Ins offne Fenster sinkt der braune Wald," appears to be a reworked version of several lines quarried from a Rimbaud (K. L. Ammer) poem: "Und boshaft warfen die Bäume durch mein / offenes Fenster ihr Laub hinein . . ." ("And angrily the trees cast / their leaves in through my open window . . .").[7] The intertextual presence of Novalis also resonates in the Trakl poem, especially in the words "blue soul" and "strangers."[8]

Countering "Melancholie's" traditional rhyme scheme and strophic structure are the emotive use of color and pronounced *Reihungstil* (serial style), both typical of German expressionism. The poem's seemingly unrelated pronouncements form a collage of imagery characteristic of the paratactic "rhetoric" Trakl learned from Rimbaud in his breakthrough phase. Each line, or sometimes line pair—and sometimes each clause within a single line—enjoys such a degree of autonomy from its surrounding context that its position within the poem would appear to be almost inconsequential. This impression is perhaps reinforced by the three-times-repeated *-ossen, -alt, -alt, -ossen* rhyme pattern. This rigid and repetitive structure suggests that word and sound configuration, as

7. See Grimm, "Georg Trakls Verhältnis," 281–82, 292.

8. Esselborn's recent essay suggests that "blue" and especially "stranger" are almost always ciphers, of varying degrees of explicitness, for a worldview and theory of poetry associated with Novalis. See Esselborn, " '*Blaue Blume*' or '*Kristallene Tränen*,' " esp. 204, 207, 209, and note 5, Chapter 7, above.

readers of Trakl's mature verse are wont to believe, might be a constitutive principle of organization in this poem. In this chapter I will investigate how this (Rimbaudian) rhetoric of word and sound configuration moves Trakl's writing subject toward a more "objective" poetic language which programmatically partakes of the paradigmatic undertones of language at the bounds of consciousness—"Le Poèt se fait voyant," wrote Rimbaud, and "Il arrive à l'inconnu."[9]

"Melancholie," in its extreme (even for Trakl) disjunction, is, like Lewis Carroll's "Jabberwocky," an exemplary modernist poem whose radical and conspicuous break with the narrational logic of representation is countered by a dense network of differential—paradigmatic—relations. It is, in other words, a "difficult" poem that would likely send Humpty Dumpty scurrying to the security of one of his patently narrative ballads. It is a difficult modernist poem which demands an appropriately modernist (and/or postmodernist) approach.

The apparent reduction of narrative-syntagmatic contiguity characteristic of a good deal of Trakl's mature work does not mean, as many critics have assumed, that "this poetry does not want to be understood in terms of content."[10] His reduction of the syntagmatic axis of language allowed him to delve into and indeed experiment with the expressive potential of a dimension of language that followed the more impersonal pulse of the paradigmatic axis. It thus opened the way for a *meaningful* word play—a *Spiel*—which, Novalis's aspirations notwithstanding, was never fully realized in the classical-romantic poem.

A good place to begin charting the paradigmatic systematics of "Melancholie" is the conspicuous use of colors. "Blue," "brown,"

9. "The poet is a seer . . . he arrives at the unconscious" (quoted by Grimm, "Georg Trakls Verhältnis," 312, from *Arthur Rimbaud: Oeuvres completes,* 270).
10. Killy, *Über Georg Trakl,* 34.

"red," "gold," and "white" are ordinarily vision-oriented words; we use them every day to talk about what we see in the panorama of the world. The sun is gold, roses are red, and violets are blue. Colors are potentially referential and are most frequently used to refer to and characterize real or plausible entities of human vision. One need not read more than three words into this poem to discover that Trakl's use of colors (often, but not always) deviates from this norm. The word "blau" (blue) is not used to describe the visual quality of some real or possible thing. It modifies, rather, something not ordinarily modified by color, an intangible "something" which is above all unseeable—"the soul." The unusual nature of the combination of "blue" and "soul," of a visual word and a conceptual term, foregrounds the abstract character of this language. "Blue" has been distanced from its visual-referential use; its significance, is, like many words in Trakl's small vocabulary, more a function of its systematic—paradigmatic—value.[11] A look at other occurrences in Trakl's work of the word *blau* reinforces this initial observation; it can modify practically anything, from a wild animal to a sound or God's breath:[12]

> A blue prey
> Bleeds quietly in a thicket of thorns (1:86)

> The blue tone of the flute in the hazel bushes (1:308)

> Quietly sink
> Blue stillness of the olive tree at bare walls (1:85)

> A blue moment is just purely soul (1:79)

> Moon, as if something dead steps
> Out of a blue cave (1:139)

11. See esp. chapter 3 of Eckhard Philipp's *Funktion des Wortes in den Gedichten Trakls* for a good analysis of Trakl's "Auflösung syntaktischer Beziehungen."
12. The original German may be found in the Appendix.

The blue rustling of a woman's gown (1:148)

The blue breath of God
Blows into the garden room (1:30)

The list could be continued for pages; "blau," after "dunkel" (dark), and "schwarz" (black) is the third most frequently occurring adjective in Trakl's work. Many of Trakl's color-commentators posit a relatively stable symbolic meaning or value for his colors, from a "mood-symbol" with which Trakl expresses directly a "mood-value"[13] to a symbol of "sensual" qualities which then either reifies an abstract notion or sets up "strange connections" with the modified noun.[14] Another critic speaks of a value, a "semantic core," which "comes to fore" when one compares the parallel occurrences of particular colors.[15] Although parallel occurrences can often be useful in determining the field of play for a particular color, the wide range of varied contexts does not yield much more than rather vague semantic generalities, whose value, not surprisingly, varies widely from critic to critic.

The second word of both the first and second stanzas of "Melancholie" is a color. A draft version of the poem shows that this regularity originally carried over to the third stanza, which began with "Die Zeit des Grüns" ("The time of green"). That all three stanzas began with colors reinforces the impression that word configuration is here an important principle of organization. Further examination of colors and draft versions bears this out: the first line of the second stanza at one point also contained the word "blau." "Upon blue horses" in an earlier version was changed to "A team of horses" in the final version. "Blue" replaced "black" in an even earlier version, demonstrating, perhaps, a certain inter-

13. Schneider, *Der bildhafte Ausdruck in den Dichtungen Georg Heyms, Georg Trakls und Ernst Stadlers,* 125.

14. Lühl-Wiese, "Georg Trakl—der blaue Reiter," 97–117.

15. Philipp, *Funktion des Wortes in den Gedichten Trakls,* 53, 51.

changeability of color words in Trakl's mature verse. This color change gives one pause to consider the appropriateness of speaking about a relatively consistent "mood-value" or "semantic core" to describe Trakl's use of colors—is Trakl quixotically switching "moods" and "semantic" values? Is he changing in such a radical way the "content" of his images? Another look at the draft versions will help to answer this question.

The following presents a line-by-line comparison of some of the variant versions as ordered by Hans Szklenar and Walther Killy in the *Historisch-Kritische Ausgabe* (2:432; italics indicates the final version; "X" denotes illegible words in manuscript draft versions, while ⟨?⟩ indicates words whose near illegibility may render the reading uncertain).

Nun ⟨?⟩ hat dein blaues Antlitz sich verschlossen
So ⟨?⟩ hat dein blaues Antlitz sich verschlossen
Die Blaue Seele hat sich stumm verschlossen

Ans offne Fenster sinkt der braune Wald,
Ins offne Fenster sinkt der braune Wald,

Die Stille sanfter Tiere, X
Die Stille dunkler Tiere, im Grunde mahlt

Im Grund die Mühle; Wolken halb zerflossen
Die Mühle; am Hügel ruhn Wolken hingegossen,
Die Mühle; am Steg ruhen Wolken hingegossen,

Die goldnen X , auf schwarzen Rossen
Die goldnen Fremdlinge, auf blauen Rossen
Die goldnen Fremdlinge. Ein Zug von Rossen

Reitet ⟨?⟩ der Abend; der Garten braun und kalt;
Zieht ⟨?⟩
Steigt
Fährt

Sprengt rot ins Dorf. Der Garten braun und kalt

Die Aster friert, am Zaun die Sonnenblume malt
Die Aster friert, am Zaun so zart gemalt

Der Sonnenblume Gold schon fast zerflossen.

Die ⟨?⟩ Zeit ⟨?⟩ des Grüns ⟨?⟩. Du ⟨?⟩ flüchte ⟨?⟩ nur zum Wein
Der Mütter Stimmen; das Gold ist ausgegossen
Der Dirnen Stimmen; Tau ist ausgegossen

Ins harte Gras und Sterne weiß und kalt.

Im tounen Schatten sieh den Tod gemalt,

Voll Tränen jedes Antlitz und verschlossen.

The first version of the first line of the third stanza was approx-
imately "The time of green. You flee indeed to wine." Just as the
"blue" of the first line of the first stanza was carried over to the first
line of the second stanza (and then deleted) so was the "goldnen"
of the first line of the second stanza carried over into first line of
the third stanza (and likewise deleted). The original version thus
showed a definite uniformity in placement of color words. In the
final version, these color correspondences have been played down;
other color correspondences, however, remain. Note the parallel
between the second lines of each stanza: "der braune Wald," "der
Garten braun und kalt," and "Sterne weiß und kalt" ("the brown
forest," "the garden brown and cold," and "stars white and cold").
The second line of the second stanza ties all three second lines
together in that the "brown" refers back to "the brown forest"
while the "cold" refers ahead to the "white and cold." These three
lines are further tied together by the directive "ins" (into)—indeed, each of these lines presents a sphere which is penetrated from
without. What we are unfolding here is a configuration of "analog-

ical"[16] relations, which, taken together, may evoke the feeling of something encroaching or closing in—the deep and expansive darkness of the woods funnels through an open window, a team of horses bursts into the village, and every countenance is closed. The past participle "verschlossen" (enclosed, closed) occurring in the first and last stanzas lends to this sense of closing in. Not surprisingly, the poem closes with "verschlossen"; a dark sense of finality pervades this line, especially if we follow the textual reference to the initial line of the poem where "verschlossen" first occurred: "The blue soul has mutely enclosed itself." The first line mentions the bright color of a singular soul which "has mutely enclosed itself," whereas the last line is without color and static in that "verschlossen" is used as a predicate adjective and not as part of an active verb. The universality of "every face full of tears and closed" serves to reinforce this finality: *every* face or countenance—that part of the body which is normally exposed and *open* to the panorama of the visual world—is tearfully closed:

> Im teuren Schatten sieh den Tod gemalt,
> Voll Tränen jedes Antlitz und verschlossen.

[Look at death painted in precious shadows, / Every face full of tears and closed.]

What appeared in the first reading to be a collage of disparate images arbitrarily joined by a fixed and repetitive rhyme scheme proves, upon closer inspection, to be a complex system of line pairs, which, because of their contextual isolation—they occur in separate stanzas—cannot be adequately characterized in syntagmatic terms. Through similarity and difference, we have constructed paradigmatic pairs which complement and delimit each other. Take, for example, the first and last lines. The finality of the last line's "tearful closure" (of a face) is heightened, as we saw, by

16. See Kemper, *Georg Trakls Entwürfe*, 21–44.

its contrast to the "action" and color of the first line's "blue soul." Once again, a look at the draft versions of the poem provides further clues to the structural principles of this paradigmatic play: "the blue soul," we find, was originally "your face." This direct reference of "face-face" gives way in the final version to the "blue soul–face" pair, a paradigm that both intensifies the contrast and lends to the development of the poem's process of "tearful closure" in general.

Clemens Heselhaus sees this play of opposites and contrasts ("Gegenbildlichkeit"), along with the relative independence of consecutive lines of construction ("Zeilenkomposition" or "Reihungstil"), as one of the basic structural traits in Trakl's poetry. Kemper further elaborates this "Gegenbildlichkeit" with his heuristic concepts of "construction-form" (*Bauform*) and "process-form" (*Vorgangsform*). "Construction-form," he posits, is a general ordering principle whereby structural and semantic analogies and contrasts—*intra*textual relationships—can be organized. To this he opposes the "process-form," a structural principle that organizes certain changes, gradations, or developments taking place in any particular poem. The "process-form," Kemper argues, also sets up a basic poem pattern which frequently occurs in Trakl's poetry—what he terms "circle-" or "goal-composition" (*Kreis-* or *Zielkomposition*)—poems. Poems that repeat an earlier image, motif, or word constellation in a varied form at the conclusion— a variation on a theme—he labels "circle-composition" poems, whereas those that exhibit image development fall into the "goal-composition" category.[17] Indeed, "Melancholie" would be a likely candidate for a goal- or circle-composition structuration in that it both circles back upon itself, returning to an original structure, as seen in the "face (soul)—face-closed" scheme, and exhibits a thematic development, what I have called the "thematic of closure."

17. Ibid., 136–59.

The other words, lines, images, and motifs—and even stanzas—of "Melancholie" can be investigated along similar lines. What comes into view (and is underscored by the many and varied draft versions) is a dense, cross-referential web or field of placed, displaced, and replaced differential—often contradictory—terms. In his repeated attempts to forge unified and "depersonalized" images, Trakl had, in effect, to submit to the more freely associating paradigmatic under*tones* of language. Commenting on his compulsive attempts to "depersonalize" his writing, Trakl wrote to his friend Erhard Buschbeck: "You must believe me that it is not easy for me, nor will it ever be, to subordinate myself unconditionally to that which is to be represented, and I will always and again and again have to correct myself in order to give truth its due" (1:486). Trakl's wish unconditionally to subordinate himself to the object of his poetry—"to that which is to be represented"—pushes him deeper into a sub- or preconscious level of paradigmatically linked signifiers, in which, in poststructuralist terms, "desire . . . moves ceaselessly on . . . from signifier to signifier, and will never find full and present satisfaction just as meaning can never be fully seized as full presence."[18] In other words, the uncontrollable flux of linguistic desire will forever thwart, as I argued in Chapters 6 and 7, Trakl's (mimetic) desire to establish a (surrogate) unity that might counter the constitutional fragmentation which is itself associated with the alienating acquisition of language.

Wolfgang Preisendanz ventures (in reference to Trakl's late poem "Landschaft" [Landscape]) that that to which the poet strove to subordinate himself so unconditionally is the linguistic "essence of all things."[19] Trakl's poetry, he claims, can be measured against neither reality nor the poet's personal experience but only

18. Moi, *Sexual/Textual Politics*, 101.
19. Preisendanz, "Auflösung und Verdinglichung," 251. Further references are given in the text. Trakl's paradigmatic modernist status is emphasized in this volume in that he is one of the only poets to whom a single essay is devoted.

against language "as the condition for the possibility of things" (245). Trakl's (mature) poetry, he argues, is reflexive through and through, it is multifaceted, ambiguous language consisting of "self-referential signs," which (like so much modernist poetry) forms "reflections upon reflections upon the linguistic essence of all cognition" (245). While I agree that Trakl's mature verse is an intense encounter with language and that it, in a way, foregrounds the reflexive and self-referential—differential—character of language, I think that Preisendanz's observation has slightly missed the mark. There is something more at stake in Trakl's mature verse than the "linguistic essence of all cognition," something like the problem of linguistic experience in general, which, when compounded by Trakl's own narcissistic tendencies, bounds on the pathological. It is a psycholinguistic condition that motivates Trakl's search for a more potent and more appropriate "depersonalized" poetic idiom which might compensate for the failure of mimetic desire to establish an Imaginary unity and cohesion.

Let us return again to analysis of "Melancholie."

> Die blaue Seele hat sich stumm verschlossen,
> Ins offne Fenster sinkt der braune Wald,
> Die Stille dunkler Tiere; im Grunde mahlt
> Die Mühle, am Steg ruhn Wolken hingegossen,
>
> Die goldnen Fremdlinge. Ein Zug von Rossen
> Sprengt rot ins Dorf. Der Garten braun und kalt.
> Die Aster friert, am Zaun so zart gemalt
> Der Sonnenblume Gold schon fast zerflossen.
>
> Der Dirnen Stimmen; Tau ist ausgegossen
> Ins harte Gras und Sterne weiß und kalt.
> Im teuren Schatten sieh den Tod gemalt,
> Voll Tränen jedes Antlitz und verschlossen. (1:332)

[The blue soul has mutely enclosed itself, / In through the open window sinks the brown forest, / The silence of dark animals; in the depths grinds / The mill, clouds rest spilled out upon the footbridge, // The golden strangers. A team of horses / Bursts red into the village. The garden brown and cold. / The aster freezes, painted so delicately upon a fence / Nearly dissolved already is the gold of the sunflower. // Voices of prostitutes; dew is spilled / Into hard grass and stars white and cold. / Look at death painted in precious shadows, / Every face full of tears and closed.]

Thus far we have briefly examined several line pairs and their relation to the thematic of closure. Taken as wholes, stanzas 1 and 2 present roughly two perpendicular axes, the vertical (downward) axis of "sinken-hingegossen" (sink-spilled out) and the horizontal axis of "sprengen-zerflossen" (burst-dissolved). The overall movement of the first stanza can be organized around the "sinken"; the stanza begins with "blue," paradigmatically related to the blue of the heavens, and sinks down to the dark depths (paradigmatic attributes) of the "Grunde" (depths) of a grinding mill. Even though the stanza then ends with a reference to the sky ("clouds"—itself a darkening element), it is a sky that has fittingly sunk and rests upon the "footbridge." The second stanza, by contrast, suggests the horizontal plane and ends with an image evocative, perhaps, of the endlessness of this axis—"zer-fließen," literally, to flow away or dissolve. The color of "golden" strangers (which originally rode blue horses into the evening) and the team of horses which bursts *red* into the village seem to melt and dissipate like the gold of the sunflower, leaving—if we glance at the final stanza—only the white of the stars in the shadows of a cold night. These stanzas form a pair: whereas the first stanza announces the foreboding sinking and darkening closure, the second stanza shows a colorful and contrastive horizontal plane against which this closure defines itself. The horizontal-vertical distinction accentuates the paradig-

matic relationship by which these stanzas develop their significance. The darkening closing in of the first stanza then finds ana-
logic expression in the second stanza's dissipating colors, a process
that begins already with the brown garden. "The brown garden" is
dull compared to the gold, red (and blue) preceding it; it is a
transitional stage between darkness and color. Yet the garden is not
only brown—associating with autumn—it is also cold—associating with (colorless) winter. The following line then shows the
resulting cold rigidity of winter in the freezing aster. Life's colorful
display has been stopped in its tracks; what was once a brilliant
aster is now merely a rigid image painted fragilely against a fence.
The wintery rigidity of this flower, the cold, and the shadows
(implied in the second stanza and spoken in the final stanza) all
evoke the proximity of Hölderlin, especially the second stanza of
his "Hälfte des Lebens" (The Middle of Life):

> Weh mir, wo nehm' ich, wenn
> Es Winter ist, die Blumen, und wo
> Den Sonnenschein
> Und Schatten der Erde?
> Die Mauern stehen
> Sprachlos und kalt, im Winde
> Klirren die Fahnen.[20]

[Woe to me, where shall I find flowers, / When it is winter, and where
/ The sunshine / And shadows of earth? / The walls stand / Speechless
and cold, in the wind / Rattle the banners.]

The "Blumen" and "Sonnenschein" vanishing into the winter in
Hölderlin's poem are displaced (and metonymically present) in
Trakl's poem in the image of a "Sonnenblume" whose dissipating
"gold" has (metonymically) displaced the "Gelb" (yellow) of the
first line of Hölderlin's poem: "Mit gelben Birnen hänget." It is

20. Hölderlin, *Sämtliche Werke,* 2:117.

hard also to miss the metallic rattle ("klirren") of Hölderlin's banners in the rigidity of Trakl's cold and lifeless "aster" (rattling against a fence in the winter wind). Hölderlin's "sprachlos and kalt" (speechless and cold), as we shall see below, also reemerges (as do many more ciphers of this poet-brother) in Trakl's "stumm" (mute), "Stille" (still, quiet), and "Stimme" (voice). Perhaps even the word "footbridge" ("Steg") in line 4 of "Melancholie," signals, as Peucker believes, the nearness of Hölderlin.[21]

Hölderlin's subtextual presence in (especially) the "Sonnenblume" helps to support the claim that the first two stanzas form a pair of complementary darkening-closing elements. This pair now takes on fuller significance when contrasted with the colorless, cold, and dark shadow of the final stanza. This stanza represents the poem's "goal"; what preceded was preparation for the pronouncement "Look at death painted in precious shadows." All the preceding images, representing the natural and human spheres, culminate here. If the preceding stanzas suggest the foreboding autumn and encroaching winter, this stanza, with its shadow and death, hard—frozen?—grasses, and cold certainly evokes the dark stasis of winter, indeed a cold, clear winter night. If one compares the wintery third line of the second stanza (with its painted image of a frozen aster) to the third line of the final stanza, one will find that these lines have more than an identical rhyme in common. It is actually in the final stanza where the "painted' (*gemalt*) of the second stanza comes into full force. The winter and cold prefigured in the painting of frozen flowers becomes in the final stanza the singular image of death. Whereas death is only connoted in the lifelessness of a two-dimensional image of frozen flowers, it is emphatically stated in the imperative of the concluding stanza: "Look at death painted. . . ." Here the poetic persona steps out of the web of images to address the reader directly. It is thus altogether fitting

21. Peucker, *Lyric Descent in the German Romantic Tradition*, 188–89.

that it is also in this stanza, above all in the final line, that the human sphere is most directly brought into play. "Every face full of tears" applies to *all* humans and refers at the same time to the human element in the poem's title—"Melancholie." That "face" metonymically represents humanity is significant, especially when one considers that these faces are not only full of tears but "closed" as well. These are not countenances which are open to and see a "leuchtende Natur" (radiant nature) or a reciprocating "blinkendes Auge" (sparkling eye) (Goethe; "Maifest") or a landscape "full of wild roses" and "yellow pears" (Hölderlin; "The Middle of Life," stanza 1). What they see they are commanded to see in the costly shadows of death-in-life: "Im teuren Schatten sieh den Tod gemalt." These faces are the second generation of those bad faces that haunted Don Juan[22] and those extinguished eyes that peered at Catalinon; here, however, there is no manic reversal (or transfiguring power of poetry) to rekindle their brilliance, which, it would seem, only flickers as a distant star in the cold winter of night.

The human element of the concluding stanza is perhaps most strikingly addressed in the first three words: "voices of prostitutes." The stark isolation of this fragment is accentuated by the semicolon that follows it and, in effect, punctuates its conspicuous lack of syntagmatic determination. Were this perplexing fragment not part of a paradigm which encompasses all three stanzas—paradigmatically related to the opening words of the preceding two stanzas— its presence would be even more troublesome. These three words ("voices of prostitutes"), however, terms from the human realm, occur in the same position as do the human elements "the blue soul" and "the golden strangers" in the preceding two stanzas.

Before considering further this constellation of human elements, it would be helpful to return to the draft versions of the first line of the concluding stanza. The first version, "Die Zeit des

22. See the section "*Don Juans Tod*" in Chapter 5 above.

Grüns, du flüchte nur zum Wein," ("The time of green. You flee indeed to wine,") contained in the *du,* likewise, a human element, which also referred back to the original, second-person singular "your face" ("dein Antlitz") of the first line. Its *fleeing* to *wine* presents a double figure for escape and relates to the effect of the impinging darkness upon the human sphere in the preceding stanzas. The encroaching darkness sent the *du* scurrying for shelter. "Green," however, is a potentially positive color within the systematics of this poem and for this reason probably was deleted from the final version to strengthen this stanza's contrastive force. The sense of refuge or escape is, nonetheless, maintained in the transitional version of "voices of mothers." Mothers' voices evoke the comfort of maternal security, a pre-Oedipal security untouched by the exigencies of the empirical world and human desire instituted by the acquisition of language. "Voices of prostitutes" then replaces this maternal refuge with an antithetical expression. While maintaining the feminine element, "prostitute" negates the positive connotations of motherhood and underscores a contrary: prostitution. Moreover, the connotation of the creative force of the natural sphere contained in "green" is likewise negated. The fallen state of "prostitute" is thus a poignant modernist figure for the oppressingly fallen state of a patrocentric world of denied and deferred desire.

It must by now be clear that these alterations involve more than just removing the color from the first line of the concluding stanza. The ominous dark of winter hinted at in the preceding stanzas forms half of a paradigm which is completed in the *Dirne* motif of this stanza. The dark, cold, and lifeless unproductivity of winter strikes at the heart of the human realm, transforming "the eternal feminine" (Goethe) into the depravity of fallen women, whores. One could, of course, also argue as I did in Chapter 6—in conjunction with the line from "Dämmerung," which aggressively denigrates the world by making it into a "whore, ugly, sick, and pale with decay!"—that a certain paranoiac alienation and aggressive retaliation also motivate this "prostitute." Here, however, there is much less aggressivity, the world is not wildly prophaned with a string of pejorative epithets; we have, rather, a single Rimbaudian vocabulary item "Dirne" (prostitute) in a controlled and sober comment—under, no doubt, the influence of Hölderlin. Here is enunciation, not excoriation.

The fuller significance of the constellation "blue soul—golden strangers—voices of prostitutes" now comes into focus. Not only do all three signal the human sphere, but they also suggest a general progression. "The blue soul" can, within the systematics of this poem, be taken as a neutral, if not positive, image. "Golden strangers," by contrast, has both positive and negative implications, whereas "voices of prostitutes" is almost certainly negative. As to the latter, the syntactic isolation of the mysterious voices of whores underscores the emptiness of these voices; they are no more than voices, human sound without sense, that pure but denigrated "feminine rhetoric" idealized in Trakl's review of Streicher's play (1:208); they are, in short, the voices of an inappropriate, defunct literary tradition that remains when "the blue soul" of Novalis "has mutely enclosed itself," which is all that remains when a *blaue Blume* is forced to dwell "in the nighttime house of pain."23

23. Version 2a of Trakl's poem "An Novalis" ("To Novalis") reads as follows:

In dunkler Erde ruht der heilige Fremdling
Es nahm von sanftem Munde ihm die Klage der Gott,
Da er in seiner Blüte hinsank.
Eine blaue Blume
Fortlebt sein Lied im nächtlichen Haus der Schmerzen. (1:325)

[In dark earth rests the holy stranger. / God took from his soft mouth the lament, / As he sank down in the flourishing prime of his life. / A blue flower / His song lives on in the nighttime house of pain.]

Note that Novalis is alluded to as a "Fremdling," a stranger.

We are now in a good position to consider three prominent words in "Melancholie" which signify quiet: "stumm" (mute), "Stille" (stillness, silence), and "ruhn" (to rest [quietly]). The first stanza of "Melancholie" contains all of these terms.

> Die blaue Seele hat sich stumm verschlossen,
> Ins offne Fenster sinkt der braune Wald,
> Die Stille dunkler Tiere; im Grunde mahlt
> Die Mühle, am Steg ruhn Wolken hingegossen,

[The blue soul has mutely enclosed itself, / In through the open window sinks the brown forest, / The silence of dark animals; in the depths grinds / The mill, clouds rest out upon the footbridge,]

The quiet pervading this stanza is then augmented by the darkness of both the mill's "depths" and the figure "the silence [*Stille*] of *dark* animals." The latter is replete with quiet, explicitly in "Stille," paradigmatically in "dark" (as we shall see below), and associatively, if one considers the speechless quietude in which animals carry out their lives. Interestingly, the poem's only explicit mention of the opposite of quiet (*Stille*) is the alliterative and assonating "Stimmen" (voices) of fallen women. "S̲t̲i̲mme" and "S̲t̲i̲lle" evince a structural paradigmatic tie which underscores their complementary connection and suggests, as we shall see in Chapter 9, that they may be a variation of the frequently occurring "Schweigen-Tönen" pair paradigm.

Kemper's important work on the structural principles underlying Trakl's verse can help to illuminate what we have thus far explored in "Melancholie." By comparing the many and often perplexing substitutions found in the draft versions of Trakl's poems, he elaborates a number of patterns, what he terms "motifs," which "form a word-field of significance specific to this poetry."[24] These motifs consist of series of words which both frequently occur to-

24. Kemper, *Georg Trakls Entwürfe*, 61.

gether and can substitute for one another. Kemper demonstrates that these word series are related by a common "idea" (*Vorstellung*) or "semantic aspect" (*Bedeutungsaspekt*) which delineates a "clearly delineated, isolated, and absolutized word-content" (61). Without doubt, one of the most important of these motifs is what might be called the "Schweigen-schwarz-Kühle" group. Such words, Kemper shows, are tied to a whole string of related words—"schwarz" (black), "dunkel" (dark), "Schatten" (shadow), "Schweigen" (silence, not speaking), "Stille" (stillness), "leise" (quiet), "stumm" (mute), "ruhen" (rest), "lautlos" (soundless), "Kühle" (coolness), "Kälte" (cold), "schneeig" (snowy), "eisig" (icy), "hart" (hard), "Härte" (hardness), "steinern" (stony), "metallen" (metallic), "kristallen" (crystalline). Kemper reasons: "The connection of all these concepts from various sensory fields . . . may be found in the fact that they all express a limit—the highest or a very high degree—of sensory perception, which, in short, relates them in an analogical function" (36).

The words that align with the "limit-concept" "Schweigen," Kemper postulates, express "Nicht-Sehen" (not-seeing), as we saw above in Chapter 7, whereas "Kälte" and "Härte" express a limit of tactile sensation. Kemper also observes that Trakl prefers the words "knöchern" (bony), "steinern," "kristallen," over "hart"— "schneeig" and "eisig" over "kalt"—because these words have synaesthetic potential. This is an important point because such synaesthetic potential allows Trakl to condense more into each word and thereby "forge" images that will fuse two (or more) paradigmatic parameters and, ultimately, expand the expressive potential of that image. Thus all of the terms aligned with these three "limit-concepts" can be related and organized along paradigmatic lines. "Eisig" and "kristallen," for example, are related by virtue of a shared attribute of hardness, "schneeig" and "steinern" by coldness, and so on. Furthermore, the connotations of coolness, darkness, blackness, and quiet of night—a high-frequency word in Trakl's vocabulary which is often modified by the above limit-concept terms—would suggest that "Schweigen" and "schwarz" could themselves be construed as a paradigm. Kemper comes close to this conclusion when he remarks that "each motif 'refers' associatively at the same time to the other terms. One can thus see how Trakl would try out in a variant version to any particular image one or more of these terms" (37). We are now close to a very important structural nodal point in Trakl's autumnal verse.[25] The centrality of darkness and darkening elements in Trakl's small vocabulary can now be directly linked to "Schweigen" and hence language, that is, its absence in some form ("stumm," "Stille," "ruhig," "Schweigen," and so on). This alignment of darkness and silence is a point of psycholinguistic fixation, a conduit of sorts for sub- or preconscious desire, which is again and again displaced in the numerous permutations of the "Schweigen-motif" elements. That "Schweigen" and "Nicht-Sehen" align (as Kemper has pointed out) suggests that this nodal point is closely related—if not rooted—in the visuality problematic manifested in Trakl's struggle with the narcissistic allure of mimetic desire. This would help to explain why Trakl's early and transparent piece of psychological exploration, *Don Juans Tod,* would align "Schweigen" and "dunkel" in a denigration of "the indolent word" ("The indolent word is always grasping / In vain at the ineffable / Which rests in dark silence at the last bounds of the spirit" [1:449]); language was in *Don Juan* a brutish and obscuring agency which engendered compensatory Imaginary fantasies of (prelinguistic) sensory integration.

Though "Melancholie" does not contain the manic reversals

25. The "Schweigen" motif also has, according to Kemper, an emotional component, in that it is often used in conjunction with "suffering," "lament," and "sorrow." "Schweigen" can even be the attribute of "sorrow" (Trauer) (ibid., 37).

seen in Trakl's earlier writing, its constellation of terms revolving around a nodal point of silence (*Schweigen*) and not-seeing (*Nicht-Sehen*) suggests that the Traklian language problematic is also manifest here. Less explicit than his earlier lamentations about the insufficiency of words, this problem is nonetheless an integral (subtextual) part of this poem, which is displaced here through the terms "Schatten," "stumm," "Stille," and the "Dirnen Stimmen" (voices of prostitutes), and its dark closures (i.e., "Every face full of tears and closed"). One could add to these indications the image of horses bursting into the village, which immediately follows the "golden strangers," an allusion to the idealized poet-brother Novalis. Here, horses carry a strong masculine connotation—especially in view of their violent, penetrating action at this crucial juncture in the darkening development of the poem—which functions as, among other things, a metaphoric displacement of the darkening, paternal effects of words onto the brutish force of bursting horses. The harsh consonants of "A team of horses / Burst red into the village" would accentuate the violence of this line and contrast with the soft and quiet assonances of the preceding lines: "Die Stille dunkler Tiere; im Grunde mahlt / Die Mühle, am Steg ruhn Wolken hingegegossen." It is not surprising that "dunkler" was, in an earlier version, "sanfter" (softer).

Thus far nothing has been said about the three rhyming words which signify flowing: "hingegossen," "zerflossen," and "ausgegossen" (which I translated as "spilled out," "dissolved," and "spilled"). One of these words is present in each stanza and, in stanzas 1 and 3, is closely associated with water. Since water is essential to all living things, the word "water" has often served poets as a figure for life. This is clearly the case in "Melancholie," where water is an integral part of both the natural and human spheres and is explicitly tied to each in the final stanza's "Tau" (dew) and "Tränen" (tears)—the initial "T" of these words reveals, perhaps, the play of another paradigmatic tie. It is in light of this constellation that the function of the unusual image of *spilled* dew ("Tau ist ausgegossen") may be grasped. By giving "Tau" the attribute of "ausgegossen," which would be empirically more appropriate to "Tränen," these two water words are pulled closer together so that their respective semantic valences may be interplayed—forged. The structural link between "ausgegossen" (spilled) and the "zerflossen" (dissolved) of the preceding line gives further evidence of the "Tau-Tränen" link, if one considers the telltale expression "in Tränen zerfließen" (to dissolve into tears). "Tränen," thus, is tied to the "zerfließen" (to dissolve) of life's color figured in the brown garden, the frozen aster, and the fading sunflower and thus also to the general decay (in the natural sphere) which is signified by the cold and darkening falltime images of the second stanza. (It could be argued that the frozen aster signifies death, in that cold has rendered the flowing water of life incapable of sustaining life; water's life-giving force is frozen, stopped.)

The interplay of human and natural realms underlying the "Tau-Tränen-zerfließen" configuration is further articulated in the "Garten-Aster-Sonnenblume" constellation of the second stanza. The garden is man's realm, yet it is also nature; it is the place where man and nature work together and as such signifies a mutual and productive relationship. The flower bed is a special kind of garden; here, the beauty of nature is cultivated and celebrated. In Trakl's "Melancholie" the time of celebration has passed, the aster is frozen, and color is fading. Mutual productivity has turned into a typically modernist antagonism; death impinges upon and threatens life. "The brown garden," as was observed above, is half of a paradigm initiated in "the brown forest" of the first stanza. It now becomes clear that this paradigm can also be viewed as part of a man-nature thematic in that the "forest" implies nature before and "garden" after human cultivation. That is, however, not a summer forest but a portentous "brown forest," which descends upon (into) man's realm—"In through the open window." It might be interesting to note here that the function of this window is exactly the opposite of the one in the *Don Juan* fragment where the window provided a way out of darkening enclosure into the bright synaesthesia of an (Imaginary) daylight world. In any case, the *open* window may be read as a synecdoche for *man*'s unhappy realm ("Tränen"); it is then through this window on the world that the darkening and closing nature ("the brown forest") "sinks" ("hingießen," "ausgießen"). The sinking sadness of autumn has descended upon the pastoral scene that once inspired the romantic poet to celebrate the felicitous unity of man and nature, where the flowers of nature were the flowers of the garden and also the flowers of poetry. A foreboding and pervasive autumnal shadow of encroaching darkness and decay dwells now within the seed of the prettiest aster and has infected and deformed the *blaue Blume* of poetry. As the shadow of the brown forest descends and penetrates man's space through the open window, tears fall. In a sense, and especially in view of Trakl's portrayal of Novalis elsewhere as a "holy stranger" (1:325), these "golden strangers"—which physically precede the brutish herd of horses and are set off by a punctuating period—are the idealized but estranged poets (most notably Novalis and Hölderlin) of a bygone golden era of poetry. This observation would corroborate Hans Esselborn's recent work on Novalis and Trakl; his conclusion deserves to be quoted at length:

> [Trakl] certainly was not interested in delineating a figure of literary history [Novalis], but rather felt himself closely akin to the romantic poet. . . . Novalis' life and poetry, as Trakl understood them, served as a kind of orientation—particularly as a counterimage to modernity—as a source of ideals, motivation, and consolation. The contrast between past and present, reality and ideality, allowed Trakl a more precise determination of his

own position. . . . It is . . . often a matter of the portrayal of human longing in terms of more beautiful and happier possibilities than those vouchsafed modern poets in their precarious situation. . . . In a psychological sense Novalis, like Hölderlin, is indeed a guarantor of the poetic tradition, a sort of literary ego-ideal, or even superego whose speech, problems, and norms provided him with both help and a contrastive sense of obligation with regard to his present state.[26]

We begin to realize that "Melancholie," like so much of Trakl's mature verse, contains subtle psychopoetological reflection upon its position vis-à-vis the precursors of tradition. One could thus conclude—using the language of the poem—that, as man's mill grinds on in the dark nether regions with the water of life, the sky has become clouded, the gold of Hölderlin's *Sonnen-Blume* has "dissolved" and Novalis's *blaue Seele* "has mutely enclosed itself": the Edenic (romantic) garden of life and poetry now stands brown and fallow in "the precious shadow" (in the paternal "shadow of the tree"?[27]). The hauntingly empty and deromanticized image of "Dirnen Stimmen" (voices of prostitutes) sounding out in the "silence" of a world darkened by a (paternal) "shadow" are the second generation of Trakl's *fleurs du mal,* his "sick flowers of melancholy" (1:218). They are a poetological cipher for an estranged modernist poet who is forced to repeat over and over again his dark, autumnal melancholy in a closed circularity of resonating differential signifiers. Indeed, the poem's structural circularity, which begins in line 1 with the quiet closure ("Die Blaue Seele hat sich stumm verschlossen") and ends with the very same word signifying closure in the last line ("Voll Tränen jedes Antlitz und verschlossen"), figures the closed and self-contained circuitry of poetry, a modern-

26. Esselborn, " *'Blaue Blume'* or *'Kristallene Träne,'* " 231.
27. See the above discussion of the "Kaspar Hauser Lied" in Chapter 7 above.

ist poetry which continues to *sound* in spite of the tearful closure of *every face*.

"The pastoral impulse of lyric has died," Brigitte Peucker remarks about the poem "Rondel," a poem very similar to "Melancholie."[28] Written about a year before "Melancholie," "Rondel" reads in its resonating simplicity:

> Verflossen ist das Gold der Tage,
> Des Abends braun und blaue Farben:
> Des Hirten sanfte Flöten starben
> Des Abends blau und braune Farben
> Verflossen ist das Gold der Tage. (1:21)

[Dissipated is the gold of the days, / The brown and blue colors of the evening: / The shepherd's soft flutes died out / The blue and brown colors of the evening / Dissipated is the gold of the days.]

Indeed, both poems evince a structural circularity and repetition of sounds, rhymes, and colors, which, as Peucker suggests about "Rondel," "seems to release the last two lines from the responsibility of meaning into pure self-declaration as language and sound."[29] Both poems, it would seem, counter the melancholy that motivates them with a densely forged richness of the "endlessly pleasing sound" (1:472) beyond the word's "content and meaning" (1:208). They seem to encircle with their rich aesthetics of sound the dark and quiet sadness which has afflicted the "blue soul" of poetry and exemplify as such the aesthetic self-sufficiency of Trakl's writing before he turned to the hymnic mode in his later poetry.

Though we have only charted out a small area of the dense structural and semantic relations whose alluring paradigmatic play and cross-referentiality seem to be almost endless, it must be evident at this point that this piece of difficult verse has not been com-

28. Peucker, *Lyric Descent in the German Romantic Tradition*, 182.
29. Ibid., 183.

pletely "released from the responsibility of meaning into pure self-declaration as language and sound" which "does not want to be understood in terms of content."[30] All its aesthetic self-sufficiency notwithstanding, the poem "Melancholie" seems to push at the edge of what can be said with its complexly urgent undulation of sound, sense, and image. In an attempt to fuse and forge compensatory unitary images, Trakl has created a dense linguistic network which encompasses and plays off a very wide range of semantic values. Melding often disparate semantic fields not ordinarily associated (as, for example, the "Tau-Tränen" paradigm), these paradigmatic relationships—with their (frequent) synaesthetic character, their "limit-concept" intensity, their contrasts of extreme, and their cross-referential, polyfunctional overlapping—seek to give expression to an indeterminate and language-resistant emotional state.[31] The poem softly gropes, I would venture, to say something

30. Killy, *Über Georg Trakl*, 34. Albert Hellmich's astute and perceptive study seems to be under the sway of Killy's unintelligibility thesis when he (over)states his case with such remarks as "Trakl's poetry becomes word-music, autonomous language par excellence" (*Klang und Erlösung*, 131). An alternate version of Killy's thesis is found in Maire Kurrik's otherwise insightful monograph on Trakl. Comparing his language to dream language and schizophrenic speech, she writes, in reference to the later poems: "But a poem that is a dream composed of words . . . is one that we cannot possibly hope to understand. . . . In the poem the word is cut off both from the images that the unconscious could bring it and from the concrete idea that consciousness could contribute. It is a language excommunicated from the interior and the exterior world; it designates nothing in any direction. But it is powerfully dynamic and dramatic, nonetheless, because it is naked primary process" (Georg Trakl, 44).

31. In a way it makes sense to say that this verse "seeks to give expression," because its complexly "depersonalized" structures reach a level of linguistic objectivity which lies to a large degree beyond the censuring and controlling function of the conscious empirical self. In submitting to the "demons" of his tormented psyche to conjure and momentarily appease (and sublimate, ultimately, in the aesthetic act) their insistent dark forces, Trakl is afforded access to the primary linguistic processes of a dementia where, to speak with Lacan, "the symptom is itself structured like a language" and "desire is a metonymy" (*Ecrits*, 59, 175).

about the deep-seated melancholy that quietly haunts human subjects inhabiting a world of increasing technical-rational efficiency
and spiritual groundlessness. The poem "Melancholie" is, in a
sense, the modern realization of an elegy foretold by Friedrich
Schlegel, the *Elegie* of "absolute difference between the ideal and
real":[32] it is a lament that issues from the dark and unbridgeable
abyss which remains when the romantic (divine) mediation between man and nature, sign and signified, word and vision has
been removed. It is an autumnal lament about the impossibility of
achieving Imaginary oneness in an era that senses more poignantly
than before the reductive and manipulating effects of language
of the estranging intellectual agency which may be repressed but
not reversed.

Trakl has not created merely a disjunctive or distorted (schizophrenic or drug-induced[33]) imagistic collage, nor has he painted a
falltime landscape that would, as in the case of *Erlebnislyrik,* impart
to a (sympathetic) reader a sense of the connectedness of all things
spiritual and physical. His signs do not point to the elements of
nature. These signs point the reader, if anything, to the other
elements of language which reside in the linguistic dimension of
the psyche, where, to speak with Novalis, "everything is united in
the most intimate, pleasing, and lively fashion," where "everything
alludes to everything else; everything becomes the sign of many
other things and is in turn signified and conjured by many other

32. See Chapter 2 above.

33. Some commentators have tried to derive Trakl's strange imagery from his
healthy "appetite" for drugs. Clemens Heselhaus claims, for example, that "Trakl's
conscious creativity follows more or less the model of drug-induced dream images"
("Das metaphorische Gedicht von Georg Trakl," 228). Though drugs were no
doubt responsible in part for his Rimbaudian derangement of the senses, it should
be clear by now Trakl was not merely transforming chaotic visions, whatever their
cause, into poetic visions. Drugs, if anything, helped Trakl to break with the "lingua
franca of sanity" so that he could explore another linguistic dimension.

signs."[34] Trakl has, in a way, disassembled our ordinary and potentially referential language whose elements certainly may be used to refer to our visual experience—even to the dark panorama of an autumn day—and then reassembled it according to the rules of another game plan, a game the reader can play by the indeterminate rules of the paradigm.

What comes into view as the attentive reader moves about within this poem and its variant versions is a grid of often repetitive *intra*textually related—condensed, displaced, and replaced paradigmatically related—terms, words, phrases, and images.[35] The repetitive nature of this constellation of shifting elements, the product of Trakl's compulsion to revise, highlights and isolates, in a sense, certain terms that seem to be invested with a special psycholinguistic value ("Antlitz," "schweigen," "dunkel," "still," and so on). The nature of these investments will become clearer in Chapter 9, when we take several small detours outside individual poems to the "self-plagiaristic"[36] field of Trakl's repetitive verse. What we have mapped out here within the confines of the poem "Melancholie" are the textual traces of part of a larger (isolated, semi-idiosyncratic) field of psycholinguistic play, a kind of "intertextual unconscious,"[37] to borrow Michael Riffatterre's term, in which my reading has followed a compulsion to repeat that which "is not simply 'in the text' nor wholly the fabrication of the

34. Novalis, *Schriften*, 3:318.
35. Hellmich's use of the (rather vague) musical concept leitmotif to characterize Trakl's language complements the process of reading which I have advanced in this chapter. He argues: "The leitmotif connects seemingly unrelated images, thoughts, and moods . . . and establishes flowing subliminal connections which affect the reader on the emotional rather than rational level" (*Klang und Erlösung*, 71).
36. Hamburger, "Georg Trakl," 204.
37. See Riffatterre's "Intertextual Unconscious," 211–25. Further references to this article appear in the text.

reader."[38] Although Riffatterre's discussion of how unconscious displacements and repetitions run through the "subtexts," "intertexts," and "textual homologues" applies to an analysis of reading narrative prose, I think it can also reinforce the sense and method of the reading I have offered of the poem "Melancholie." Riffatterre writes:

> Any subtext, or, more broadly still, any unit of significance . . . may serve as an intertext to some further such unit, if the latter has features in common with the former. Such features make it possible or necessary for the reader to see the two units as different versions . . . or two variants of the same structure. Components of the second will thus acquire a meaning other than what they convey in context because they will be perceived as referring also or primarily to their homologues in the first. On the other hand, the meaning of such a homologue may be retrospectively modified by our rethinking it in the light of the second version, in which case the latter now functions as the intertext to the first. (220–21)

Such a reading process, which Riffaterre says "contradicts the basic rule of any narrative" and offers a "nonsequential and nonnarrative reading . . . of selected links," seems especially well suited for exploring the many paradigmatically linked homologues of which Trakl's poetry is so rich. Nonsequential rereading, Riffaterre continues, "bespeaks an exploratory, inquisitive, questioning approach quite like psychoanalytical procedures—and no wonder, for it must be obvious that the writer rewrites or tries variations because he obeys a repetition compulsion" (221), which I would add, is similar to the one that motivates the reader.

"Melancholie" is a difficult poem. Its language is, for the reader

38. Brooks, "The Idea of Psychoanalytic Literary Criticism," 156; see the discussion of Brooks's ideas in the section *"Don Juans Tod"* in Chapter 5 above.

who comes from the speech of everyday communication (or from the poet "Confiteor"), obtrusive, dense, and unaccommodating—but not unintelligible. This poem's difficulty demands more work of its reader; its almost endlessly proliferating constellation of words, phrases, and images transforms the reader into an active producer, who must be willing to trace back the tracks of a criss-crossing paradigmatic play that will never yield semantic determinacy. Trakl evinces in his later work a sustained effort to overcome the limitations of this representation-confessional mode of expression, a mode he felt was disingenuous and illusory. "Communicating," his friend Karl Röck reports him to have said, "is not possible in poems. Communication is not possible at all. It's all just fancy phrases." Further, "Goethe is often shameless, full of fancy phrases, full of confession . . . he's totally superficial and always stays on surface. He's heartless. His kind [of poetry?] lies."[39] Was Goethe so superficial, was his confession so shallow, a lie? Did it not also strive for a universal validity (*das Ideale, das Allgemeine*)? Were Trakl's outrageously profane remarks about Goethe's confessional poetry perhaps also motivated by some deep-seated filial defiance to the father's imposing presence—one more infuriating paternal agency that issues from the disconcerting linguistic *other* of the psyche? Was he perhaps, in Harold Bloom's words, "emptying the precursor of *his* divinity"?[40] Or, as his remarks might also suggest, had the model of language grounded in representation and speaker intention turned darkly opaque, having become the lie or illusion of the inherited Goethean past?

Trakl's fascination with "colorful images" (1:246) of visuality and visual reciprocity (its absence or disruption as well) led him early on to fantasize an Imaginary realm of integration and lumi-

39. See Szklenar, "Beiträge zur Chronologie und Anordnung von Georg Trakls Gedichte," 227.

40. Bloom, *Anxiety of Influence*, 91.

nous visual reciprocity. This luminous realm constitutes a light background against which the dark and melodious later poems such as "Melancholie" take form. His earlier poetry was, paradoxically, motivated, as was so clearly manifest in Catalinon's "song to himself," by a subliminal aversion to language, a sentiment that is clear in the letter he wrote at about this time (July 1910; 1:477) lamenting the "terrible insufficiency" of words. This aversion brought him to valorize the presignificative "sweet feminine rhetoric" which "seduces us to listen to the *melos* of the word and ignore its content and meaning" (1:208). I think that it would be safe to refine Sharp's assertion that "the act of writing brought Trakl into increasingly intimate contact with the stress points of this shell [of the empirical self]" so that his "poetry delved more deeply into the shifting structures of this shell"[41] by stating that these "shifting structures" are essentially linguistic in nature, that they are, in postmodern terms, the shifting signifiers of the unconscious—the linguistic other—which always shadow and underlie consciousness and the linear discourse of rational speech. Though Trakl's early verse may fancifully valorize a presignificative dimension of *melos,* his poetic explorations never get beyond the terribly insufficient words nor do they proceed "primarily in the mind space anterior to language." Trakl's explorations are inherently linguistic, they are a struggle *in* and *with* language itself—a torturous struggle that exceeded any poetic rendition of an intellectual fashion. No doubt colored by the "commonly held intellectual property of poets, scientists, and philosophers in Vienna around the turn of the century,"[42] Trakl's writing gave expression to and registered, as poignantly as any of the other thinkers and writers of his era, the intellectual crisis of linguistic representation and the not unrelated psychological discourse of mirrors.

41. Sharp, *Poet's Madness,* 82.
42. Ibid., 45, 58–59.

Trakl's struggle with language was doomed to (personal) failure from the start. He could neither transcend the "paternal" authority of words to achieve a maternal "feminine rhetoric"—a quasi-mystical prelinguistic world, a "beautiful world full of endless pleasing sound" whose "images . . . are more beautiful than all of reality" (1:472)—nor could he compensate for his constitutional fragmentation through his compulsive revisions and repeated attempts forcefully to forge "in four lines of verse, four individual image-parts into one" unitary image.[43] Here, his poetry bounds on the pathological; he is fighting fire with fire, words with words. He must court and embrace not only "howling demons" (and the menacing paternal authorities of his guilty conscience) but also an anonymously reverberating and repetitive circuitry of shifting signifiers which will forever decenter his desperate longing for the reassuring experience of a stable and unified center, self. One could argue, granting a certain validity to the psychobiographical "facts," that Trakl's writing subject was more susceptible to the decentering textuality of the human psyche because it had never been able to construct the "armor" of defense which normally enables other human beings to ward off the disconcerting message of the unconscious other. He, by contrast to Goethe, did not have the "imaginary defenses"[44] with which he could happily renounce the "golden" dreams of mimetic desire.[45] Trakl, it would appear, was lacking in this healthy censorship: he was afforded a disturbing view, as he wrote his sister Minna, "as if I could see . . . life as it is without any personal interpretation, naked without preconceptions, as if I were perceiving all the voices, which reality speaks. . . . I think that it must be terrible to always live like this, to be com-

43. See Trakl's letter from July 1910 to his friend Buschbeck (1:478).

44. The ego, Lacan contends, is a "construct of imaginary defenses," whose *mesconnaissance* function ordinarily censures the message of the "unconscious of the subject," the "discourse of the other" (*Ecrits*, 55, 7, 40–56).

45. See the discussion of Goethe's "Auf dem See" in Chapter 5 above.

pletely in touch with all of the animalistic drives. . . . What a horrible nightmare" (1:472). Trakl was unarmored, relentlessly and "without preconceptions" exposed to and overwhelmed by those frightening and fragmenting "voices" of reality which produced a surging chiaroscuro welter of images, faces, and visions. "I have been plagued by far too much lately (what an infernal chaos of rhythms and images)," Trakl wrote to his friend Buschbeck in the summer of 1910, "so that I have had little time for anything other than giving form to these things in some small measure." And one line later: "What a senselessly fragmented life we lead!" (1:479). His poetry—his obsessively repetitive transcription of the insistent and chaotic "rhythms" of pulsing images—cannot center or give a stabilizing meaning to a "fragmented life."

CHAPTER 9

The Dark Flutes of Fall

Trakl had too much imagination. For this reason
he couldn't stand war, which arises above all from
a monstrous lack of imagination.[1]—Franz Kafka

A poem is an event and makes no attempt to record an event.—Robert Lowell

Grodek

IN THE SUMMER OF 1914, shortly after the outbreak of World
War I, twenty-seven-year-old Georg Trakl enlisted in the Austrian
army. In the fall of that year his field hospital unit was sent to the
Austrian-occupied Polish province of Galicia. There, in the gruesome aftermath of a battle near the town of Grodek, he witnessed
what must have seemed the prophetic truth of his poetry of doom,
death, and decay. Without adequate training or medical supplies,
Trakl was assigned to a makeshift hospital barn where ninety seriously wounded soldiers lay. He could do little to alleviate their suffering; some even begged to be shot. When one soldier ended his
torment by sending a bullet through his skull, the sight of his splat-
tered brains on the wall sent Trakl fleeing outside only to be re-
pulsed by yet another gruesome scene of death: dangling from the

1. "Er hatte zuviel Phantasie. Darum konnte er den Krieg nicht ertragen, der
vor allem aus einem ungeheuren Mangel an Phantasie entstanden ist" (Janouch,
Gespräche mit Kafka, 65).

surrounding oak trees were the limp bodies of hanged partisans. After attempting suicide, Trakl was transferred to the army psychiatric ward in Cracow. There, before he died of a self-administered overdose of cocaine, he wrote his final poems, of which the following Hölderlinian hymn[2] is thought to be his last.

Grodek

1   Am Abend tönen die herbstlichen Wälder
Von tödlichen Waffen, die goldnen Ebenen
Und blauen Seen, darüber die Sonne
Düstrer hinrollt; umfängt die Nacht
5   Sterbende Krieger, die wilde Klage
Ihrer zerbrochenen Münder.
Doch stille sammelt im Weidengrund
Rotes Gewölk, darin ein zürnender Gott wohnt
Das vergossne Blut sich, mondne Kühle;
10   Alle Straßen münden in schwarze Verwesung.
Unter goldnem Gezweig der Nacht und Sternen
Es schwankt der Schwester Schatten durch den
    schweigenden Hain,
Zu grüßen die Geister der Helden, die blutenden
    Häupter;
Und leise tönen im Rohr die dunkeln Flöten des
    Herbstes.
15   O stolzere Trauer! ihr ehernen Altäre
Die heiße Flamme des Geistes nährt heute ein gewaltiger
    Schmerz,
Die ungebornen Enkel. (1:167)

[In the evening the falltime woods sound / With deadly weapons, the golden plains / And the blue lakes, above which the sun / More darkly

2. Cf. Patrick Bridgwater's analysis of "Grodek" and the genre of war poetry: "Georg Trakl and the Poetry of the First World War," 96–113.

rolls; the night envelops / Dying warriors, the wild lament / Of their shattered mouths. / Yet quietly building in the willow dell / Red clouds, in which a wrathful god dwells / The spilled blood, lunar coolness; / All roads lead to black decay. / Beneath the golden bough of night and stars / The shadow of the sister sways through the silent grove, / To greet the spirits of the heroes, the bleeding heads; / And the dark flutes of fall softly sound in the reeds. / Oh prouder grief! You brazen altars / Today a great pain feeds the hot flame of the spirit, / The unborn grandchildren.]

The title "Grodek" immediately brings to mind a number of ineluctable yet intriguing questions. What does this poem have to do with the town where Georg Trakl saw his poetic visions of doom and decay become a concrete reality, where inner and outer world, image and event, frightfully converged? Does the specificity of this geographical proper name mean that the despairing poet was attempting to break out of the self-contained circularity of his indeterminate verse and say something determinate about the horrible reality of Grodek's bloody battlefield? Should the reader refer "Grodek" to Grodek? Did Trakl return at the very end of his life to a form of that lyrical genre—*Erlebnislyrik*—from which he had previously struggled to extricate himself?

To be sure, the undeniably high referential potential of this proper name (combined, of course, with biographical foreknowledge) tempts the reader to refer the ensuing imagery of resounding deadly weapons, of dying warriors crying out with fractured mouths, of spilled blood, of bleeding heads, to the events Georg Trakl witnessed at a place called Grodek. Even if one knew nothing of these events or of Trakl's experience at the front, one might still wonder after reading these violent images whether this peculiar title is a proper name that refers to a place where such images might have originated. In a way, "Grodek" offers a tempting invitation to stabilize and ground the play of a (difficult) poetic event with the truth of a real event. Indeed, the urgency of its "referential allure" is intensified by the fact that the poem's overall development generally conforms to the *Erlebnislyrik* pattern, which moves from a particular (personal) experience to a more general—abstract—level. "Grodek" contains four periods, each of which punctuates a "sentence" with a particular narrative function. Lines 1 through 6 (the first "sentence") provide the particular setting: time (evening), place (woods, plains, and so on), and event (war, battle). In lines 7 though 10, the second "sentence," the poet appears to step back from the battlefield scene to relate his more subjective response to the "spilled blood." The horrific scene is transformed into the potent metaphor of a wrathful god in a blood-red cloud and then summarized with the apocalyptic pronouncement: "All roads lead to black decay." The narrative function of the third sentence, lines 11 through 14, is, however, not so readily apparent, and although its imagery does not appear to lend itself to a very specific recapitulation, one could argue that this "sentence" presents another subjective, somewhat dreamy and distanced response to the battlefield horrors. The open and indeterminate quality of the imagery in these final lines seems more typical of Trakl's later work. Line 12 is probably the most typical with at least three "primal" Trakl words—"Schwester," "Schatten," and "schweigend"—and its rich alliterations and assonances. The declamatory tone of the final "sentence" suggests that these lines may contain a concluding generalization about both the immediate effects of this battlefield experience upon the passionate spirit of man ("heiße Flamme des Geistes") and the longer-term effects upon mankind's posterity ("die ungebornen Enkel"). One cannot, however, be certain, and though "Grodek" appears to move from the experiential to the general, an uncertainty and corresponding tension mount as the poem progresses. This tension, which derives at least in part from a pull between the reader's mimetic desire for referential determinacy and the poem's figural indeterminacy,[3] focuses attention on the uneasy affiliation between poet and poem, language and world—and, in a more general sense, between reader and text. The poem "Grodek" is, as its commentators have often pointed out,[4] not without the usual Traklean difficulties. Which element in lines 7 through 9, for example, is the subject for "(sich) sammelt"? Is it the "rotes Gewölk," "das vergossne Blut," or "mondne Kühle"? The poem's syntax at this point is conspicuously open; indeed, the characteristically polyfunctional "sammelt" could have any of the three elements as its subject. The poem's first verb, "tönen" (to sound), is likewise polyfunctional. Does it have one subject ("die herbstlichen Wälder") or three ("die herbstlichen Wälder," "die goldnen Ebenen," and "die blauen Seen")? What, an uninitiated Trakl reader might query, is the shadow of the sister doing swaying through a silent grove? And what do the "brazen altars" have to do with the battlefield? What is, moreover, their grammatical-syntactical function? Are they an appositive for the preceding "prouder sorrow"? The following "ihr" is, after all, not capitalized and suggests that these altars may belong to the sorrow. But why the second-person plural (*ihr*)? "Trauer" (sorrow), the would-be antecedent for the appositive, is an uncountable substantive and as such a grammatically singular term.

The indeterminate character of these syntactic idiosyncrasies, when combined with the rather open character of the poem's second and third "sentences," reinforces the impression that this verse

3. Peter von Matt discusses a similar tension between "two contrary ways of understanding" or "means of reception" which underlie the various approaches to Trakl's poetry. Readers either engage in an analysis of the poem as "pure montage and/or lyrical-musical arrangement" or in a " 'secondary revision' of the text into a homogenous and coherent semantic context" ("Die Dynamik von Trakls Gedicht," 58). The process of secondary revision, he argues with the aid of the Freudian concept ("Sekundäre Bearbeitung"), attempts to rearrange apparent incoherence of any given difficult poem into a comprehensive scenario.

4. See Ritzer, *Neue Trakl-Bibliographie*, 171–74.

might be more than a despairing poet's anguished portrayal (*Erleb-nislyrik* expression) of his front-line experience. "Grodek's" strong "referential allure," is countered, as we shall see, by a more typically open and polyvalent structure. Though not as patently self-contained as a poem such as "Melancholie," "Grodek" is every bit as complex and richly significant.

"Grodek's" Psychoparadigmatic Infrastructure

Not unlike the poem "Melancholie," color epithets—golden, blue, red, black—figure prominently in this poem. "Golden," for example, occurs in two lines, 2 and 11, and in both cases modifies an element from the natural sphere: "the plains" and "bough." Both of these elements then contrast with elements connoting either darkening—"evening" and "falltime woods" (line 1)—or dark— "night" (line 11). "Falltime woods" is of particular interest here because it contains already both epithets of dark and golden, in that "falltime" connotes both the approach of winter's darkness and the colorful autumnal display of turning leaves ("golden bough") and fields of golden grain ("golden plains"). The phrase "Beneath the golden bough of night and stars" both reiterates and develops this gold-dark interplay: the (connoted) darkness of night is directly linked (by the genitive case of "der Nacht") to the golden bough. Looking to the following line (line 12) one notices that the darker aspect of woods and bough (of the night) is further articulated in that "grove" (as a variation of woods) is modified by a form of *schweigen* (to be silent, not speak) a word which, as discussed in the preceding chapters, functions in Trakl's work as a psycholinguistic nodal point with paradigmatic affiliations to darkness. In its development, the golden of the first part of the poem has given way (as was also the case in the poem "Melancholie") to darkness in the latter part. This in turn is reflected in the transformation of evening into night. The golden sun, moreover, which "more darkly rolls," and "the night," which "umfängt," both suggest an enveloping-obscuring action that likewise plays into this darkening development. The oxymoronic image of a sun which "more darkly rolls" lends a catastrophic quality to this darkening trend. The comparative form "darker" (*düstrer*) would mean that the ultimate source of color, light, and energy, the sun, is darker or has grown darker. But the word *düster* can have an emotional component as well and can signify "gloomy," "sinister," "melancholy," or "depressing," which would play into and reinforce the poem's emotional tone of lament. It is also important that "düster" can modify the noun *Schweigen* (i.e., "düsteres Schweigen," sinister silence) indicating that the darkness evoked by the "schweigender Hain" is reinforced and further differentiated by the word "schweigen" itself.

"Falltime woods" and "silent grove" form a pair of homologues whose subtextual similarities and differences paradigmatically modify each other.[5] Both share a primary semantic feature—"woods"—and both are modified by an epithet of darkness, which, in both cases is indirectly linked to falltime gold. It is, however, their contrast with respect to degrees of darkness which plays into the poem's thematic of darkening. This (homologue) contrast involves other immediate contextual elements as well. "Falltime woods" and "silent grove" are both syntactically linked to an element signifying horizontal movement—the rolling of the sun and the "swaying" shadow of the sister—but contrast with respect to light: the brighter element, "sun," versus the darker element, "shadow." This contrast is intensified by the syntactical linkage of the sun (itself a golden element) with the brightness of

5. See Riffatterre's discussion of homologues and intertexts at the end of Chapter 8 above. See also Hildegard Steinkamp's similar, though more purely structural-linguistic analysis of the "isotopic polysemy" as it pertains to "Hain" in "Grodek" ("Trakl's Landscape Code," 158).

blue lakes and golden plains (over which it rolls). The "stars" of line 11, however, represent a reduction in the intensity of light—the sun (in line 3) signifying a brighter light source than stars.

Reinforcing the sense of darkness in line 12 is the mystifying shadow of the sister, an element that brings more darkness to the nighttime panorama of the "silent grove." As the cacophony of the battleground fades into the dreamy nightscape of the silent woods, a mysterious shadow of the sister sways (*schwankt*) through the scene. Conjured, perhaps, by the menacing lethal weapons (*tödliche Waffen*), the potentially reassuring familial presence of *the sister*—signaling the counterpart of the brother and the shared sibling connection to the maternal—ushers in a feminine element that quietly opposes the wrathful god of war ("zürnender Gott"). Here is, however, neither a manic *Don Juan* reversal of bright synaesthesia nor a redemptive transfiguration, but rather the wistful shadowy vestige of a feminine ground whose unifying potential has arrived too late. The wrathful god of war, the destructive masculine agency, appears to have won, for the sister, reduced to a dark shadow, connects only with the deceased heroes and bloody heads:[6]

Es schwankt der Schwester Schatten durch den schweigenden Hain,
Zu grüßen die Geister der Helden, die blutenden Häupter;

[The shadow of the sister sways through the silent grove, / To greet the spirits of the heroes, the bleeding heads;]

This dark sister signals the last glimmers of a fading hope for an indirect, at best, connection to a significant other; its darkness indicates a weakened link to the potentially stabilizing Imaginary

6. Bridgwater remarks: "In line 12 the ubiquitous sister is transformed into a Valkyrie-figure receiving the spirits of the slain into Valhalla, an allusion to the fascination which Wagner's *Die Walküre* held for Trakl" ("Georg Trakl and the Poetry of the First World War," 109).

dimension that figures in various ways throughout Trakl's work. "The sister has been radically dematerialized," as Aurnhammer puts it, "in the last phase of Trakl's work; she has been relegated to the realm of the dead where she leads a shadowy existence."[7] Aurnhammer also points out (270) that the relative frequency of *Schwester* increases in Trakl's later work, especially after 1912. That she should occur in both of Trakl's final poems shows how important this psychoparadigmatic nodal point has become for the poet in the desperation of his last days.

The homologue contrast in which the swaying sister (reduced to a silenced two-dimensional shadow) is overshadowed by the obscuring force of a raging god—a loud and destructive paternal agency—further elaborates the darkening thematic. In a sense, the combined shadows of the many trees signified by the falltime woods of line 1 is a foreboding image that raises exponentially the potential (paternal) menace of the single "shadow of the tree" threatening Kaspar Hauser's Edenic world. Just as the latent menace of *Schatten des Baums* was figurally transformed into the *Schatten des Mörders* by Kaspar Hauser's fateful entry into language and society, the latent menace of these trees' shadows is likewise transformed, in this case by man's resounding weapons, into a murderer of exponential proportions. Resounding weapons—guns, cannons, and the like—are themselves a violent image which suggests an underlying masculine (phallic) aggressivity. In any case, the murderous aggressivity in both poems has a strikingly similar figural result: the final line of both poems contains a form of the unusual term "unborn." To be sure, the "Silver, the head of the unborn sank down" ("Kaspar Hauser Lied") and the "unborn grandchildren" ("Grodek") would invite lengthy critical speculation; suffice it to say at this point that the plural sense of "unborn

7. Aurnhammer, *Androgynie*, 269. Further references to this work appear in the text.

grandchildren" as opposed to the singular sense of "the head of the unborn [one]," is analogically related to the multiplication of tree into woods discussed here.

Returning again to the woods-grove homologue pair, we notice that the "grove" contrasts in another way with the "woods," that is, with respect to sound:

Am Abend tönen die herbstlichen Wälder (line 1)
Es schwank der Schwester Schatten durch den schweigenden Hain,
  (line 12)

[In the evening the falltime woods sound // The shadow of the sister sways through the silent grove,]

The falltime "woods" sound (*tönen*) while the "grove" is quiet (*schweigend*). "Schweigend" signals, in opposition to the "falltime woods," not only reduction of color and light but also the absence of sound. This play between *Tönen* and *Schweigen* is more than coincidental—indeed, the frequent occurrence of this pair in Trakl's poetry led an earlier critic to characterize *Schweigen* as "negatively expressed" *Tönen*.[8] Because this pair of contrary terms occurs so frequently in poems and poem versions (variant transformations), one could posit, as a subcategory of Kemper's general *Schweigen-Motif*, a *Schweigen-Tönen* paradigm or homologue pair.[9] Looking now two lines past "silent grove" (*schweigender Hain*), one will find a configuration that repeats and varies both the dark and quiet elements while at the same time reiterating the "falltime" and "tönen" as well: "Und leise tönen im Rohr die dunkeln Flöten des Herbstes." (line 14) ("And the dark flutes of fall softly sound in the reeds."). This line presents a kind of summation of the paradigmatic play discussed up to this point. Not only does it repeat "Herbst" (autumn) and "tönen" but it also contains elements—

8. See Simon, *Traum und Orpheus*, 77.
9. See Kemper, *Georg Trakls Entwürfe*, 34.

"leise" (quiet) and "dunkel" (dark)—which play into the thematic of darkening decline. In addition to its similarity to other words denoting quiet, "leise" can, as we saw in Chapters 7 and 8, also align paradigmatically with "dunkel." "Leise," and "dunkel," along with "still" and "Nacht," belong to what Kemper calls the *Schweigen-Motif.* Indeed, it is not hard to see how the quiet stillness associated with night could be the paradigmatic link that relates the semantically disparate "leise" and "dunkel." Lines 1, 2, 11, and 12 thus set up a homologic network of relations which converge in line 14.

Line 14's Poetological Valence

Adding to the conspicuous quality of line 14 is the verb "tönen." Perhaps the single most significant word of the poem, this verb serves a dual function: not only is it an important syntactic element in the first three lines, but it is also the first verb to occur in the poem and the only verb to occur more than once. Before addressing this polyfunctionality, it would be helpful to consider a pair of lines from another late Trakl poem which bears a striking similarity to the imagery of "Grodek"'s line 14. Compare "Und leise tönen im Rohr die dunkeln Flöten des Herbstes" with the following lines from "Geistliche Dämmerung" (Spiritual Twilight), written more than a year before Trakl was sent to the front: "Und die sanften Flöten des Herbstes / Schweigen im Rohr" ("And the soft flutes of fall / Are silent in the reeds"). The variation or difference between the above lines exhibits typical Trakl substitutions and involves, most important, the play of the *Schweigen-Tönen* paradigm: the flutes of fall *schweigen* in the earlier poem and *tönen* in the later. Rather than substituting contraries in variant *draft* versions, Trakl, it would seem, has, whether deliberately or not, reversed the epithets of images occurring in different *poems* themselves. Indeed, the *Tönen-Schweigen* reversal itself involves homologic play, for it is the paradigmatic relation inhering between contrary terms which makes such a switch possible and perhaps even intelligible.

"Grodek" is in an important way typical of Trakl's mature work in that it exhibits his unique method of "self-plagiarism." Trakl not only quarried imagery (lifted and "plagiarized") from other poets, but he also borrowed from his own work.[10] "Grodek" contains so many bits and pieces—image fragments—from other poems that it seems at times almost to be a collage of his own "already written" phraseology. "Zerbrochene Münder" ("shattered mouths"), so poignantly appropriate to the carnage of a battlefield or the horrible reality of a soldier who has shattered his own skull with a bullet, shows close ties to phrases such as "der Purpur ihrer zerbrochenen Münder ("the crimson of their shattered mouths"; 1:314), "zerbrochenen Augen in schwarzen Mündern" ("shattered eyes in black mouths"; 1:73), or "zerbrochene Stirne im Munde der Nacht" ("shattered forehead in the mouth of night"; 1:308)—lines written before Trakl experienced the horrors of Grodek. "War is but the summation," writes Patrick Bridgwater of Trakl's reiteration of such imagery in "Grodek," concluding that "the whole war-situation was already implicit in his work."[11]

In any case, the recognition of this intratextual *Schweigen-Tönen* reversal adds to our understanding of the paradigmatic relations at play in "Grodek" by revealing, in effect, an absence of "Schweigen" in line 14. Not only does this absence underscore the importance of "tönen" in this line, but it also accentuates the presence of silence in line 12's "Schweigender Hain," which, as we already know, opposes the violently loud *tönen* in the falltime woods of lines 1 and 2:

---

10. Otto Basil, for example, considers the "subliminal" relatedness of Trakl's imagery to be one of its salient characteristics (*Georg Trakl*, 98).

11. Bridgwater, "Georg Trakl and the Poetry of the First World War," 98, 101.

Am Abend tönen die herbstlichen Wälder.
Von tödlichen Waffen. . . .

[In the evening the falltime woods sound / With deadly weapons. . . .]

A look at the other variations or differences between line 14 of
"Grodek" and the two lines from "Geistliche Dämmerung"—the
substitutions involving "Sanft," "dunkel," and "leise"—supports
and furthers what has been discussed above. Although "sanft" per
se is absent in "Grodek," its primary sense—softness—is still (paradigmatically) present in "leise." This softness, however, is more
specific because the word "leise" is primarily an acoustic epithet
whereas "sanft" can be tactile as well as acoustic. The absence of
this tactile-acoustic ambiguity in "leise" stresses the acoustic sense
and accentuates the presence of *tönen*. This emphasis is in turn
reinforced by the fact that "leise" is an adverb that modifies a verb
of sound, whereas the adjective "sanft" modifies an object-noun—
Flöten—a noun which only implies, metonymically, sound. The
change from "sanfte Flöten" to "dunkele Flöten," for example,

Und die sanften Flöten des Herbstes / Schweigen im Rohr
Und leise tönen im Rohr die dunkeln Flöten des Herbstes.

is equally revealing. In substituting "dunkel" for "sanft" Trakl has
eliminated the tactile sense of softness, emphasized the acoustical,
and also brought a dark element into play. Moreover, if one recalls
that "leise" is paradigmatically related to "dunkel," the change
from "sanft" to "dunkel" will make even more sense: "leise" is, so
to speak, a paradigmatic *tertium* which made the "sanft-dunkel"
displacement possible in the first place.

Just as the comparison of the variants found in the manuscript
draft versions yields, as Kemper remarks, "criteria . . . with which
completed texts may be interpreted,"[12] the comparison of recur-

12. Kemper, *Georg Trakls Entwürfe*, 30.

rent intertextual imagery can likewise yield, and for similar reasons, helpful criteria which then aid in the interpretation of individual poems. Because of the unusually reiterative character of Trakl's imagery, any given poem is, in a way, a variation or version of any number of "already written" poems or poem parts. This is clearly the case in the two poems discussed here. By comparing just one example of parallel imagery we have gained insight into the particular homologic relations that converge in line 14. As the striking parallels and variations between "Grodek" and "Geistliche Dämmerung" suggest, the "intertextual" context of Trakl's later poems is perhaps as important as the biographical context in which "Grodek" was written.

Now we are in a better position to address the polyfunctionality of *tönen* in "Grodek." Comparing its respective environments, we notice, in addition to the differences and similarities already discussed in conjunction with the *Wälder-Hain* pair, another very important contrast: the (loud) *tönen* of "weapons" in the first occurrence, as opposed to a quiet *tönen* of "flutes" in the second. What now emerges is yet another, interrelated constellation of terms, what might be characterized as a *Waffen-Flöten* paradigm. But what is the function of this constellation's play of difference and similarity with respect to the pivotal *tönen*? And what bearing does it have on the import of "Grodek's" line 14? Could the second *tönen* be construed as the "goal" of the thematic of darkening decline developing within the poem, an example of *Zielkomposition,* or is it a variation of the first line (the first image) of the poem, *Kreiskomposition?*[13] Is, in other words, the sounding of *Flöten* a return to the original image of the poem, as, for example, a quietly resounding echo of the louder daytime weapons which now recede into the quiet darkness of night (*Kreiskomposition*)? Or might these quietly sounding flutes be read as something different, as, perhaps,

13. See ibid., 136–59.

a metonymic mention of music which sounds out in spite of, or as a result of, the horrible and loud sound of weapons (*Zielkomposition*)?

Once again, a look at "Geistliche Dämmerung" can be of help. In its entirety, the stanza in which *die sanften Flöten des Herbstes* occurs, reads:

Verstummt die Klage der Amsel,
Und die sanften Flöten des Herbstes
Schweigen im Rohr.

[The lament of the blackbird ceases to sound / And the soft flutes of fall / Are silent in the reeds]

If one can talk of a poet's "primal vocabulary," "Amsel" (blackbird), along with "Drossel" (thrush) and "Vogel" (bird), would certainly have to be placed near the top of Trakl's list. Together, these words occur ninety-eight times in his work, as compared to, for example, sixty-eight occurrences each for "Herbst" (autumn) and *tönen*. If one were to include composite words such as "Vögelchen," "Vogelflug," "Vogelmund," "Vogelstimme," "Vogelzeichen," "Vogelzug," the number of occurrences would be nearly twice as high. Though the contexts in which these birds appear are varied and many, a comparison of the following examples may reveal some instructive tendencies or "criteria":[14]

Quietly the flight of birds sound (1:57)
In the evening I follow the wonderful flight of birds (1:59)
Ineffable is the flight of birds, encounter
    With dying ones; this is followed by dark years. (1:108)
The flight of birds is sounding with old legends (1:109)
The monk listens for a long time to the dying bird at the edge
    of the woods (1:368)

14. The original German may be found in the Appendix.

Elis, whenever the blackbird calls in the black woods,
 This is your demise. (1:84)
The bird sings for a long time at the edge of the woods of your
 demise. (1:304)
Listening to the soft lament of the blackbird. (1:126)
The blackbird is lamenting in the defoliated branches (1:59)
In the evening the lament
 Of the cuckoo has become silent. (1:136)
Perhaps the unspeakable flight of birds, of the unborn one
 (1:80)
Or a nighttime bird in the woods
 Endless lament (1:328)
Ancient legends
 And the dark significance of the flight of birds (1:373)
Lament of thrushes. (1:425)

Although it is impossible to abstract from the foregoing list any single common denominator, it seems safe to say that these bird words are part of a constellation of overlapping and interrelated phrases and images which often prefigure (and lament) future events (especially foreboding ones). Indeed, the southerly flight of birds, which "entschwinden in den herbstlich klaren Weiten" ("disappear in the autumnally clear vastness" 1:219), can be taken as a natural sign of fall, decay, and decline.[15] Furthermore, because bird words occur very often in conjunction with sound (or its absence) and with elements denoting (or connoting) darkness, one can also say that birds, very generally, are paradigmatically related to the *Schweigen-Tönen* paradigm. The most intriguing aspect of this constellation, however, is what one might term a music sub-complex. Often associated with birds are various elements that

15. Emil Staiger assumes that Trakl, like Novalis, believed birds and the flight of birds to be natural signs whose meaning has become obscure and inaccessible. See Staiger, "Zu einem Gedicht Georg Trakls," 288.

connote the art form of music—"singen," "musizieren," "Gesang," "flöten," and "Harmonien." Compare the following examples:[16]

> The blackbird makes music in the hazel bush (1:279)
> Full of harmony is the flight of birds (1:144)
> Loudly a bird sang wondrous tales (1:267)
> Where perhaps the thrush still sings. (1:70)
> A black bird sings in autumn trees (1:429)
> He truly loved . . . the singing black bird (1:95)
> Evening, when the blackbird sang at a dusky wall (1:117)
> The song of a captive blackbird (1:135)
> Lamentfully a blackbird flutes (1:12)
> Oh quiet! The blind thrush is singing (1:289)

Birds thus sometimes, but not always, metonymically represent—are paradigmatically linked to—music or art and in a few instances are even connected via the *blaue Blume* with poetry:[17]

> Indeed, the black flight of birds moves
>   The looking one, the holiness of blue flowers, (1:113)
> The shadows of the old ones cross the flight of a small bird;
>   The secret of blue flowers on their temples. (1:315)
> A blue a red of flowers dull
>
> . . . .
>
> A call of the blackbird lost and dull (1:318)

If one is not convinced that the *blaue Blume* is in itself sufficient to link these lines to poetry, one need only consider the poem "An Novalis" (To Novalis), the only poem Trakl wrote whose title is dedicated to another poet, to see that blue flowers can have a strong poetological valence:

16. The original German may be found in the Appendix.
17. The original German may be found in the Appendix.

An Novalis

In dunkler Erde ruht der heilige Fremdling.
Es nahm von sanftem Munde ihm die Klage der Gott,
Da er in seiner Blüte hinsank.
Eine blaue Blume
Fortlebt sein Lied im nächtlichen Haus der Schmerzen. (1:325)

[In dark earth rests the holy stranger. / God took from his soft mouth
the lament, / As he sank down in the flourishing prime of his life. / A
blue flower / His song lives on in the night house of pain.]

Note also that "Klage," and "Lied" (music) as well as numerous
Schweigen-Motif elements occur in this poetological poem. The
bird constellation, in any event, contains, in addition to the music subcomplex, a (albeit smaller) poetry (or poetological) sub-
complex. Blue flowers are, moreover, often themselves capable of
sounding—"tönen," "klingen," or "läuten"—which, in effect,
links them to the music subcomplex, as well as to birds more generally (this is likely what led Pfisterer-Burger to assert: "All sounding
figures [*alle tönenden Gestalten*] in Trakl's poetry meet in his metaphors for poetic speech"[18]). Some examples:

Blaue Blume
Die leise tönt in vergilbtem Gestein (1:120)

[Blue flower / That quietly sounds in the yellowed stone]

Umfängt den Tönenden mit purpurnen Armen sein Stern
Und das Läuten bläulicher Blumen (1:376)

[His star enveloped with crimson arms the sounding one / And the
sounding of bluish flowers]

Klangen leise ihm blaue Blumen nach (1:425)

18. Pfisterer-Burger, *Zeichen und Sterne,* 108.

[Blue flowers sounded lightly after him]

O, das Blut, das aus der Kehle des Tönenden rinnt,
  Blaue Blume; (1:117)

[Oh, the blood that runs from the throat of the sounding one, A blue flower;]

The Venn diagrams on page 302 schematically represent the paradigmatic contiguity of "birds," "music," and "blue flowers" in their peripheral relationship to the dark and quiet elements of the *Schweigen-Motif*. I would venture to say that the self-referential or poetological value of any image or poem is highest when all circles intersect, that is, when elements from each of the general categories are present.[19] Note the presence, for example, of birds, music, and blue flowers in "Gesang einer gefangenen Amsel" (Song of a Captive Blackbird), a poem Trakl dedicated to his friend and mentor Ludwig von Ficker:

Gesang einer gefangenen Amsel
für Ludwig von Ficker

Dunkler Odem im grünen Gezweig.
Blaue Blümchen umschweben das Antlitz
Des Einsamen, den goldnen Schritt
Ersterbend unter dem Ölbaum.
Aufflattert mit trunknem Flügel die Nacht.
So leise blutet Demut,
Tau, der langsam tropft vom blühenden Dorn.
Strahlender Arme Erbarmen
Umfängt ein brechendes Herz.

19. The claim that birds (and music) can have poetological value is strengthened by the fact that the only explicit mention of the poet ("Der Dichter" [The Poet; 1:285]) in all of Trakl's work occurs in a stanza of an earlier poem (1910) in which "Vögel" and "Flötenklängen" also occur. Cf. "An Angela" (To Angela; 1:286–88).

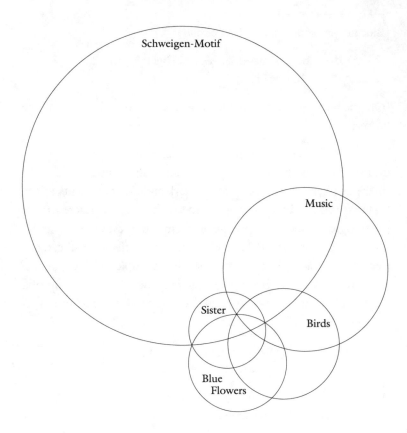

[Dark breath in the green bough. / Little blue blossoms waft around the face / Of the lonely one, the golden footstep / Dying under the olive tree. / Night flutters up on a drunken wing. / Humility bleeds so gently, / Dew, dripping slowly from the blossoming thorn. / The mercy of radiant arms / Embraces a breaking heart.]

The occurrence of all of these elements likely contributed to Wolfgang Preisendanz's groping conjecture: "It might not go too far to construe the little blue flower as a metaphor for the poetic existence of the lonesome one, and his golden step as a metaphor for his song which is connected to . . . the song of the blackbird."[20] It is interesting that Trakl's friend and mentor Ludwig von Ficker early on alluded to this poem as an aestheticized statement about poetry in which the singing blackbird is closely aligned with the poet.[21] This singing blackbird recalls the captive blind thrush in a stanza of an unnamed and fragmentary poem written sometime in 1912:

> O still! Die blinde Drossel singt
> Im Käfig ihre trunkne Weise
> Dem goldnen Helios zum Preise— (1:289)

[Quiet! The blind thrush is singing / In its drunken way in the cage / In praise of the golden Helios—]

Isolated from its natural habitat, this bird still manages to sing despite its incarceration and blindness. It sings an intoxicated song in praise of the golden sun god, a song about the brilliant visual experience which it either lacks or has been denied. In view of my discussion of the poetological significance of the "not-seeing" in Chapter 7, it should come as no surprise that blindness should also figure in this poetological constellation.

20. Preisendanz, "Auflösung und Verdinglichung," 253.
21. See Ficker, "Erinnerungen an Georg Trakl," 114–19. Ficker reports that Trakl never "grew tired of hearing the voice of the lonely bird" (117–18).

Given that words denoting birds have long served poetic traditions as a figure for the poet, we begin to sense that a mention of a
singing blackbird is, in Trakl's work, a paradigmatic mention, with
varying degrees of explicitness—relative to other contextual elements—of the poet or poetry. One might argue that the word
"Amsel" is doubly poetological, for "Amsel" (*turdus merlus*) is a
European *black* bird noted for its melodious and variable song; it
would be especially well suited to function as a self-referential
figure for a poet who, like Georg Trakl, writes such dark, sensuous poetry of rich, *melo*dious assonance, alliteration, rhythm, and
rhyme. Meld to this the sense of foreboding associated with the
autumnal flight of birds in general, and to the frequent connection
in Trakl's verse of the *Amsel* with lament, and one has a poignantly
appropriate poetological figure for a poet who sings of the darkening decline of the West, the *Abend-land*. To what degree Trakl was
conscious of this poetological valence is open to speculation. *Amsel*
signals, at least, a subliminal or unconscious level of aesthetic reflexivity. It is, perhaps, an example of what Peter von Matt has
termed an "opus-fantasy," a meta-figure or image which is engendered by and in the artist's preconscious fantasizing about his or
her artistic creativity.[22]

It should by now be clear that the stanza

> Verstummt die Klage der Amsel,
> Und die sanften Flöten des Herbstes
> Schweigen im Rohr.

22. See Matt, "Die Opus-Phantasie," 200. See also Kleefeld's use of the concept, *Das Gedicht als Sühne,* 318–20. Kleefeld's exploration of the poetological
undercurrent in Trakl's work, which makes use of the concept of the "Opus-Phantasie," claims that such words as "Stern," "Auge," or "Blume" often have a decidedly poetological value. A "tönende Blume," has, in his view, an explicitly poetological value: "In the Trakl's opus phantasy the poem occurs as a sounding flower"
(322).

[The lament of the blackbird ceases to sound / And the soft flutes of fall / Are silent in the reeds]

from "Geistliche Dämmerung" (Spiritual Twilight) has a pronounced poetological value and that "Grodek's" line 14, by virtue of its close affiliation with this line, also has, within the psychoparadigmatic infrastructure of Trakl's small and concentrated oeuvre, a poetological valence. Looking back to line 12 of "Grodek," it should now also be clear why the sister sways so close to line 14: "Es schwankt der Schwester Schatten durch den schweigenden Hain," ("And the shadow of the sister sways through the silent grove,"). Her presence here—especially a dark "shadow of the sister" with its ties to the dark and quiet elements of the *Schweigen-Motif*—suggests that this line also has deep poetological implications, because she, as we know,[23] is part of a larger psycholinguistic dimension in which both art and poetry figure. The alliteration of "<u>Sch</u>wester" and a form of "<u>Sch</u>weigen" forge here a structural link that emphasizes their strong subliminal ties to both poetry and significant elements associated in the *Schweigen-Tönen* paradigm. That "Amsel," "Flöten," and "Schweigen" should all occur in the above lines from "Geistliche Dämmerung" further underscores the poetological valence of their variation in line 14 of "Grodek": "Und leise tönen im Rohr die dunkeln Flöten des Herbstes." ("And the dark flutes of fall softly sound in the reeds"). The sister's dreamy appearance in the final stanzas of "Geistliche Dämmerung" in an image associated with the obscured specularity of a water surface and, hence, with Trakl's aesthetic of mirrors, provides further evidence of the deep psychopoetological significance of these two poems:

> Verstummt die Klage der Amsel,
> Und die sanften Flöten des Herbstes
> Schweigen im Rohr.

23. See the second and third sections in Chapter 7.

Auf schwarzer Wolke
Befährst du trunken von Mohn
Den nächtigen Weiher,

Den Sternenhimmel.
Immer tönt der Schwester mondene Stimme
Durch die geistliche Nacht.

[The lament of the blackbird ceases to sound / And the soft flutes of fall / Are silent in the reeds. / Upon a black cloud / You travel drunken with poppy / Across the night pond, // The starry heavens. / The lunar voice of the sister always sounds / Through the spiritual night.]

Interestingly, even the paradigmatic counterpart of "Schweigen" ("Tönen") occurs in the final stanza as the sister's "linguistic" attribute: "Immer tönt der Schwester mondene Stimme."[24]

Weapons and Flutes: Figure and Reflexivity

As we saw in the preceding section, the second occurrence of "tönen" in "Grodek" can be construed as both a reiteration and a variation of the first. Read as a reiteration, the second "tönen" plays into a *Kreiskomposition* structuring by aligning the two kinds of "tönen." Construed as a variation, however, it plays into a *Zielkomposition* structuring and sets up a contrast between the two "tönen" and makes possible the reflexive-figural reading by contrasting the two. This pivotal verb is the semantic-structural unit that both differentiates and connects the potentially referential weapons of war with the potentially poetological flutes of fall.

24. It is perhaps not coincidental that one of Trakl's last letters—likely his last letter—which was written to Ludwig von Ficker, contained his last two poems, "Grodek" and "Klage," and an important reference to his sister. Trakl concluded his short letter, writing "should I die, it is my wish and will that my dear sister Grete shall receive all money and anything else which I might have" (1:546). As mentioned above, both poems also contain a "Schwester."

The imagery of the first part of the poem, lines 1 through 10, contains all of the poem's loud and violent imagery and is thus linked to the first kind of *tönen,* the loud and violent sounding of weapons. This sequence of images, from the expansive image of lakes, plains, and woods all resounding with the sound of deadly weapons, to the series of gruesome and haunting resultant images (the wild lament, shattered mouths, and so on) then culminates in the devastating simplicity of line 10:

> Alle Straßen münden in schwarze Verwesung.

Black decay is ineluctable; there is no way of escaping the horror and destruction, the murderous paternal aggressivity of "tönende Waffen." With the period at the end of this medially situated pronouncement, the "loud" battlefield imagery of the first part of the poem is concluded. The following three lines (11 through 13) are transitional in that they continue the battlefield imagery but are also pervaded by quiet. This pervasive quiet—which points ahead to the "quiet" sounding of flutes—contrasts with the preceding loud cacophony of dying warriors' wild lament and resounding weapons. In a sense, these lines present the aftermath of battle; "evening" has turned to "night," "tönen" has turned into "schweigend," and "sterbende Krieger" (dying warriors) into heroic "Geister" (ghosts). Because the imagery of the poem's final section, from line 14 on, is neither loud nor violent, it aligns more easily with the second kind of "tönen," the quiet (and soft) sound of flutes. It is here amid the dark and quiet imagery converging in line 14 that the dark flutes of fall sound. Line 14 is, then, the point at which the alluringly referential weapons of war (and all that they entail) give way to (and become) their figural and thematic goal, the alluringly poetological *Flöten des Herbstes.* In other words, the sounding of flutes is the figural end point for the first kind of *tönen.* Indeed, the connection between the "tönen" of "tödliche Waffen" (deadly weapons) and "tönen" of "Flöten" (flutes) is more than fortuitous, for there is a symmetry of "ö" words between the first two lines of the poem, "tönen/tödlich," and line 14, "tönen/ Flöten." "Tönen" is thus a paradigmatic *tertium* which links deathly "tödlich" to musical "Flöten." In any case, the weapons and flutes of "Grodek" are structurally, thematically, and figurally juxtaposed and interrelated. Their pivotal function accentuates the poem's referential-figural tension, which, in the specific terms of "Grodek," correlates the quiet sounding of music (or poetry) to the loud aggressivity of war and, more generally, to the darkening negativities of a Kaspar Hauserian *Abend-land*. In an important way, the *Flöten des Herbstes* are similar to the "hearty" poetological "sick flowers of melancholy" of the poem "Dämmerung,"[25] which spring from a shattered harp. Like those *fleurs du mal* these flutes call attention to the existence of poetry in a world darkened by adversity and alienation; they sound out in spite of and as a result of the cacophony of deadly weapons and impinging words.

Like the poem "Melancholie," "Grodek" is "depersonalized" verse; it contains neither *du* nor *ich* nor any other oblique personal references such as a shattered harp or a singing "Amsel." The flutes of fall—the music of fall—are not played by anyone or anything in particular. Here the blackbird is, by contrast to the parallel lines in "Geistliche Dämmerung," conspicuously absent. In a way this absence accentuates these flutes' anonymity and purity; they are the figural realization of a presignificative feminine rhetoric of *melos,* a musical response to the darkness of the *Evening-land,* not a manic reversal of bright synaesthesia à la Don Juan. That the sister "sounds" (tönt) in "Geistliche Dämmerung" and the "Schwester Schatten" in "Grodek's" "Schweigenden Hain" are closely associated with the *tönen* of the flutes of fall in line 14 suggests that this musical response, these *Flöten des Herbstes,* have a strong tie to the

25. See Chapter 6.

feminine, which has been fused or transfigured into the impersonal music of these flutes; this is not unlike the metaphorical transformation in the final lines of a poem written in 1912 called "Kleines Konzert" (Small Concert) where one of the few explicit references in Trakl's work to Narcissus occurs:

> Im Hader dunkle Stimmen starben,
> Narziß im Endakkord von Flöten. (1:42).

[Dark voices died in strife, / Narcissus in the final chord of flutes.]

In the death associated with the strife of dark voices—language—Narcissus appears, only to be transfigured into (the sound of) flutes. This passage seems to conflate the myth of Narcissus and Echo with that of the forest-dwelling Earth-god Pan, who is said to have invented the flute ("Panflöte") when the nymph Syrinx[26] was converted into a tuft of reeds to avoid his amorous embrace. As he sighed in disappointment, his breath sounded in the reeds, producing a plaintive melody, an expression of loss whereby the feminine object of desire has been transformed into the music of flutes. Narcissus, who, we should recall, always has in Trakl's work subliminal, psychoparadigmatic ties to the sister, thus represents in "Kleines Konzert" the vestige of a "depersonalized" psychic longing, that is, a manifestation of mimetic desire, for a prelinguistic existence of Imaginary oneness. Interestingly, the pre-Fall Kaspar Hauser figure in Trakl's Hauser poem appears to have enjoyed both luminous Imaginary visions and a "feminine rhetoric" of *melos* before his entry into society, before his alienating acquisition of the "content and meaning" of words.[27] The idyllic scenery of that poem's opening lines contains, in addition to its

26. "Syrinx" is a name derived from the Greek word meaning pipe and signifies, both in English and German, "the vocal organs of birds."

27. See 1:208 and my discussion of Trakl's review of Gustav Streicher's play in Chapter 5 above.

colors and images of brightness and purity, a singing bird, a pure melody untainted by human language:

Er wahrlich liebte die Sonne, die purpurn den Hügel hinabstieg,
Die Wege des Walds, den singenden Schwarzvogel
Und die Freude des Grüns.

[He truly loved the sun, which, crimson, descended the hill, / The paths of the forest, the singing blackbird / And the joy of green.]

A. F. Bance notes that Kaspar Hauser "was a particularly productive" motif for Trakl and that it "was easily assimilated to such figures of his last years as Endymion, Helian, Elis, and Sebastian, all representing innocence preserved by early death."[28] The figure of Elis is of particular interest here, not only because he appears in both versions of Trakl's poem "An den Knaben Elis" (To the Boy Elis[29]) in close proximity to "Amsel," "tönen," and "Schweigen," but also because of his ties to the legendary-literary Elis figure in E. T. A. Hoffmann's and Hugo von Hofmannsthal's renditions of the mine of Falun story. Both authors used Elis's attraction to the dark depths of the mine as a figure for the dangerous allure of the subconscious. In the Hofmannsthal version, the figure takes on a decidedly poetological character and represents, as Hofmannsthal noted in his diary in 1894, an "analysis of poetic existence."[30] Trakl's interest in Elis not only underscores the claim that he was particularly interested in the connection between poetry and psychology, but also that this interest manifested itself in a wide range of his poetry, be it either a more deliberate and explicit thematization of the process of poetic creativity, or, as is likely the case in

28. Bance, "The Kaspar Hauser Legend," 209.
29. Trakl's Elis poems ("Elis" and "An den Knaben Elis") have generated a prodigious amount of secondary criticism. See esp. Sharp, *Poet's Madness*, 110–23, and the works by Lindenberger, Pfisterer-Burger, and Heselhaus.
30. Wunberg, *Der frühe Hofmannsthal*, 90.

"Grodek," a subliminal "opus-fantasy." Indeed, Kathrin Pfisterer-Burger is right to claim that Elis is an "evocation of poetic imagina-tion . . . which can only mean that seeing and sounding ["tönen"] are the fundamental forces of the poet's lyrical existence."[31]

One significant feature in line 14 of "Grodek" remains to be discussed: the "reeds" (*das Rohr*), the location of the anonymously sounding flutes of fall: "Und leise tönen im Rohr die dunkeln Flöten des Herbstes." ("And the dark flutes of fall softly sound in the reeds.") Though not one of Trakl's "primal" words, "Rohr" does appear in fourteen poems. It is invariably part of landscape imagery; in six poems it is directly linked (syntactically) to verbs of sound, and in five poems it is found in close proximity with birds. In one intriguingly similar occurrence from a poem of late 1912, "Rohr" is also the place where "dark flutes" sound:

> Da sie [die kranke Seele] am Abend dem Wahnsinn der Nymphe lauscht,
> Den dunklen Flöten des ⟨ . . . ⟩ im dürren Rohr; (1:421)

[As it [the sick soul] listens in the evening to the insanity of the nymph, / To the dark flutes of ⟨ . . . ⟩ in the dry reeds;]

Here, "nymph," "reed," and "flutes" again evoke the mythic origin of the flute in a "depersonalized" passage in which a feminine object of desire has been transformed into the music of flutes.

The occurrence of "Rohr" in the explicitly poetological poem "Passion"—a poem which, along with "Grodek" and "Geistliche Dämmerung," could be read as a trilogy of interrelated poetolog-ical poems—is similarly significant. The second version of the poem begins with a mention of Orpheus, whose doomed back-ward glance and yearning for a lost feminine counterpart, as we saw in Chapter 7, gave rise to beautiful melody:

31. Pfisterer-Burger, *Zeichen und Sterne*, 128.

Wenn silbern Orpheus die Laute rührt,
Beklagend ein Totes im Abendgarten—
Wer bist du Ruhendes unter hohen Bäumen?
Es rauscht die Klage das herbstliche Rohr,
Der blaue Teich. (1:125)

[When Orpheus touches silver his lyre, / Lamenting something dead in the evening garden— / Who are you, resting one, beneath tall trees? / Lament rustles in the autumnal reeds, / The blue pond.]

Orpheus's plaintive singing here is a variation on Pan's lament of disunion and loss. It might be interesting to note in this context that according to the legend, the nightingale sings nowhere in Europe more beautifully than above the grave of Orpheus. ("Nachtigal," German for "nightingale," means "night singer." It should not surprise us that "nightingale," "the sound of flutes," "reeds," "nymph," and "Orpheus" should all occur in another explicitly poetological poem, "Leuchtende Stunde" [Radiant Hour].) In any event, it is significant that *die Schwester* displaces Euridice as the lost lover in Trakl's treatment of the Orpheus myth in the "Passion" poems; as we know, she occurs in the fourth stanza in a question that parallels the rhetorical question of the Orphic first stanza, "Who are you, resting one, beneath tall trees?":

Wen weinst du unter dämmernden Bäumen?
Die Schwester, dunkle Liebe
Eines wilden Geschlechts[32]

[For whom are you crying beneath dusking trees? / The sister, dark love / Of a wild race]

The conspicuously repetitive occurrence of trees in seven of the eighteen stanzas of the poem's first version, for example, "beneath

32. Interestingly, "die Schwester" becomes "dem Schatten der Schwester" (the shadow of the sister) in the final version of the poem, suggesting a closer tie between this sister and "der Schwester Schatten" of "Grodek."

tall trees," "beneath dusking trees," "beneath black trees," "beneath greening trees," "in dark woods," "a snowy tree," and "beneath dark olive trees," recalls the exponential intensification of the menacing "Kaspar Hauser tree" in the woods of "Grodek" (discussed above). These trees evoke a pervasive and overshadowing (paternal) agency whose uncompromising law has been transgressed (conjured?) and then expiated or transfigured in the creation of poetry. The tenuous peace achieved in the concluding stanzas of "Passion," where "beneath dark olive trees" (the music of the soul sounding at the feet of a feminine penitent) is followed by quiet images of Christian resurrection and poetic transfiguration,[33] seems not to be possible for the poet of "Grodek." That resolution which overcomes *in death* all earthly struggle and the disunion of male and female would entail the cessation of human desire, which is, ultimately, the dark (and problematic) origin of the flutes of fall, the wellspring of poetry. The complete absence of redemptive images of transfiguration in "Grodek" suggests that such overcoming of human desire is an unfulfillable poetic dream wish.

In "Grodek's" final pronouncements—the three lines immediately following "the dark flutes of fall"—the poem's figural-referential tension reaches a zenith.

O stolzere Trauer! ihr ehernen Altäre
Die heiße Flamme des Geistes nährt heute ein gewaltiger Schmerz,
Die ungebornen Enkel.

[Oh prouder grief! You brazen altars / Today a great pain feeds the hot flame of the spirit, / The unborn grandchildren.]

The exclamation mark that follows "Trauer"—the only one in the poem—and the final three lines' general tone of proclamation suggest that this section (the fourth "sentence") should be read as a

33. See the discussion of "Passion" in Chapter 7.

conclusion. To be sure, "sorrow," an expression of the living's lament for those who have recently died, is an appropriate response for a survivor who looks back and reflects upon the death and horror of the battlefield. But this is a special "sorrow," a "prouder" sorrow—prouder, perhaps, because it exceeds all that came before. It is the prouder, outstanding lament of sounding flutes (of art and poetry) which is opposed to and greater than all the grief that the (false) pride of war sounding in deadly weapons can cause.

Immediately following the grammatically singular "Oh prouder grief" ("Trauer") is a plural image (you brazen altars) whose syntactic function is perplexingly indeterminate. Strictly speaking, it cannot, in its plurality, be an appositive for the preceding "sorrow" nor can it be the antecedent for the following singular "hot flame." The plurality of "altars" can, however, be tied in to the plural flutes of fall that precede the vocative exclamation of "Oh prouder grief." Semantically, the brazen altars would be a fitting place for expressing the grief caused by the "deadly weapons." Indeed, these "brazen altars" also have a specific referential significance, as Patrick Bridgwater has recently pointed out, in that this image, "is not only a general reference to war, it is a more specific reference to the phrase 'auf dem Altar des Vaterlandes sterben' [to die upon the altar of the fatherland] which was almost invariably used to announce death at the front, and the pride mixed with sorrow with which such announcements were made."[34] The word "altar" has, moreover, a certain archaic ring, which, when linked to the distinctly archaic "warriors," "heroes," and "wrathful god," conjures not only the vindictive Old Testament God[35] and the uncompromising

34. Bridgwater, "Georg Trakl and the Poetry of the First World War," 109.

35. Bridgwater aptly remarks: "Whether the god is . . . [the] demonic war-god (i.e., Mars), or the Christian god reduced to wrath by man's brutish behaviour, or Moloch, the god to whom children . . . are sacrificed, is best left open, for any poem by Trakl is the sum total of its probable interpretations" (ibid., 108).

demands of the "fatherland," but also notions of the battlefields of antiquity, where, after the battle, the dead heroes were ceremoniously placed onto funeral pyres and burned. Is, then, the "hot flame of the spirit," the flame of the funeral pyre, a flame fanned by the "deadly weapons" and ultimately by the "great pain"[36] of the departed "spirits of the heroes"? We should take careful note of the all-important syntax of line 16, for it indicates that "ein gewaltiger Schmerz" (a great pain) is the grammatical subject of the verb "nährt" (feeds): pain is that which feeds "the hot flame of the spirit." It is the pain that transformed a survivor of Grodek named Georg Trakl into an *Amsel*, to borrow the poet's reflexive image, who/which sang of the sounding "weapons" of the evening-fatherland, as well as his/its own "flutes of fall" and their origins in the dark realm of human desire which pulses through a labyrinth of paradigmatic displacements.

"Grodek's" "dark flutes of fall," when read in the larger psycho-paradigmatic infrastructure of Trakl's small and reiterative work, becomes a pregnant, reflexive figure that points beyond the confines of this one poem to the ethical-aesthetic *response*-ibility of Georg Trakl's poetry, to an irrepressible compulsion to sound out—to make music—in the face of ineffably horrible suffering and pain. This is a timeless pain associated with the "shattered mouths" and "bloody heads" of the "dying warriors" who perished at Thermopylae, but it is also the pain of those who lay suffering in a makeshift hospital-barn near the town of Grodek. The violence and carnage of Grodek are more than convenient props, objective correlatives simply used by the poet to enact a per-

36. Höllerer's impressionistic reading of "Grodek" relates the "great pain" and "brazen altars" to the "music of another [sphere of] time, against which the sorrow can be prouder than all depression and cataclysm, because this sorrow belongs to that other sphere. The poem ends with a call to the 'brazen altars' which have been removed from the cataclysm. The great pain bridges the gap [to that other sphere]" ("Georg Trakl," 423).

sonal psychodrama of sin and expiation; they are real events that indeterminately exerted their force on the poetic *response*-ibility of this poem. The poem beneath the specific title "Grodek" thematizes this figural-poetic response to weapons and war, which have become here the symptomatic essence of man's fallen state, the collective expression of the insatiable rapacity and aggression of Western man. Though one can argue that Trakl's writing was influenced, colored, or motivated by his dementia praecox and his specular (narcissistic) fixations, or that his poetry is even a convergence of symptom and symbol, a ritualistic enactment of psychic conflict in search of compensatory atonement, one cannot subtract the specific pain of Grodek from Trakl's last poetic gestures. As long as there is history, the reader cannot take the Grodek out of "Grodek," nor can the reader overlook the poem's archaic dimension, its rootedness in the patriarchal history of the *Abend-land*.

In that Trakl managed—despite his personal trauma, his frustration with the "indolent word," and his deep uneasiness with the demands of mimetic desire—to create beautiful "sick" and "poisonous" flowers (to borrow again from his imagery) which engage the modern reader confirms, in a sense, Hans Magnus Enzensberger's remark that " 'negative' behavior is poetically impossible; the reverse side of any literary destruction is the construction of a new poetics."[37] The "construction" of Trakl's poetics seems to have been born of the negativities of a weakened ego that apparently was incapable of conjuring the healthy defense mechanisms necessary for maintaining the illusion of a stable and unified subject. This vulnerability exposed him to the distressing linguistic "message of the unconscious" and allowed him, in his poetry of self-analysis, to delve ever further into the impersonal symbolic matrix of the linguistic other. Trakl's vulnerability, in other words, provided him with an Orphic access to the melodious underworld of

37. Enzensberger, *Museum der modernen Poesie*, 11.

the unconscious, where desire is forever channeled through the under*tones* of language. Here his poetic fusions, displacements, and identifications carefully followed the repetitive, paradigmatic pulse of words, the combinatory laws of the primary process of signifiers themselves, where the grammatical, narrative force of conscious speech had loosened its grip on the words he used. The reverse side of Trakl's negativity is the positive implications of a deromanticized romanticism, a modernist poetry (and poetics) that fills the gap between words and world with the rich play of paradigmatic resonances, a poetry that ensues when words are played, to speak with Novalis, like the keys of a piano. The musical keys Trakl played—the words, metaphors, images, motifs, allusions, mythemes—strike tonal chords whose harmonic intra- and intertextual vibrations resonate through a psychomythic arena of almost unlimited paradigmatic possibilities. The dense weave of Trakl's interconnected and polyfunctional imagery, we have also come to understand in the last four chapters, often involves with varying degrees of explicitness a reflexive and/or poetological level of significance which connects the problematics of narcissistic self-reflection to the creation of its own "dark flutes of fall." In so "turning back" upon itself, it becomes in more abstract terms, a kind of *Transzendentalpoesie* postulated in Friedrich Schlegel's romantic speculations,[38] a *Poesie der Poesie,* which "considers" and accentuates the conditions under which it comes into being. It is, moreover, a conspicuous linguistic event that puts the inherent reflexivity of all language—even "Grodek's" alluringly referential images—on display and presents, in a way, an exaggerated picture of the complex paradigmatic underside of words. Trakl's mature work thus thrives in the space between words and things, intention and expression that began to open in the philosophical-aesthetic tracts of the mid to late eighteenth century. It is a *Poesie der Poesie*

38. See Chapter 3 above.

that is not only a realization of a meaningful word play envisioned by the German early romantic theorists but also a poetic articulation of a modernist understanding of language which underwrites much of the philosophy of language and semiotic analysis of postmodern critical theory. His work points to a "new poetics" (of writing *and* reading) which uses the representational insufficiency of the word but also celebrates the limitation "of the word in its impotent power"[39] as the possibility of stretching the limits of what can be said; it is a poetics which, Trakl's disparaging remarks notwithstanding, pushes at the "ineffable" resting "in dark silence at the last bounds of the spirit."

Trakl's intense confrontation with the "deepest terrors and desires" at the end of language's "tentacular roots"[40] began, ironically, as a poetic flight from language, a flight from a deep-seated aversion to the socializing, self-alienating influence of language. This aversion manifested itself in his earlier writing in manic reversals and in a dramatic juxtaposition of light and dark imagery as well as in an idealized feminine rhetoric of "pleasing sound" and "melos" beyond the semantic constraints of rational, syntagmatic discourse. These manic reversals gave way in his middle period to a more subtle (Kaspar Hauserian) imagery of visuality and its denigration. In his later work Trakl's Imaginary longing finds poignant expression in the redemptive reversals of various images figuring an androgynous transcendence whose impossibility in this life adumbrated Trakl's ultimate escape in a lethal overdose of cocaine.

One must wonder how such an involuted verse so rich in melancholy and insanity, so rich in compulsive, self-plagiaristic homologue repetitions and "microscopic variations," yet so "poor in melodic invention,"[41] has managed to captivate the imagination of

39. Foucault, *Order of Things,* 300.
40. Eliot, *Selected Essays,* 135.
41. Hamburger, "Georg Trakl," 204.

generations of readers, critics, and poets. His work is bizarre and unique, to be sure, but it is a uniqueness whose "insanity outsounds itself" (*sich selbst übertönt*), sounding beyond itself and its own *Wohllaut* (1:495). Trakl strove, as we have seen, to forge a more objective verse which would both "say and mean more" (1:485), and in so doing, was able to create a semiautonomous *Zwischenreich* in which the psycholinguistic "investments" of the poet and reader meet. He achieved, in other words, a level of psycholinguistic objectivity which, among other things, speaks to the alienations of an increasingly rationalized and textualized era, an era which, in philosophical terms, theorizes about the *crisis of representation* and the shifting signifiers of the Symbolic Other. But this is also an era in which—and for similar reasons—the myths of the past still exerted their psychic allure, an allure that resounds in the many classic, pagan, and Judeo-Christian elements interwoven in the fabric of Trakl's texts. His work is an intertextual weave that includes the archaic paternal tree of knowledge (*Baum der Erkenntnis*) alongside the more recent legendary figure of Kaspar Hauser. It is a weave that also contains the psychomythic dimension in which Pan, Orpheus, and the pre-Christian wedlock of Zeus and Hera stand near or next to a sister named Grete, who in turn stands not far from the sister seen by Narcissus as he gazed at his own reflection in a pool of water.

Trakl's breakthrough in the second decade of this century is part of a larger epistemological transformation whose roots reach back 250 years to the philosophical and aesthetic speculations in the Enlightenment about *ut pictura poesis* and absolute visual mimesis. His aesthetic of mirrors registers a profoundly modern psycholinguistic problematic which exceeds any personal psychological trauma or melodramatic disaffection with words; it is intimately connected to a deeper psychological discourse taking form at that time, which culminated in the next decades in the work of such writers and thinkers as Hofmannsthal, Freud, Rank, Kassner, and Lacan. In his incessant problematizing of visual reciprocity, Trakl's writing subject seemed to conjure or imagine the narcissistic security of a noncontingent, specular link with the world, only to recognize this as a wishful projection—a beautiful but impossible myth.

Appendix

Passages and translations from pages 212–13 of Chapter 7

Silbern schaut ihr Bild im Spiegel
  Fremd sie an im Zwielichtscheine (1:12)

[Silver her mirror image looks / Strangely at her in the glowing twilight]

Der Knabe streichelt der Katze Haar,
  Verzaubert von ihrer Augen Spiegel (1:271)

[The boy strokes the cat's hair, / Spellbound by the mirror of its eyes]

Es sind Schatten, die sich vor einem erblindeten Spiegel
  umarmen (1:55)

[There are shadows which embrace before a blinded mirror]

Und in silbernen Augen
  Spiegeln sich die schwarzen Schatten unserer Wildnis, (1:393)

[And in silver eyes / Is mirrored the black shadows of our wildness,]

Aus eines Spiegels trügerischer Leere
  Hebt langsam sich . . . ein Antlitz: Kain! (1:220)

[From the mirror's deceptive emptiness / Arose slowly . . . a face: Cain!]

Laut zerspringt der Weiherspiegel (1:27)

[Loudly the pond-mirror shatters]

Rosiger Spiegel: ein häßliches Bild,
  Das im schwarzen Rücken erscheint, (1:302)

[Rosy mirror: an ugly image, / Which blackly appears from behind,]

Und seh' gleich einem Sabbath toller Hexen //
Blutfarbene Blüten in der Spiegel Hellen (1:222)

[And I see, like a sabbath of mad witches, // Blood-colored blossoms in the brightness of the mirror]

Blindet sacht der Weiherspiegel, (1:107)

[Softly blinds the mirror-pond,]

Aus geisterhaftem Weiherspiegel
Winken Früchte (1:265)

[From a ghostly mirror-pond / Wave fruits]

In schwarzen Wassern spiegeln sich Aussätzige (1:72)

[In the black waters are mirrored leprous ones]

Bessessene spiegeln sich in kalten Metallen (1:301)

[Possessed ones are mirrored in cold metals]

O! Ihr stillen Spiegel der Wahrheit.
. . . Erscheint der Abglanz gefallener Engel. (1:68)

[Oh! You quiet mirrors of truth. / . . . There appears the reflection of fallen angels.]

Ins kahle Zimmer sinken blaue Firne,
Die Liebender erstorbene Spiegel sind. (1:501)

[Blue firn sink into a barren room, / Which are the deceased mirrors of lovers.]

Passages and translations from pages 224–26 of Chapter 7

Aus blauem Spiegel trat die schmale Gestalt der Schwester und er stürzte wie tot ins Dunkel. (1:147)

[The slender figure of the sister steps out of the blue mirror and he falls as if dead into darkness.]

Die fremde Schwester erscheint wieder in jemands bösen Träumen.

. . . .

Der Student, vielleicht ein Doppelgänger, schaut ihr lange vom Fenster nach. (1:55)

[The strange sister appears again in someone's evil dreams. / . . . / The student, perhaps a *Doppelgänger*, watches her for a long time. / Behind him stands his dead brother.]

Die Hände rühren das Alter bläulicher Wasser
Oder in kalter Nacht die weißen Wangen der Schwestern. (1:70)

[His hands touch the age of bluish waters / Or in the cold night the white cheeks of the sisters.]

Da die Augen der Schwester sich rund und dunkel im Bruder aufgetan, (1:314)

[As the eyes of the sister open round and dark in the brother]

Sprichst du von deiner Schwester! Ihr Antlitz sah ich heut'
nacht im Sternenweiher, gehüllt in blutende Schleier. (1:455)

[Are you speaking of your sister! I saw her face last night in a starry pond shrouded in bloody veils.]

Purpurne Wolke umwölkte sein Haupt, daß er schweigend über sein eigenes Blut und Bildnis herfiel, ein mondenes Antlitz; steinern ins Leere hinsank, da in zerbrochenem Spiegel, ein sterbender Jüngling, die Schwester erschien; die Nacht das verfluchte Geschlecht verschlang. (1:150)

[A crimson cloud shrouded his head, so that he fell silently upon his own blood and image, a lunar face; and he fell stonily into emptiness, when in a shattered mirror there appeared a dying youth, the sister; and the night devoured the accursed race.]

Am Abend ward zum Greis der Vater; in dunklen Zimmern versteinerte das Antlitz der Mutter und auf dem Knaben lastete der Fluch des entarteten Geschlechts. Manchmal erinnerte er sich seiner

Kindheit, erfüllt von Krankheit, Schrecken und Finsternis . . . .
Aus blauem Spiegel trat die schmale Gestalt der Schwester und er
stürzte wie tot ins Dunkel. Nachts brach sein Mund gleich einer
roten Frucht auf und die Sterne erglänzten über seiner sprachlosen
Trauer. Seine Träume erfüllten das alte Haus der Väter. (1:147)

[In the evening the father became an old man; in dark rooms the
face of his mother turned to stone and the curse of the fallen race fell
heavily upon the boy. At times he remembered his childhood, filled
with sickness, terror and darkness. . . . The slender figure of the
sister stepped out of a blue mirror and he fell as if dead into darkness. At night his mouth broke open like a red fruit and the stars
shimmered above his speechless sorrow. His dreams filled the old
house of the fathers.]

Passages and translations from pages 252–53 of Chapter 8

Ein blaues Wild
   Blutet leise im Dornengestrüpp, (1:86)

[A blue prey / Bleeds quietly in a thicket of thorns,]

Der blaue Ton der Flöte im Haselgebüsch (1:308)

[The blue tone of the flute in the hazel bushes]

Leise sinkt
   An kahlen Mauern des Ölbaums blaue Stille, (1:85)

[Quietly sink / Blue stillness of the olive tree at bare walls,]

Ein blauer Augenblick ist nur mehr Seele. (1:79)

[A blue moment is just purely soul.]

Mond, als träte ein Totes
   Aus blauer Höhle (1:139)

[Moon, as if something dead steps / Out of a blue cave]

Das blaue Rauschen eines Frauengewandes (1:148)

[The blue rustling of a woman's gown]

Gottes blauer Odem weht
In den Gartensaal herein, (1:30)
[The blue breath of God / Blows into the garden room,]

Passages and translations from pages 297–98 of Chapter 9

Leise der Flug der Vögel tönt, (1:57)
[Quietly the flight of birds sound]

Am Abend . . . Folg ich der Vögel wundervollen Flügen, (1:59)
[In the evening . . . I follow the wonderful flight of birds]

Unsäglich ist der Vögel Flug, Begegnung
Mit Sterbenden; dem folgen dunkle Jahre. (1:108)
[Ineffable is the flight of birds, encounter / With dying ones; this is
followed by dark years.]

Der Flug der Vögel tönt von alten Sagen. (1:109)
[The flight of birds is sounding with old legends]

Lange lauscht der Mönch dem sterbenden Vogel am Waldsaum (1:368)
[The monk listens for a long time to the dying bird at the edge of the
woods]

Elis, wenn die Amsel im schwarzen Wald ruft,
Dieses ist dein Untergang. (1:84)
[Elis, whenever the blackbird calls in the black woods, / This is your
demise.]

Lange singt ein Vogel am Waldsaum deinen Untergang. (1:304)
[The bird sings for a long time at the edge of the woods of your demise.]

Lauschend der sanften Klage der Amsel. (1:126)
[Listening to the soft lament of the blackbird.]

Die Amsel klagt in den entlaubten Zweigen. (1:59)
[The blackbird is lamenting in the defoliated branches.]

Am Abend schweigt die Klage
    Des Kuckucks im Wald. (1:136)
[In the evening the lament / Of the cuckoo has become silent.]

Vielleicht unsäglichen Vogelflug, des Ungeborenen (1:80)
[Perhaps the unspeakable flight of birds, of the unborn one]

Oder ein nächtlicher Vogel im Wald
    Unendliche Klage (1:328)
[Or a nighttime bird in the woods / Endless lament]

Uralte Legenden
    Und dunkle Deutung des Vogelflugs. (1:373)
[Ancient legends / And the dark significance of the flight of birds]

Klage der Drossel. (1:425)
[Lament of thrushes.]

Passages and translations from page 299 of Chapter 9

Im Haselstrauch die Amsel musiziert (1:279)
[The blackbird makes music in the hazel bush]

Voll Harmonien ist der Flug der Vögel. (1:144)
[Full of harmony is the flight of birds.]

Laut sang ein Vogel Wundermär, (1:267)

Appendix

[Loudly a bird sang wondrous tales,]

Wo vielleicht noch die Drossel singt. (1:70)
[Where perhaps the thrush still sings.]

Ein schwarzer Vogel singt in Herbstesbäumen (1:429)
[A black bird sings in autumn trees]

Er wahrlich liebte . . .
    den singenden Schwarzvogel (1:95)
[He truly loved . . . / the singing blackbird]

Abend, da an dämmernder Mauer die Amsel sang, (1:117)
[Evening, when the blackbird sang at a dusky wall]

Gesang einer gefangenen Amsel (1:135)
[The song of a captive blackbird]

Kläglich eine Amsel flötet. (1:12)
[Lamentfully a blackbird flutes.]

O still! Die blinde Drossel singt (1:289)
[Oh quiet! The blind thrush is singing]

Passages and translations from page 299 of Chapter 9

Doch immer rührt der schwarze Flug der Vögel
    den Schauenden, das Heilige blauer Blumen, (1:113)
[Indeed, the black flight of birds moves / The looking one, the holiness of
    blue flowers,]

Die Schatten der Alten kreuzen den Flug eines kleinen Vogels;
    Geheimnis blauer Blumen auf ihren Schläfen. (1:315)

327

[The shadows of the old ones cross the flight of a small bird; / The secret of blue flowers on their temples.]

Ein Blau ein Rot von Blumen spat

. . . .

    Ein Amselruf verirrt und spat (1:318)

[A blue a red of flowers dull / . . . . / A call of the blackbird lost and dull]

Bibliography

Abrams, M. H. *The Mirror and the Lamp*. New York: Oxford University Press, 1953.

Adams, Jeffrey. "*Literaturpsychologie* Today." *German Quarterly* 61 (Fall 1988): 540–55.

———. "The Scene of Instruction." *Deutsche Vierteljahresschrift* 3 (1988): 467–513.

Aurnhammer, Achim. *Androgynie*. Cologne: Böhlau, 1986.

Bance, A. F. "The Kaspar Hauser Legend and Its Literary Survival." *German Life and Letters* 28 (1974–75): 199–210.

Barthes, Roland. "Death of the Author." In *The Rustle of Language*, translated by R. Howard. New York: Hill & Wang, 1986.

———. *S/Z: An Essay*. Translated by Richard Miller. New York: Hill & Wang, 1974.

———. *Writing Degree Zero*. Translated by Annette Lavers. New York: Hill & Wang, 1969.

Basil, Otto. *Georg Trakl in Selbstzeugnissen und Bilddokumenten*. Reinbek bei Hamburg: Rowohlt Taschenbuch, 1965.

Beardsley, M. C., and W. K. Wimmsatt. "The Intentional Fallacy." *Sewanee Review* 54 (1946): 469–88.

Benn, Gottfried. *Gottfried Benn: Das Hauptwerk*. 4 vols. Wiesbaden: Limes Verlag, 1980.

Birke, Joachim. "Gottscheds Neuorientierung der deutschen Poetik an der Philosophie Wolffs." *Zeitschrift für deutsche Philologie* 85 (1966): 550–82.

Black, Max. *Models and Metaphors.* Ithaca: Cornell University Press, 1962.

Bloom, Harold. *The Anxiety of Influence: A Theory of Poetry.* 1973. Reprint. New York: Oxford University Press, 1975.

——. "The Breaking of Form." In Harold Bloom, Paul de Man, et al., *Deconstruction and Criticism.* New York: Continuum, 1979.

——. *Poetry and Repression.* New Haven: Yale University Press, 1976.

——, ed. *Sigmund Freud.* New York: Chelsea House, 1985.

Blumenberg, Hans. "'Nachahmung der Natur': Zur Vorgeschichte der Idee des schöpferischen Menschen." In *Studium Generale,* 10:265–83. Berlin: Springer Verlag, 1957.

Blümner, J. Hugo. *Lessing's Laokoon.* 2d ed. Berlin: Bong, 1880.

Bodmer, Johann Jacob, and Johann Jacob Breitinger. *Von dem Einfluß und Gebrauche der Einbildungs-Krafft: Zur Ausbesserung des Geschmackes: Oder Genaue Untersuchung Aller Arten Beschreibungen, Worinnen die ausserlesensten Stellen der berühmtesten Poeten dieser Zeit mit grundtlicher Freyheit beurtheilt werden.* Zurich: Conrad Orell, 1727.

Bonaventura. *Die Nachtwachen von Bonaventura.* Stuttgart: Reclam Universal-Bibliothek (No.8926/27), 1964.

Böschenstein, Bernhard. "Hölderlin und Rimbaud, simultane Rezeption als Quelle poetischer Innovation im Werk Georg Trakls." In *Salzburger Trakl Symposium,* edited by Walter Weiss and Hans Weichselbaum, pp.9–27. Salzburg: Otto Müller, 1978.

Bridgwater, Patrick. "Georg Trakl and the Poetry of the First World War." In *Londoner Trakl Symposion,* edited by Walter Methlagl and William E. Yuill, pp.96–113. Salzburg: Otto Müller, 1981.

Brinkmann, Richard. "'Abstrakte' Lyrik im Expressionismus und die Möglichkeit symbolischer Aussage." In *Der deutsche Expressionismus. Formen und Gestalten,* edited by Hans Steffen, pp.88–114. Göttingen: Vandenhoeck, 1965.

————. "Nachtwachen von Bonaventura: Kehrseite der Frühromantik?" In *Die deutsche Romantik*, edited by Hans Steffen, pp.134–58. Göttingen: Vandenhoeck & Ruprecht, 1978.

Brockes, Barthold Heinrich. *Auszug der vornehmsten Gedichte aus dem Irdischen Vergnügen in Gott*. Facsimile reprint of 1738 ed. Stuttgart: Reihe Texte des 18. Jahrhunderts, 1965.

Brooks, Cleanth. *The Well Wrought Urn*. 1947. Reprint. New York: Harcourt, Brace, 1975.

Brooks, Peter. "The Idea of a Psychoanalytic Literary Criticism." In *The Trial(s) of Psychoanalysis*, edited by Françoise Meltzer, pp.145–59. Chicago: University of Chicago Press, 1987.

Buch, H. C. *Ut Pictura Poesis: Die Beschreibungsliteratur und ihre Kritiker von Lessing bis Lukacs*. Munich: Carl Hanser Verlag, 1972.

Calinescu, Matei. *Five Faces of Modernity: Modernism, Avant-Garde, Decadence, Kitsch, Postmodernism*. Durham: Duke University Press, 1987.

Carroll, Lewis. *The Annotated Alice*. Edited by Martin Gardner. New York: Bramhall House, 1960.

Celan, Paul. "Der Meridan. Rede anläßlich der Verleihung des Georg-Büchner Preises." In Celan, *Ausgewählte Gedichte*, pp.131–38. 9th ed. Frankfurt am Main: Edition Suhrkamp, 1981.

Cersowski, Peter. "Georg Trakl, Oskar Wilde, und andere Ästhetiker des Schreckens." *Sprachkunst* 16 (1985): 231–45.

Culler, Jonathan. *Structuralist Poetics*. Ithaca: Cornell University Press, 1975.

Davidson, Donald. "A Coherence Theory of Truth and Knowledge." Unpublished paper.

————. "Truth and Meaning." In *Readings in the Philosophy of Language*, edited by Jay F. Rosenberg and Charles Travis, pp.450–75. Englewood Cliffs: Prentice Hall, 1971.

————. "What Metaphors Mean." In *Inquiries into Truth and Interpretation*, pp.245–64. Oxford: Clarendon Press, 1984.

Davies, Cicely. "Ut pictura Poesis." *Modern Language Review* 30 (1935): 159–69.

Denneler, Iris. *Konstruktion und Expression: Zur Strategie und Wirkung der Lyrik Georg Trakls.* Salzburg: Otto Müller, 1984.

Derrida, Jacques. *Of Grammatology.* Translated by Gayatri Chakravorty Spivak. 1974. Reprint. Baltimore: Johns Hopkins University Press, 1976.

————. "Structure, Sign and Play in the Discourse of the Human Sciences." In *The Structuralist Controversy: The Languages of Criticism and the Sciences of Man,* edited by Richard Macksey and Eugenio Donato, pp.247–72. Baltimore: Johns Hopkins University Press, 1970.

Detsch, Richard. *Georg Trakl's Poetry: Toward a Union of Opposites.* University Park: Pennsylvania State University Press, 1983.

————. "Unity and Androgyny in Trakl's Works and the Writings of Other Late Nineteenth and Early Twentieth Century Authors." In *The Dark Flutes of Fall: Critical Essays on Georg Trakl,* edited by Eric Williams, pp.115–33. Columbia, S.C.: Camden House, 1991.

Doppler, Alfred. "Georg Trakl und Otto Weininger." In *Peripherie und Zentrum, Festschrift für Adalbert Schmidt,* edited by Gerlinda Weiss and Klaus Zelewitz, pp.43–54. Salzburg: Das Berglandbuch, 1971.

————. "Orphischer und apokalyptischer Gesang." *Literaturwissenschaftliches Jahrbuch* 9 (1968): 219–42.

————. "Die Stufe der Präexistenz in den Dichtungen Georg Trakls." *Zeitschrift für deutsche Philologie* 87 (1968): 273–84.

Dowden, Stephen D. *Sympathy for the Abyss: A Study in the Novel of German Modernism.* Tübingen: Niemeyer, 1986.

Eagleton, Terry. *Literary Theory: An Introduction.* Minneapolis: University of Minnesota Press, 1983.

Eliot, T. S. *Selected Essays: New Edition.* New York: Harcourt, Brace, and World, 1960.

Enzensberger, Hans Magnus. *Museum der modernen Poesie*. Frankfurt am Main: Suhrkamp, 1960.

Erinnerung an Georg Trakl: Zeugnisse und Briefe, 2d ed. Salzburg: Otto Müller, 1959.

Esselborn, Hans. "'Blaue Blume' or 'Kristallene Tränen'? Trakl's Poetology and Relation to Novalis." In *The Dark Flutes of Fall: Critical Essays on Georg Trakl*, edited by Eric Williams, pp.203–32. Columbia, S.C.: Camden House, 1991.

———. *Georg Trakl: Die Krise der Erlebnislyrik*. Cologne: Böhlau, 1981.

Fautek, H. "Die Sprachtheorie Friedrich Hardenbergs." Dr. Phil. diss., Berlin University, 1940.

Fichte, Johann. *Über den Begriff der Wissenschaftslehre oder der sogenannten Philosophie*. Stuttgart: Reclam, 1972.

Ficker, Ludwig von. "Erinnerungen an Georg Trakl." *Études Germaniques* 15 (1960): 113–19.

Fiedler, Theodor. "Trakl and Hölderlin: A Study in Influence." Ph.D. diss. Washington University, 1969.

Firmage, Robert. *Song of the West: Selected Poems of Georg Trakl*. San Francisco: North Point, 1988.

Fischer, F. J. "Die Trakl-Handschriften im Salzburger Museum Carolino Augusteum." *Jahresschrift* 4 (1958): 147–68.

Foster, Hal. *The Anti-Aesthetic: Essays on Postmodern Culture*. Port Townsend, Wash.: Bay Press, 1983.

Foucault, Michel. *The Archaeology of Knowledge*. Translated by A. M. Sheridan Smith. New York: Harper Colophon, 1976.

———. *The Order of Things: An Archaeology of the Human Sciences*. New York: Vintage/Random House, 1973.

———. "What Is an Author?" In *Language, Counter-Memory, Practice: Selected Essays and Interviews by Michel Foucault*. Edited with an introduction by D. F. Bouchard, pp.113–38. Ithaca: Cornell University Press, 1977.

Frege, Gottlob. *Kleine Schriften*. Edited by Ignacio Angelelli. Hildesheim: Georg Olms, 1967.

Freud, Sigmund. *Standard Edition*. Translated by James Strachey. 24 vols. London: Hogarth, 1964.

Frey, Northrop. *Anatomy of Criticism*. New York: Atheneum, 1967.

Friedrich, Hugo. *Struktur der modernen Lyrik: Von der Mitte des neunzehnten bis zur Mitte des zwanzigsten Jahrhunderts*. 5th expanded ed. Hamburg: Rowohlt Taschenbuch Verlag, 1979.

Furness, Raymond. "Trakl and the Literature of Decadence." In *Londoner Trakl Symposium*, edited by Walter Methlagl and William E. Yuill, pp.82–95. Salzburg: Otto Müller, 1981.

Gallop, Jane. "Lacan's 'Mirror Stage': Where to Begin." *SubStance* 37–38 (1983): 118–28.

Goethe, Johann Wolfgang von. *Goethes Werke*. 143 vols. Weiner: Böhlau, 1887–1918. (*Weimarer Ausgabe*.)

———. *Goethes Werke*. 14 vols. Edited by Erich Trunz. Munich: C. H. Beck, 1978. (*Hamburger Ausgabe*.)

Gottsched, Johann Christoph. *Der Biedermann Zweiter Theil*. Leipzig: Wolffgang Deer, 1729.

———. *Handlexicon oder kurzgefaßtes Wörterbuch der schönen Wissenschaften und freyen Künste*. Leipzig: Caspar Fritschischen Handlung, 1760.

———. *Versuch einer Critischen Dichtkunst*. Photo-mechanical reprint of the 4th ed., 1751. Darmstadt: Wissenschaftliche Buchgesellschaft, 1962.

Graziano, Frank. "Introduction." In *Georg Trakl: A Profile*. Durango, Colo.: Logbridge-Rhodes, 1983.

Grimm, Reinhold. "Georg Trakls Verhältnis zu Rimbaud." *Germanisch-Romanische Monatsschrift* 9 (1959): 271–313.

Gruppe, Otto Friedrich. *Philosophische Werke*. Edited by Fritz Mauthner. Munich: Georg Müller, 1914.

Habermas, Jürgen. "Modernity—An Incomplete Project." In *The*

Anti-Aesthetic: Essays on Postmodern Culture, edited by Hal Foster. Port Townsend, Wash.: Bay Press, 1983.

Hacking, Ian. *Why Does Language Matter to Philosophy?* Cambridge: Cambridge University Press, 1979.

Hamburger, Michael. "Georg Trakl." In *A Proliferation of Poets,* pp.239–71. New York: St. Martin's Press, 1984.

Hardenberg, Friedrich von (Novalis). *Schriften.* Edited by Paul Kluckhohn and Richard Samuel. 4 vols. Leipzig: Bibliographisches Institut, 1929.

Hartman, Geoffrey. "Preface." In *Deconstruction and Criticism,* edited by Harold Bloom et al. New York: Continuum, 1979.

Hassan, Ihab. *The Postmodern Turn: Essays in Postmodern Theory and Culture.* Columbus: Ohio State University Press, 1987.

Heidegger, Martin. "Georg Trakl: Eine Erörterung seines Gedichts." *Merkur* 7 (1953): 226–58.

———. "Language in the Poem: A Discussion of Georg Trakl's Poetic Work." In *On the Way to Language,* pp.159–98. Translated by Peter Hertz. New York: Harper & Row, 1971.

Heine, Roland. *Transzendentalpoesie: Studien zu Friedrich Schlegel, Novalis und E. T. A. Hoffmann.* Abhandlungen zur Kunst- Musik- und Literaturwissenschaft, 144. Bonn: Bouvier Verlag, 1974.

Held, Wolfgang. "Mönch und Narziß: Hora und Spiegel in der Bild- und Bewegungsstruktur der Dichtungen Georg Trakls." Dr. Phil. diss., Freiburg University, 1960.

Hellmich Albert. *Klang und Erlösung: Das Problem musikalischer Strukturen in der Lyrik Georg Trakls.* Salzburg: Otto Müller, 1971.

Hermand, Jost. "Der Knabe Elis: Zum Problem der Existenzstufen bei Georg Trakl." *Monatshefte* 51 (1959): 225–36.

———. *Synthetisches Interpretieren: Zur Methodik der Literaturwissenschaft.* Munich: Nymphenburger, 1968.

Herrmann, Hans Peter. *Naturnachahmung und Einbildungskraft: Zur*

Entwicklung der deutschen Poetik von 1670 bis 1740. Bad Homburg
v. d. H.: Verlag Gehlen, 1970.

Heselhaus, Clemens. "Das metaphorische Gedicht von Georg Trakl."
In *Deutsche Lyrik der Moderne von Nietzsche bis Ivan Goll: Die Rück-
kehr zur Bildlichkeit der Sprache*, pp.228–57. Düsseldorf: A. Bagel,
1961.

Hoesterey, Ingeborg. "Review Essay: Literatur zur Postmoderne."
German Quarterly 62 (Fall 1989): 505–9.

Hofmannsthal, Hugo von. *Ausgewählte Werke in zwei Bänden*. Edited
by Rudolf Hirsch. Frankfurt am Main: Fischer, 1957.

Hölderlin, Friedrich. *Sämtliche Werke*. Stuttgart: Kohlhammer, 1951.

Höllerer, Walter. "Georg Trakl: Grodek," In *Die deutsche Lyrik: Form
und Geschichte*, edited by Benno von Wiese, 2:419–24. Düsseldorf:
A. Bagel, 1970.

Howard, William G. "Ut Pictura Poesis." *PMLA* 24 (1909): 40–123.

Huyssen, Andreas. *After the Great Divide: Modernism, Mass Culture,
Postmodernism*. Bloomington: Indiana University Press, 1986.

Iser, Wolfgang. *The Act of Reading: A Theory of Aesthetic Response*.
Baltimore: Johns Hopkins University Press, 1978.

———. *The Implied Reader*. Baltimore: Johns Hopkins University
Press, 1974.

Jakobson, Roman. "Linguistics and Poetics." In *Style in Language*,
edited by Thomas Sebeok, pp.350–77. Cambridge, Mass.: MIT
Press, 1960.

Jameson, Fredric. "The Imaginary and the Symbolic in Lacan: Marx-
ism, Psychoanalytic Criticism, and the Problem of the Subject."
Yale French Studies 55–56 (1977): 338–95.

———. *The Prisonhouse of Language*. Princeton: Princeton University
Press, 1972.

Janouch, Gustav. *Gespräche mit Kafka*. Frankfurt: Fischer, 1961.

Jauss, Hans Robert. *Toward an Aesthetic of Reception*. Translated by Timothy Bahti. Minneapolis: University of Minnesota Press, 1982.

Juhl, Peter D. "Intention and Literary Interpretation." *Deutsche Vierteljahresschrift* 45 (1971): 1–23.

Jung, Carl G. *Man and His Symbols*. New York: Dell, 1973.

Kant, Immanuel. *Werke in 12 Bänden*. Edited by Wilhelm Weischedel. Frankfurt am Main: Suhrkamp, 1968.

Kassner, Rudolf. *Narciss oder Mythos und Einbildungskraft*. Leipzig: Insel, 1928.

Kayser, Wolfgang. *Das sprachliche Kunstwerk*. 16th ed. Bern: Francke, 1973.

Kermode, Frank. *Romantic Image*. New York: Random House, 1964.

Kemper, Hans Georg. "Georg Trakl and His Poetic Persona: On the Relationship between Author and Work." In *The Dark Flutes of Fall: Critical Essays on Georg Trakl*, edited by Eric Williams, pp.24–37. Columbia, S.C.: Camden House, 1991.

———. *Georg Trakls Entwürfe: Aspekte zu ihrem Verständnis*. Tübingen: Niemeyer, 1970.

———. "Gestörter Traum. Georg Trakl: 'Geburt.'" In *Expressionismus*. Edited by Silvio Vietta and H. G. Kemper, pp.229–85. Munich: Fink, 1980.

Killy, Walther. "Gedichte im Gedicht. Beschäftigung mit Trakl-Handschriften." *Merkur* 12 (1958): 1108–21.

———. *Über Georg Trakl*. 3d. ed. Göttingen: Vandenhoeck & Ruprecht, 1967.

———. *Wandlungen des lyrischen Bildes*. 7th ed. Göttingen: Vandenhoeck & Ruprecht, 1978.

Kleefeld, Gunther. *Das Gedicht als Sühne: Georg Trakls Dichtung und Krankheit: Eine psychoanalytische Studie*. Tübingen: Max Niemeyer, 1985.

———. "Kaspar Hauser and the Paternal Law: The Dramaturgy of Desire in Trakl's 'Kaspar Hauser Lied.'" In *The Dark Flutes of Fall:*

Critical Essays on Georg Trakl, edited by Eric Williams, pp.38–84. Columbia, S.C.: Camden House, 1991.

Knoespel, Kenneth J. *Narcissus and the Invention of Personal History*. New York: Garland, 1985.

Krieger, Murray. *The New Apologists for Poetry*. Minneapolis: University of Minnesota Press, 1956.

Kristeva, Julia. *Desire in Language: A Semiotic Approach to Literature and Art*. Edited by Leon Roudiez. Translated by Thomas Gora et al. New York: Columbia University Press, 1980.

Kurrik, Maire. *Georg Trakl*. Columbia Essays on Modern Writers, 72. New York: Columbia University Press, 1974.

Lacan, Jacques. *Écrits*. Translated by Alan Sheridan. New York: Norton, 1977.

———. "Some Reflections on the Ego." *International Journal of Psycho-Analysis* 34 (1953): 11–17.

Lachmann, Eduard. *Kreuz und Abend: Eine Interpretation der Dichtungen Georg Trakls*. Salzburg: Otto Müller, 1954.

Lakoff, George, and Mark Johnson. *Metaphors We Live By*. Chicago: University of Chicago Press, 1980.

Latimer, Dan. *Contemporary Critical Theory*. New York: Harcourt Brace Jovanovich, 1989.

Lentricchia, Frank. *After the New Criticism*. Chicago: University of Chicago Press, 1980.

Lessing, Gotthold Ephraim. *Gotthold Ephraim Lessings Werke*. Edited by Herbert G. Göpfert. Munich: Carl Hanser Verlag, 1974.

Lévi-Strauss, Claude. *The Raw and the Cooked: Introduction to a Science of Mythology*. Translated by John Weightman and Doreen Weightman. New York: Harper & Row, 1978.

———. "The Structural Study of Myth." *Journal of American Folklore* 78 (1955): 428–44.

Lindenberger, Herbert. "The Early Poems of Georg Trakl." *Germanic Review* 32 (1957): 45–61.

————. *Georg Trakl*. New York: Twayne, 1971.

Lühl-Wiese, Brigitte. "Georg Trakl—der blaue Reiter: Form- und Farbstrukturen in Dichtung und Malerei des Expressionismus." Dr. Phil. diss., University of Münster, 1963.

————. "The Structural Study of Myth." *Journal of American Folklore* 78 (1955): 428–44.

Magee, Bryan. *Men of Ideas*. New York: Viking Press, 1978.

Mähl, Joachim. "Friedrich von Hardenberg (Novalis)." In *Deutsche Dichter der Romantik*, edited by Benno von Wiese, pp.190–224. Berlin: Erich Schmidt, 1971.

Malcolm, Norman. "Ludwig Wittgenstein." In *The Encyclopoedia of Philosophy*, 8:327–40. New York: Macmillan, 1967.

Man, Paul de. *Allegories of Reading*. New Haven: Yale University Press, 1979.

Markwardt, Bruno. *Geschichte der deutschen Poetik*. Vol.2. Berlin: Walter de Gruyter, 1956.

Marson, E. L. "Trakl's 'Grodek': Towards an Interpretation." *German Life and Letters* 26 (1972–73): 32–38.

Matt, Peter von. "Die Dynamik von Trakls Gedicht." In *Expressionismus—sozialer Wandel und künstlerische Erfahrung*, edited by Horst Meixner and Silvio Vietta, pp.58–72. Munich: Wilhelm Fink, 1982.

————. "Die Opus-Phantasie." *Psyche* 33 (1979): 193–212.

Meier, Georg Friedrich. *Auszug aus der Vernunftslehre*. Halle, 1752. Text reproduced in *Immanuel Kant, Kants Gesammelte Schriften*, edited by der Königlich-Preußischen Akademie der Wissenschaften. Vol.15. Berlin: Georg Reimer, 1914.

Meltzer, Françoise. "Reiter- (Writer- Reader-) Geschichte." *Monatshefte* 77 (1985): 38–46.

————. *Salome and the Dance of Writing*. Chicago: University of Chicago Press, 1987.

Mendelssohn, Moses. *Gesammelte Schriften*. Jubiläumsausgabe. Edited by Fritz Bamberger et al. Stuttgart-Bad Constatt: Friedrich Fromann, 1971.

Moi, Toril. *Sexual/Textual Politics: Feminist Literary Theory.* New York: Methuen, 1985.

Mukarovskí, Jan. *The Word and Verbal Art: Selected Essays by Jan Mukarovskí.* Translated and edited by John Burbank and Peter Steiner. New Haven: Yale University Press, 1977.

Muller, J. P., and W. J. Richardson. *Lacan and Language.* New York: International Universities Press, 1985.

Nägele, Rainer. "Das Imaginäre und das Symbolische." In *Goethezeit: Studien zur Erkenntnis und Rezeption Goethes und seiner Zeitgenossen; Festschrift für Stuart Atkins,* edited by Gerhart Hoffmeister, pp.45–63. Bern: Francke, 1981.

Nietzsche, Friedrich. *Werke in drei Bänden.* Edited by Karl Schlechta. Munich: Hanser, 1966.

Neumann, Erich. "Georg Trakl: Person and Mythos." In *Creative Man: Five Essays,* translated by Eugene Rolf, pp.138–231. Princeton: Princeton University Press, 1979.

Novalis. *Schriften.* Edited by P. Kluckhohn and R. Samuel. Leipzig: Bibliographisches Institut, 1929.

Ovid. *Ovid: Metamorphoses.* Translated by Rolfe Humphries. Bloomington: Indiana University Press, 1955.

Pestalozzi, Karl. *Die Entstehung des lyrischen Ich. Studien zum Motiv der Erhebung in der Lyrik.* Berlin: de Gruyter, 1970.

Peucker, Brigitte. "Goethe's Mirror of Art: The Case of 'Auf dem See.'" *Goethe Yearbook* 2 (1984): 43–49.

———. *Lyric Descent in the German Romantic Tradition.* New Haven: Yale University Press, 1987.

Pfisterer-Burger, Kathrin. *Zeichen und Sterne: Georg Trakls Evokationen lyrischen Daseins.* Salzburg: Otto Müller, 1983.

Philipp, Eckhard. *Die Funktion des Wortes in den Gedichten Georg*

Trakls: Linguistische Aspekte ihrer Interpretation. Tübingen: Niemeyer, 1971.

Pietzcker, Carl. *Trauma, Wunsch und Abwehr*. Würzburg: Königshausen & Neumann, 1985.

Poe, Edgar Allan. "The Poetic Principle." In *The Complete Works of Edgar Allen Poe*, 14:266–92. New York: Crowel, 1902.

Preisendanz, Wolfgang. "Auflösung und Verdinglichung in den Gedichten Georg Trakls." In *Immanente Ästhetik, Ästhetische Reflexion: Lyrik als Paradigma der Moderne*, edited by Wolfgang Iser, pp.227–61. Munich: Fink, 1966.

Quine, Willard van Orman. "Two Dogmas of Empiricism." In *Readings in the Philosophy of Language*, edited by Jay F. Rosenberg and Charles Travis, pp.63–81. Englewood Cliffs: Prentice-Hall, 1977.

———. *Word and Object*. Cambridge, Mass.: MIT Press, 1960.

Rank, Otto. *The Don Juan Legend*. Translated and edited with an introduction by David G. Winter. Princeton: Princeton University Press, 1975.

———. *The Double: A Psychoanalytic Study*. Translated and edited with an introduction by Harry Tucker. Chapel Hill: University of North Carolina Press, 1971.

Richards, I. A. *Principles of Literary Criticism*. London: Keegan Paul, 1924.

Rieck, Werner. *Johann Christoph Gottsched: Eine kritische Würdigung seines Werkes*. Berlin: Akademie-Verlag, 1972.

Riffaterre, Michael. "The Intertextual Unconscious." In *The Trial(s) of Psychoanalysis*, edited by Françoise Meltzer, pp.211–25. Chicago: University of Chicago Press, 1987.

Rimbaud, Arthur. *Arthur Rimbaud*. Translated by K. L. Ammer. Leipzig: Insel, 1907.

———. *Arthur Rimbaud: Oeuvres complètes*. Paris: Gallimard, 1954.

Ritzer, Walter. *Neue Trakl-Bibliographie*. Salzburg: Otto Müller, 1983.

Rorty, Richard. *Philosophy and the Mirror of Nature*. Princeton: Princeton University Press, 1980.

Saussure, Ferdinand de. *A Course in General Linguistics*. Translated by Wade Baskin. New York: McGraw-Hill, 1959.

Schier, Rudolf. "Büchner und Trakl: Zum Problem der Anspielungen im Werk Trakls." *PMLA* 87 (1972): 1052–64.

———. *Die Sprache Georg Trakls*. Heidelberg: Carl Winter, 1970.

Schlegel, A. W. "Vorlesungen über schöne Literatur und Kunst." 23rd. Vorlesung (1801–2). *Deutsche Litteraturdenkmale des 18. und 19. Jahrhunderts*. Edited by Bernhart Seuffert. 1801. Reprint. Heilbronn: Henniger, 1884.

Schlegel, Friedrich. *Friedrich Schlegel: Literary Notebooks, 1797–1801*. Edited by Hans Eichner. Toronto: Toronto University Press, 1957.

———. *Kritische Friedrich-Schlegel-Ausgabe*. 35 vols. Edited by Ernst Behler et al. Munich: Schöningh, 1958–67.

Schleiermacher, Friedrich. *Hermeneutik*. Edited by Heinz Kimmerle. Heidelberg: Carl Winter, 1959.

Schneider, Karl-Ludwig. *Der bildhafte Ausdruck in den Dichtungen Georg Heyms, Georg Trakls und Ernst Stadlers. Studien zum lyrischen Sprachstil des deutschen Expressionismus*. Probleme der Dichtung. Vol. 2. Heidelberg: Carl Winter, 1954.

Scholes, Robert. *Structuralism in Literature: An Introduction*. New Haven: Yale University Press, 1974.

Seeba, Hinrich C. "Wirkungsgeschichte der Wirkungsgeschichte." *Jahrbuch für Internationale Germanistik* 3 (1971): 145–67.

Sharp, Francis Michael. *The Poet's Madness: A Reading of Georg Trakl*. Ithaca: Cornell University Press, 1981.

———. "Trakl: Metaphors and Readers." In *The Dark Flutes of Fall: Critical Essays in Georg Trakl*, edited by Eric Williams, pp. 254–63. Columbia, S.C.: Camden House, 1991.

Simon, Klaus. *Traum und Orpheus: Eine Studie zu Georg Trakls Dichtungen.* Salzburg: Otto Müller, 1955.

Sluga, Hans. *Gottlob Frege.* London: Routledge & Keegan Paul, 1980.

Sokel, Walter. *The Writer in Extremis.* New York: McGraw-Hill, 1964.

Sorg, Bernhard. *Das lyrische Ich.* Tübingen: Niemeyer, 1985.

Spinner, Kaspar. *Zur Struktur des lyrischen Ich.* Frankfurt am Main: Akademische Verlagsgesellschaft, 1975.

Spoerri, Theodor. *Georg Trakl: Strukturen in Persönlichkeit und Werk: Eine psychiatrisch-anthropographische Untersuchung.* Bern: Francke, 1954.

Staiger, Emil. *Grundbegriffe der Poetik.* 8th ed. Zurich: Artemis, 1968.

————. "Literatur und Öffentlichkeit." *Sprache im technischen Zeitalter* 22 (1967): 90–97.

————. "Zu einem Gedicht Georg Trakls." *Euphorion* 55 (1961): 279–96.

Steinkamp, Hildegard. *Die Gedichte Georg Trakls: Vom Landschaftscode zur Mythopoesie.* Frankfurt am Main: Peter Lang, 1988.

————. "Trakl's Landscape Code: Usage and Meaning in His Later Poetry." In *The Dark Flutes of Fall: Critical Essays on Georg Trakl,* edited by Eric Williams, pp. 134–66. Columbia, S.C.: Camden House, 1991.

Storck, Joachim. "Arbeitsgespräche: Trakl und Rilke." In *Salzburger Trakl Symposion,* edited by W. Weiss and H. Weichselbaum, pp. 152–69. Salzburg: Otto Müller, 1978.

Stupp, Johann Adam. "Beobachtungen zu Georg Trakls Fragment *Don Juans Tod.*" *Südostdeutsche Semesterblätter* 22 (1968): 32–37.

Szklenar, Hans. "Beiträge zur Chronologie und Anordnung von Georg Trakls Gedichten aufgrund des Nachlasses von Karl Röck." *Euphorion* 60 (1966): 222–62.

Trakl, Georg. *Georg Trakl: Dichtungen und Briefe.* Edited by Walther Killy and Hans Szklenar. 2 vols. Salzburg: Otto Müller, 1969.

Vietta, Silvio. *Sprache und Sprachreflexion*. Berlin: Bad Homburg v. d. H., 1970.

Vordtriede, Werner. *Novalis und die französischen Symbolisten*. Stuttgart: Kohlhammer, 1963.

Wassermann, Jakob. *Caspar Hauser*. Translated by Caroline Newton. New York: Liveright, 1983.

————. *Caspar Hauser oder die Trägheit des Herzens*. Berlin: Fischer, 1929.

Wellbery, David. "Aesthetics and Semiotics in the German Enlightenment." Ph.D. diss., Yale University, 1977.

————. *Semiotics and Aesthetics in the Age of Reason*. Cambridge: Cambridge University Press, 1984.

————. "The Specular Moment: Construction of Meaning in a Poem by Goethe." *Goethe Yearbook* 1 (1982): 1–41.

White, Hayden. "The Value of Narrativity in the Representation of Reality." In *On Narrative*, edited by W. J. T. Mitchell. Chicago: University of Chicago Press, 1980.

Wilde, Oscar. *The Picture of Dorian Gray*. Edited with an introduction by I. Murray. London: Oxford University Press, 1974.

Wittgenstein, Ludwig. *On Certainty*. Edited by G. E. M. Anscombe and G. H. von Wright. New York: Harper Torchbooks, 1972.

————. *Philosophical Investigations*. 3d ed. Translated by G. E. M. Anscombe. New York: Macmillan, 1968.

————. *Schriften*. Frankfurt: Suhrkamp, 1969.

————. *Tractatus Logico-Philosophicus*. Translated by D. E. Pears and B. F. McGuinnes. Reprint. Bungay: Chaucer Press, 1974.

Wolff, Christian. *Vernünftige Gedanken von GOTT, der Welt und der Seele des Menschen, auch allen Dingen überhaupt*. Halle: Regnerische Buchhandlung, 1720.

Wunberg, Gotthart. *Der frühe Hofmannsthal: Schizophrenie als dichterische Struktur*. Stuttgart: Kohlhammer, 1965.

Index

Other volumes in the series Texts and Contexts include: